Ordinary Vices

Ordinary Vices

Judith N. Shklar

The Belknap Press of Harvard University Press

Cambridge, Massachusetts
and London, England
1984

This book is printed on acid-free paper, and its binding
materials have been chosen for strength and durability.

Library of Congress Cataloging in Publication Data

Shklar, Judith N.
Ordinary vices.

Includes index.
1. Political ethics—Addresses, essays, lectures.
2. Liberalism—Addresses, essays, lectures.
3. Vices—Addresses, essays, lectures.   I.   Title.
JA79.S44   1984   172   84-531
ISBN 0-674-64175-2 (alk. paper)

Page 261 constitutes an extension of the copyright page.

Designed by Gwen Frankfeldt

For Stanley Hoffmann

Acknowledgments

PARTS OF Chapter 1 and a version of Chapter 2 originally appeared in *Daedalus,* summer 1979 and 1982 respectively, and are here reprinted with its kind permission. I am particularly grateful to its editor, Stephen R. Graubard, for his help and encouragement. There is, of course, something silly about thanking one's friends for being one's friends, but it is very agreeable to mention their names both in private and in public. My conversations with them about this book have been the best part of writing it. Both when we agree and when we argue, it is always a great intellectual pleasure to talk to Stanley Cavell, Stephen Holmes, Harry Hirsch, Nancy Rosenblum, Michael Walzer, and Bernie Yack. Every one of them gave me some good advice and renewed my confidence in our common scholarly enterprise.

I presented a part of "Putting Cruelty First" at the Lionel Trilling Seminar of Columbia University on April 2, 1981. The comments made there, especially by the two discussants, Arthur Danto and George Kateb, were very useful and I am grateful to them, as I am to Franklin Ford, who also helped me with the original essay. Finally I would like to thank the Warden and Fellows of All Souls College, Oxford, for electing me to a Visiting Fellowship for the Trinity Term of 1983, which allowed me to complete this book under the best of working conditions.

Contents

Ordinary Vices

T*hinking about vices*

Treachery, disloyalty, cruelty, tyranny
. . . are our ordinary vices.

—Montaigne, "Of Cannibals"

ORDINARY VICES are the sort of conduct we all expect, nothing spectacular or unusual. Dishonesty should be added to
the list that Montaigne made because, like him, we are
so familiar with it. Perhaps cruelty, hypocrisy, snobbery,
and betrayal are so commonplace that they are not worth
discussing: philosophers have so little to say about cruelty,
especially, that one must suppose that everything that can
be thought about it is too obvious to mention; and virtue
has certainly claimed more of their attention. That is not,
however, a plausible guess, for historians, dramatists, and
poets in verse and prose have not ignored these vices, least
of all cruelty. It is to them that we must turn for illumination and acknowledgment of what daily experience has already taught us. One might suggest that the works of
theologians could prove useful, but their range is somewhat
limited. Offenses against the divine order—sin, to be
exact—must be their chief concern. Moreover, the seven
deadly sins of traditional Christianity do not include these
ordinary vices, which actually receive rather scant attention.
It is only if we step outside the divinely ruled moral universe that we can really put our minds to the common ills
we inflict upon one another every day. That is what Montaigne did and that is why he is the hero of this book. In
spirit he is on every one of its pages, even when his name

1

does not appear. He put cruelty first, and it is from him that I have learned just what follows from that conviction.

Cruelty, hypocrisy, snobbery, treachery, and misanthropy all share a special quality: they have both personal and public dimensions. We are cruel to children and to our political foes; hypocrisy is visible on every stage, at home and abroad; snobbery is domestic, but in a representative democracy it has serious ideological implications; and we betray our personal friends no less than our political allies—indeed, that is why love and war are so similar. Misanthropy may, moreover, afflict us if we think too much about ordinary vices and take them too much to heart. It may merely make us depressed, but it can also reduce us to political fury to the point of mass murder, which also is quite familiar to us, just now. Because these vices flaw our character so deeply, they are a common sight everywhere. As such, they pose complicated puzzles for liberal democrats, who have notorious difficulties in settling the boundaries between private and public spheres of conduct. Some personal vices, which may be completely revolting to a free people, must nevertheless, as a matter of principle or prudence, be overlooked. That is especially difficult with the vices that I have in mind—cruelty, misanthropy, hypocrisy, snobbery, and treachery. They are not like unpopular views or obnoxious ideologies, to which people have a constitutional right, nor do they encompass merely specific acts or decisions. These vices may involve our whole character, and our responses to them are therefore far deeper, both emotionally and speculatively. Cruelty, to begin with, is often utterly intolerable for liberals, because fear destroys freedom. Next in line, hypocrisy and betrayal have always been despised. How can we be free to get on with our lives if we cannot trust our friends and fellow citizens? How can we be expected to endure the humiliations inflicted by an uncontained snobbery? Our only consolation may well be that without moral aspirations there would be no hypocrisy, and that without trust there would be no betrayals. But there is nothing to redeem cruelty and humiliation.

Though we may talk calmly about the private and public

boundaries of disloyalty and dishonesty, we tend to be reticent about cruelty. Cruelty is different—and not, I think, just because we are too squeamish. This is the twentieth century, after all. Cruelty is baffling because we can live neither with nor without it. Moreover, it puts us face to face with our irrationality as nothing else does. And that is not all. We have trouble grading the vices generally, even if we tend to agree on what is vicious; but when we put cruelty at the head of the vices, which liberal theory may well do, we may become politically disoriented and deeply confused. That is not the least important reason for investigating it and the other common vices. They have to be ranked, and that opens the whole question of the implications of our moral choices, in private and in public.

An experienced and worldly person might, in spite of all this, say, quite wisely, that it will not do to talk so much about vice, because it makes one hate men. We become misanthropic if we contemplate dishonesty, infidelity, and cruelty, especially, for too long a time. Better, perhaps, to change the topic. Who, after all, can bear the nag and the scold? More seriously, it is undeniable that misanthropy has the most destructive political possibilities. To hate men as they are enough to do anything for the sake of a new and improved humanity; to clean up the human race until only the strong and handsome are left—these are projects about which we know all that we need to know by now. And the private misanthrope who cannot bear the errors and defects of his neighbors is a poor friend and a domestic tyrant in his little sphere. Here again the ranking of the vices makes a difference. If one puts cruelty first, one will be careful to control one's misanthropy, lest it become rage. Nevertheless, liberalism owes a deep and enduring debt to misanthropy, or, to be exact, to a suspicious temper that does not think that any set of officials is fit to do more than to inhibit, within strict legal limits, the grosser forms of violence and fraud. Misanthropy is itself a vice that liberals need to think about, especially if they do not wish to succumb to its more threatening and cynical forms. If one puts dishonesty or betrayal first, then there is no built-in restraint upon fury, which did indeed inspire unstable outbursts and violent misanthropy in the early modern period and again in the years immediately after World War I.

Not only does it matter politically how we rank the vices, but freedom demands that as a matter of liberal policy we must learn to endure enormous differences in the relative importance that various individuals and groups attach to the vices. There is a vast gulf between the seven deadly sins, with their emphasis on pride and self-indulgence, and putting cruelty first. These choices are not casual or due merely to the variety of our purely personal dispositions and emotional inclinations. These different ranking orders are parts of very dissimilar systems of values. Some may be extremely old, for the structure of beliefs does not alter nearly as quickly as the more tangible conditions of life. In fact, they do not die at all; they just accumulate one on top of the other. Europe has always had a tradition of traditions, as our demographic and religious history makes amply clear. It is no use looking back to some imaginary classical or medieval utopia of moral and political unanimity, not to mention the horror of planning one for the future. Thinking about the vices has, indeed, the effect of showing precisely to what extent ours is a culture of many subcultures, of layer upon layer of ancient religious and class rituals, ethnic inheritances of sensibility and manners, and ideological residues whose original purpose has by now been utterly forgotten. With this in view, liberal democracy becomes more a recipe for survival than a project for the perfectibility of mankind.

Since the eighteenth century, clerical and military critics of liberalism have pictured it as a doctrine that achieves its public goods, peace, prosperity, and security by encouraging private vice. Selfishness in all its possible forms is said to be its essence, purpose, and outcome. This, it is said now as then, is inevitable once martial virtue and the discipline imposed by God are discarded. Nothing could be more remote from the truth. The very refusal to use public coercion to impose creedal unanimity and uniform standards of behavior demands an enormous degree of self-control. Tolerance consistently applied is more difficult and morally more demanding than repression. Moreover, the liberalism of fear, which makes cruelty the first vice, quite rightly recognizes that fear reduces us to mere reactive units of sensation and that this does impose a public ethos on us. One begins with what is to be avoided, as Montaigne feared being afraid most of all. Courage is to be prized, since it both prevents us from being cruel, as cowards so often are, and fortifies us against fear from threats, both physical and moral. This is, to be sure, not the courage of the armed, but that of their likely victims. This is a liberalism that was born out of the cruelties of the religious civil wars, which forever rendered the claims of Christian charity a rebuke to all religious institutions and parties. If the faith was to survive at all, it would do so privately. The alternative then set, and still before us, is not one between classical virtue and liberal self-indulgence, but between cruel military and moral repression and violence, and a self-restraining tolerance that fences in the powerful to protect the freedom and safety of every citizen, old or young, male or female, black or white. Far from being an amoral free-for-all, liberalism is, in fact, extremely difficult and constraining, far too much so for those who cannot endure contradiction, complexity, diversity, and the risks of freedom. The habits of freedom are developed, moreover, both in private and in public, and a liberal character can readily be imagined. It is, however, by definition not to be forced or even promoted by the use of political authority. That does not render the tasks of liberalism any easier, but it does not undermine its ethical structure.

In putting Montaigne and our ordinary vices in their private and public places, I have looked to literature to find those characters and situations that can tell us most about these vices. Tudor drama, so close to Montaigne in its responses to cruelty and treachery and indeed also to Machiavelli, proved particularly helpful. It is so telling because of both its differences from and far deeper similarities to and affinities with that most recent past which we call the present. I shall go on to tell stories, many very familiar, to show some of the ways (by no means all) in which the common vices are displayed and what they do to agents and patients in as many settings as possible. That is clearly not history. And it may not be philosophy in any exact way. It is too close to psychology and too remote from those arguments and counterarguments designed to avoid contradiction and exception, which define the style of philosophical discourse, to be more than prephilosophical. Nothing I have to say depends on jurisdictional disputes about intellectual territories. It may well be that the vices, and especially cruelty, escape rationalizing so completely that only stories can catch their meaning. Of this I am not entirely sure, again in keeping with Montaigne's caution and skepticism.

Cruelty, hypocrisy, snobbery, and treachery will certainly never go away. My purpose has not been to celebrate or to extirpate them, but to explore the difficulties of thinking about them. Each one has ambiguities, not least betrayal because it wounds us so deeply and yet may be insignificant in its causes and general consequences. The same may be said of snobbery, while hypocrisy is not without its social functions. This is, in short, a ramble through a moral minefield, not a march toward a destination, and these essays ought to be read in that spirit. Each one deals with one of the ordinary vices. The final chapter is a theoretical review and analysis of the whole, designed for those who have a taste for political theory; but the preceding chapters do not depend on it, and can be read separately.

P<u>utting cruelty first</u>

Everything is plundered, betrayed,
  sold,
Death's great black wing scrapes the
  air,
Misery gnaws at the bone.
Why do we not despair?

—Akhmatova

1

PHILOSOPHERS rarely talk about cruelty. They have left it to the dramatists and historians, who have not neglected it. Classical tragedy is unthinkable without physical cruelty, and comedy depends on moral cruelty, but one looks in vain for a Platonic dialogue on cruelty. Aristotle discusses only pathological bestiality, not cruelty. Cruelty is not one of the seven deadly sins, of which pride is by far the worst. The many manifestations of cupidity seem, to Saint Augustine, more important than cruelty. Revenge as part of the capital sin of anger is noted frequently by theologians in the Middle Ages. Cruel tyrants are duly reproved, and they are especially punished in Dante's *Inferno*. But the only cruelties shown in Giotto's *Vices* in Padua's Arena Chapel occur at the feet of a cold and negligent figure of Injustice. If one really wants to know what cruelty looks like, one can, of course, look at Giotto's *Last Judgment*, where every conceivable instrument of physical torture is used against the damned. One can also read Dante for such descriptions. Suffering was, to be sure, thought to be good for us and even to be a sign of blessedness. The faces of the martyrs

7

imply as much. Perhaps the extent of divinely sanctioned cruelty made it impossible to think of human cruelty as a distinct and unmitigated evil. Certainly those Christians who came to doubt the literal accounts of physical torment in hell also worried about the cruelty and vindictiveness ascribed to God.[1] By the eighteenth century these were very common concerns, especially in England, where secular humanitarianism had begun its extraordinary career. It was never to be without its enemies. Religious rigor, the theory of the survival of the fittest, revolutionary radicalism, military atavism, masculine athleticism, and other causes hostile to humanitarianism never abated. Nevertheless, taking cruelty seriously became and remained an important part of Europe's accepted morality, even in the midst of unlimited massacres. Putting cruelty *first* is, however, a matter very different from mere humaneness. To hate cruelty more than any other evil involves a radical rejection of both religious and political conventions. It dooms one to a life of skepticism, indecision, disgust, and often misanthropy. Putting cruelty first has therefore been tried only rarely, and it is not often discussed. It is too deep a threat to reason for most philosophers to contemplate it at all.

Most of us may intuitively agree about right and wrong, but we also, and far more significantly, differ enormously in the ways in which we rank the virtues and the vices. Very few people have chosen to run the emotional and social risks of putting cruelty first, to regard it as unconditionally the *summum malum*. Among moralists only Montaigne and his disciple Montesquieu can be said to have done so consistently, and it is not difficult to see why they remain rather isolated examples. To put cruelty first is to disregard the idea of sin as it is understood by revealed religion. Sins are transgressions of a divine rule and offenses against God; pride—the rejection of God—must always be the worst one, which gives rise to all the others. However, cruelty—the willful inflicting of physical pain on a weaker being in order to cause anguish and fear—is a wrong done entirely to *another creature*. When it is marked as the supreme evil it is judged so in and of itself, and not because it signifies a denial of God or any other higher norm. It is a judgment made from within the world in which cruelty occurs as part of our normal private life and our daily public practices. By putting it unconditionally first, with nothing above us to excuse or to forgive acts of cruelty, one closes off any appeal to any order other than that of actuality. To hate cruelty with utmost intensity is perfectly compatible with Biblical religiosity, but to put it *first* does place one irrevocably outside the sphere of revealed religion. For it is a purely human verdict upon human conduct and so puts religion at a certain distance. The decision to put cruelty first is not, however, prompted merely by religious skepticism. It emerges, rather, from the recognition that the habits of the faithful do not differ from those of the faithless in their brutalities, and that Machiavelli had triumphed long before he had ever written a line. To put cruelty first therefore is to be at odds not only with religion but with normal politics as well.

Why should one hate cruelty with the utmost intensity? Montaigne thought it an entirely psychological question. He looked first of all into himself and found that the sight of cruelty instantly filled him with revulsion. It was a wholly negative reaction, for, as he put it, "the horror of cruelty impels me more to clemency than any model of clemency could draw me on."[2] Pity, indeed, is often mean-spirited. It has nothing positive in it, no particular approval of charity or humane feeling except as restraints upon our cruel impulses. Montaigne distrusted soft men: they tend to be unstable and easily become cruel. Cruelty, like lying, repels instantly and easily because it is "ugly." It is a vice that disfigures human character, not a transgression of a divine or human rule. We need not doubt Montaigne's word that he simply hated cruelty, and, as he put it, "what we hate we take seriously."[3] But although his loathing of cruelty was a personal choice, it was not a random one; neither did it occur in an intellectual or historical vacuum.

ORDINARY VICES

Cruelty and Christian Practices

It is clear that well before he began to write his *Essays* Montaigne had lost most of his faith in established Christianity, though perhaps not in God. The next step for him and his contemporaries was a return to the philosophers of classical antiquity, and Montaigne never ceased to depend on their wisdom. There was, however, a danger in this neo-paganism that he could not ignore. Given his sensibilities, he was bound to recognize that Machiavelli was also a refugee from Christian restraints, that this most outspoken of enemies of revealed religion was the foremost teacher of cruelty, and that his misanthropy posed a constant moral threat. It must have seemed to Montaigne that cruelty was everywhere—the ubiquitous moral disease of Europe. He put it first among the vices because it had become the most conspicuous and the least reformed evil, especially in the course of the then-current wars of religion. The first three of the *Essays* are, therefore, not surprisingly aimed at Machiavelli. The opening one turns Machiavelli upside down. In *The Prince* Machiavelli had asked whether it was more efficient for a self-made ruler to govern cruelly or leniently, and had decided that, on the whole, cruelty worked best. Montaigne raised the question that the prince's victims might ask: Is it better to plead for pity or to display defiance in the face of cruelty? There are no certain answers, he concluded. Victims have no certainties. They must cope without guidebooks to help them. The second of the *Essays* deals with the sadness of those whose children and friends die. And the third suggests that one might take precautions against the terrors of princes. If there were an established review of the deeds of princes as soon as they died, their passion for posthumous fame might restrain them here and now. Indeed, Machiavelli had noted that an indiscriminate butcher was not likely to enjoy the best of reputations in history, even if he should have succeeded in all his enterprises. He would be cheated of his full share of glory. Machiavelli did not say whether this warning would prove effective; but if one considers Marlowe's Tamburlaine, driven by his passion for fame from slaughter to slaughter, one doubts that the fear of a blemished record might have restrained him. Montaigne was only too aware of the cruelty of ambitious princes who were driven by the passion for fame, and he did not really place much hope in any restraining devices. But by reading *The Prince* as a victim of princely cruelty might read it, Montaigne set a great distance between his own and Machiavelli's classicism. Putting cruelty first was thus an instant reaction to the new science of politics. It did not reconcile Montaigne to revealed religion. Indeed, it reinforced his conviction that Christianity had done nothing to inhibit cruelty. He could not even admit that his hatred of cruelty was a residual form of Christian morality. On the contrary, putting cruelty first exacerbated his antagonism to an established religiosity that seemed to him hypocritical at best, and actively cruel at worst.

For both Montaigne and Montesquieu after him, the failure of Christianity from a moral point of view was made perfectly manifest by the conduct of the Spaniards in the New World. These conquerors were no longer mere historical figures, but actors in a timeless morality play. Montaigne regarded them as the supreme example of the failure of Christianity. It preached a purer doctrine than any other religion but had less influence on human conduct. Mohammedans and pagans tended to behave better than Christians. What an opportunity was lost when the New World was discovered by Spaniards! How might the New World have flourished if Greek and Roman virtues had been introduced to the natives! Instead there was unexampled slaughter for the sake of gold, with hypocritical talk of conversions to Christianity; for hypocrisy and cruelty go together and are, as it were, unified in zeal. Zeal had taken the place of both religion and philosophy, and it works wonders "when it seconds our propensity to hatred, cruelty, ambition, avarice, detraction, rebellion," and the like.[4] This indictment went well beyond the tradition of Christian reformers, who had always invoked the memory of Christ and the Apostles to rebuke a wayward Church. To Montaigne the distance between profession and behavior appeared unbridgeable. Montesquieu did use the image of a charitable Christ to shame a cruel Inquisitor, but only ironically, for he put the argument into the mouth of an Iberian Jew. For Montesquieu the overt professions of religiosity no longer mattered. All religions were to be treated as forms of social control—necessary but not, on the whole, admirable. The deluded Spaniards were, to be sure, "superbly Christian" as they went about their slaughter; but in fact they were like all other conquerors, past and present. We are meant to feel more than a touch of disgust at this species of cruelty so liberally laced with piety.

The Spaniards, as Montesquieu saw them, had created a new nightmare world. They had not only through prejudice "renounced all gentle and humane feelings," but they had also contrived to reorder reality. When they encountered a population with habits and an appearance unlike their own, they found it easy to say that God could not have put souls into such ugly bodies, that clearly those creatures lacked the higher rational qualities. Once the Spaniards had begun their cruelties, it became especially important to say that "it is impossible to suppose these creatures to be men, because allowing them to be men a suspicion might arise that we were not Christian."[5] For both Montesquieu and Montaigne the Spaniards in the New World served as the ultimate example of public cruelty. It was the triumph of Machiavellianism by those who claimed to be its chief opponents. Here cruelty and pious pretense had joined to prove Machiavelli right.

Because cruelty is made easier by hypocrisy and self-deception, these two vices are bound to stand high on the list that begins with cruelty. And in fact Uzbek, the intelligent and cruel tyrant of Montesquieu's *Persian Letters,* is typically self-deceived. He believes that the women who are tormented in his seraglio all love him, since they are all so unlike him. Dishonesty becomes here less a violation of truth than an aid to cruelty. And other traditional vices that are remote from cruelty did not shock Montesquieu at all. He was not disturbed by any manifestation of genuine affection, even if it was incestuous. This was a radical intellectual gesture, which signaled how far putting cruelty first had taken him from all traditions. And Montaigne regarded the knot of lying, treachery, malice, and cruelty as far worse than adultery, so much berated by other moralists. Lust, in fact, was not a fault at all. We are, Montaigne argued, made infinitely worse by our self-hatred in performing the most natural and necessary of acts. What could be more appalling than to hide in the dark as we create a new life, while we destroy life with whoops of joy in broad daylight as we cry "kill, rob, betray"?[6] It was this transvaluation of values that took Montaigne well beyond the mere rejection of Christian doctrine. Indeed, it put him outside most of the conventions of his world. The contempt that Europeans felt for their physical nature was, in his view, just one more sign of mankind's general moral imbecility.

In spite of their own advice and habitual good humor, hatred of cruelty reduced both Montaigne and Montesquieu to a profound philosophical misanthropy. Montesquieu was a master of black humor and satire, while Montaigne gave way to outbursts of loathing for his fellow men. It was in such a moment of concentrated disgust that he decided it was better to laugh than to cry at mankind, because the former "expresses more disdain"—which is appropriate, since "we can never be despised more than we deserve."[7] It is not even a matter of intelligent evil, but of inanity. Misanthropy is surely one of the hazards of putting cruelty first. If cruelty horrifies us we must, given the facts of daily life, always be in a state of outrage, overwhelmed like Hamlet by the density of evil. Montaigne was neither so paralyzed nor so desperate as to hope that mankind might simply stop reproducing itself, as Hamlet suggested to Ophelia, but at times he could not think of a single thing to say in favor of humanity. For positive qualities he therefore looked to those ultimate victims of human cruelty, the animals. The immediate impulse and strategy of those who put cruelty first is to look to the victims for moral reassurance.

Animals are our moral superiors in every significant way, according to Montaigne. They seek only "tangible" and

13

"attainable" goods, whereas we have only "wind and smoke" as our portion.[8] They have an unimpaired sense of reality, seeking only repose, security, health, and peace, whereas we pursue reason, knowledge, and renown, which bring us nothing but grief. With the exception of the bees, they want only to preserve themselves, and know nothing of war or terror. Pyrrho's pig, untroubled by a storm at sea, had no more ardent admirer than Montaigne. Montesquieu thought that compared to the animals we are nature's step-children, because animals do not seem "to make so bad a use of their passions" as we do.[9] But Montaigne thought that nature was entirely fair. We have only ourselves to blame for our follies and cruelties. Although he was de-voted to Lucretius, he could not accept the latter's melan-choly picture of nature's mindless destructiveness. That would have taken cruelty entirely out of the realm of human choice and morality and would have made it our fate—that is, an invitation to complacency. Montaigne compared men to animals not to condemn nature but to re-veal human folly, especially the sort that looks down on sentient, physical life. No greater mark of idiocy seemed imaginable than the doctrine that man was the best of crea-tures, destined to lord it over the vegetable and animal kingdoms. The result is that we are encouraged from our earliest years to be cruel to plants and beasts. What, in fact, could be more absurd than that "this miserable and puny creature, who is not so much as master of himself . . . should call himself master and emperor of the universe?"[10] Such is the extremity of misanthropy to which one is driven if one looks at people through the eyes of our chief victims, plants and animals.

The need to escape from such a degree of misanthropy is particularly obvious if one is led to it by the hatred of cru-elty. Surely, loathing one's kind and oneself is hardly the best cure for cruelty. It leads us into Machiavelli's realm. The temptation is therefore great not only to identify wholly with the victims, but to idealize them and to attrib-ute improbable virtues to them. That is how Montaigne came to overrate the animals and the peasants. Montesquieu overestimated the Jews, at least for the purposes of political argument. Dickens idolized children, and Euripides' women are too superb. It is, of course, a perfect way to shame the cruel, but more significantly it is the only way to avoid the nausea of misanthropy. The victims must redeem mankind. The virtues most becoming to them are fortitude and pride, and it is these that are usually ascribed to them. Pride may be a deadly sin for those who preach faith and meekness, but it recommends itself to those who put cruelty first. They appreciate the magnificent pride of Webster's tortured Duchess of Malfi, for whom "integrity of life" was everything. In Montesquieu's *Persian Letters*, Roxanne, one of Uzbek's wives in the harem, commits suicide as a final act of defiance and as a means of escaping from the seraglio. In this she demonstrates not only her own courage but also her superiority to her owner, who contemplates suicide because he is bored and frustrated—a despot desiring to quit this life because his existence has no cosmic significance. His chatter is typical of a tyrant's self-importance, whereas Roxanne's death is an act of heroism and liberation.

Thinking about the Victims: Then and Now

Valor was for Montaigne a great virtue, even though he was often unsure of even that. He could dissociate it from aggression by recognizing its perfection only in the dignity of defeated soldiers, not in victorious ones. Only the Indian kings conquered by the marauding Spaniards displayed valor as a spiritual rather than as a merely physical quality. Their invincible courage was a dignified refusal to placate their conquerors, and not just a desire to triumph. Peasants, always victimized, lived in resignation and died without making a fuss. That, to Montaigne, was also a form of valor. Montesquieu's Jews held philosophical discourses in sight of the stake and openly held fast to the faith of their fathers, without deceit. That was not their only virtue. They, and they alone, engaged in commercial activities in spite of

Christian persecutions and prohibitions. They thus preserved for Europe the social activity most likely to save it
from war and Machiavellianism. For the spirit of commerce
is the spirit of peace. It may destroy the highest Platonic
virtues and create awful individuals, but it was all for the
public good, and a great civilizing force. Montaigne, who
lived in an earlier age, would not have understood this improbable hope. As an aristocrat he found it peculiarly horrible that the Spaniards had turned a beautiful country
upside down merely "for a traffic in pearls and pepper."[11]

For Montaigne only pure aristocratic valor, courage as a
style of life, deserved admiration and a claim to noble
standing. It is the obverse of cruelty—the expression of
cowardice—for valor is generous. We must note, however,
how often valor appears to make people indifferent to
others, for its aim is self-perfection. It serves to satisfy a heroic self-image. Valor can be an extreme of individualism.
In its military context, Montaigne could see it occasionally
as the comradeship among brave men, and he admired it as
he valued the company of his peers. He could do this without considering the purpose that brought them together:
war, which he despised. "War," he wrote, is "the testimony
of our imbecility and imperfection."[12] Montaigne was not
the first or last man to be puzzled by the fact that the most
brutal of all social enterprises should also be the occasion of
so much personal nobility, fellowship, and courage. Montaigne not only detested war; he particularly did not admire
victors. Winning wars, to him, was entirely a matter of Fortune. Unlike Machiavelli, he did not think that Fortune was
a woman to be manhandled by determined and aggressive
princes. Fortune, he thought, was the sum of uncontrollable
and unpredictable circumstances. Alexander the Great and
Julius Caesar were merely its beneficiaries. Conquerors, in
short, are deprived of all merit. Their victories are not due
to their efforts or character. Only victims can rise to true
fortitude, because Fortune has obviously deserted them.
The glamour of glory is quite gone. What matters is how
bravely one endures defeat. Putting cruelty first may in this
way lead one to an ideology of heroic self-destruction. And

indeed Socrates as the dignified suicide was Montaigne's ideal figure. Cato's showy act seemed to him very inferior.

There is surely something disturbing about idealizing the defeated as Montaigne did. They, too, are pawns of Fortune, no better than her favorites. They are just losers. To favor them extravagantly is, however, a way of escaping from misanthropy and of finding an ethos that, unlike revealed religion, leads neither to zeal nor to cruelty. Valor as a defiant refusal to live as a slave or a victim may be a recipe for isolation and potential suicide. It is also the pride that saves without attacking. But to think thus may be unfair to the victims. They are being used untruthfully, as a means to nourish our self-esteem and to control our own fears. They are forced to serve the onlookers. Who indeed knows how best to think about victims? Since anyone can become a victim, they are merely a fair sample of all mankind. Victimhood happens to us: it is not a quality. What, moreover, can one do for or to those victims who are killed, not merely injured? With so many occasions and so much time to consider victims, we have not really improved upon Montaigne and Montesquieu. Victimhood may have become an inescapable category of political thought, but it remains an intractable notion. We are often not even sure who the victims are. Are the tormentors who may once have suffered some injustice or deprivation also victims? Are only those whom they torment victims? Are we all victims of our circumstances? Can we all be divided into victims and victimizers at any moment? And may we not all change parts in an eternal drama of mutual cruelty? Every question about responsibility, history, personal independence, and public freedom and every mental disposition haunts us when we begin to think about victims. That has become especially so thanks to the great massacres of our age. We too have been driven to adopt some of the expedients to which Montaigne and Montesquieu resorted, to protect ourselves against utter despondency.

The extent of the more recent slaughters, however, has made it particularly difficult to single out the heroic few and to ignore the silent millions. To forget the many would be to falsify the experiences of the survivors by embellishing the past. The victims were, like all of us, ordinary people who suffered extraordinary cruelties. How are we to think about them? One way of making them useful is to remember them abusively. Why did the Jews go to their death like sheep? Put that way, it is a shocking and false charge. One might as well ask why there are any victims at all. This is, to be sure, not meant as a question, but to evoke a necessary response: "never again!" Nevertheless, as Bruno Bettelheim has reminded us, it is simply unacceptable to speak of these people as dumb beasts.[13] It is an intolerable insult to their friends and relations and it shows an unseeing, retrospective malice. Once the Jews were in the camps, only an outside force could have saved them, and none was forthcoming. Nevertheless, Bettelheim does blame those individuals and groups that did not do as much as they could have to make things more difficult for the Germans. Some lives might have been saved by obstructive behavior. He presses these charges against the victims because he does not want to absolve them of all responsibility. To do so would be to remember them as less than human, as beings without will or intelligence. As long as they were alive they had responsibilities, and to deny that, or to ignore their errors and to speak only of those who did act heroically, would be unjust to the dead and to the survivors. If the victims could not fail, they were not human, and one might as well call them sheep. To say less than Bettelheim does would be demeaning, but to claim more can be utterly wrong. In the end it is not the victims but the torturers and persecutors who are guilty. To blame the victims for their own suffering is simply an easy way to distance oneself from them. Blaming the victims is just like idealizing them—at best superfluous, perhaps a sign of the difficulty of facing cruelty at all.

It is, however, not only undignified to idealize political victims; it is also very dangerous. One of our political actualities is that the victims of political torture and injustice are often no better than their tormentors. They are only waiting to change places with the latter. Of course, if one puts cruelty first this makes no difference. It does not matter whether the victim of torture is a decent man or a villain. No one deserves to be subjected to the appalling instruments of cruelty. Nevertheless, even at the cost of misanthropy, one cannot afford to pretend that victimhood improves anyone in any way. If we do not remember that anyone can be a victim, and if we allow hatred for torture, or pity for pain, to blind us, we will unwittingly aid the torturers of tomorrow by overrating the victims of today. One may be too easily tempted to think of all victims as equally innocent because there cannot, by definition, be a voluntary victim. That may have the consequence of promoting an endless exchange of cruelties between alternating tormentors and victims.

Unreasonable as this may seem, there actually is a serious philosophical justification for such a scenario. Jean-Paul Sartre, in his early writings, saw this as the true situation of mankind. He began with the incontrovertible fact that victims are created by their tormentors. The Jews, in this view, are entirely the creations of anti-Semitism.[14] That is not, of course, meant as a historical account, but as a definition of Jews as the victims of the moment (in 1946 they surely were, but there have been many others since then). One could do worse than attend to Sartre's account of the anti-Semite as a "cowardly malcontent" who has "chosen to be terrifying." Thanks to the stereotype that he forces upon the Jew, the latter is so overdetermined by his social definition that he has no choice except either to flee from reality or to accept himself as a Jew and act his part as a victim authentically. That, as Sartre notes, takes courage, and more than courage. It seems that Sartre had, in fact, simply returned to Montaigne and to the whole stoic tradition that made valor the highest virtue, the glory of the victims—indeed, their moral triumph over adversity and their craven tormentors. The victim's courage cannot help him out of his doom, but he can transform himself within his situation by bravely asserting his worth—in this case as a Jew, in another age as an Indian warrior. Likewise, the slave may yet overcome the master by revolt or suicide. The victim as hero represents the possibility of universal human freedom, even in chains.

There is, however, a great difference between Sartre's and Montaigne's views on victimhood. Sartre believed in a transforming future. Helpless though Sartre's Jew is, even he will eventually be liberated by the war to end all classes. Of this Montaigne had not yet heard; but he had read the same historians as Machiavelli and shared the classical view that all states rise, decay, and fall. Unlike Machiavelli, he did not suggest that one interfere with this cycle by dominating Fortune. Like all enterprises that are in some way dependent on the forces of history, Machiavelli's plot against its ups and downs was marked by cruel enormities. Montaigne thought such schemes to be as futile as they were cruel. Fortune was to limit us, not encourage us, in our zeal. When the clerical authorities asked him to take out all references to Fortune, he simply refused.[15] Sartre's victims, however, are crushed by a historic force as exigent as Machiavelli's Fortune. The passive courage of Sartre's Jews is only a present necessity. They, and all other victims, are not meant to be the enduring moral monuments or the personal heroes that Montaigne's Indian victims were made to be. The hope at the end of the historical tunnel is, in fact, the alleviation of a misanthropy far deeper than that of even the darkest of Montaigne's pages. Especially if one knows that the road to liberation is endless and littered with cruelties that are self-perpetuating, this is a grim sort of hope.

The darkness of Sartre's picture deepens when one looks beyond the anti-Semite and the Jew. These two are merely examples of the universal cognitive situation of all human beings. We are all victims and victimizers in that we perceive one another as objects of observation; we all look upon one another as things. Some, to escape this uneasy subjugation, turn to sadism. They become the fear they inspire. They see themselves as they have forced others to see them, as cruel. The anti-Semite is merely an extreme case of this self-escaping ploy. In either case, it is an inauthentic effort to run away from oneself as both victim and victimizer, slave and master. The sadist simply cannot bear the double burden of limits and possibilities. A more honest relationship between authentic beings would appear to be one of complete mutual indifference. For we are all alike in being obstacles to one another. This misanthropic egoism is what Montaigne might have come to without friendship. In Sartre it was relieved by a theory of action imported from the doctrine of class war. Although we are indeed less than nothing to one another as individuals, we must take sides historically among the classes. Of these, there are now only two— the victims and the other oppressors, easily recognized as such. No one has any alternative except to be for one or the other. There is no escape from this Manichaean situation: either for us or against us. And in such struggles everything is permitted. The victim can learn to respect himself only through violence if he is not to remain an individual overdetermined by another, as the Jew is by the anti-Semite and the slave by the master. As a "world-historical" class victim he must learn to play his part, cruelly. Is this meant to be an escape from the nausea, indifference, and misanthropy which is our lot as individuals? That can be the case. At best we shall be able to live peacefully in mutual contempt at the end of class-dominated history.[16] Nevertheless, revolutionary rage is a response to human cruelty, even if it is a self-immolating fantasy. It is one way to "hate cruelty cruelly," but in a way very remote from that of Montaigne, who first used the phrase. Those who now claim to hate cruelty cruelly do so in the Machiavellian manner and in the belief that cruelty is endlessly effective, even in putting an end to itself. The strength of this view, and of Sartre's, is its unwavering concentration on the torturers, on the victimizers both in private and public life. No one who takes cruelty seriously can forget about them. But like Montaigne, one will not be tempted to accept those ideological distortions that make it easy to become zealously cruel. It is nevertheless extraordinary how easily misanthropy moves even the most determined loners to a worship of violent collective public action. That is the work of ideology, and like Fortune and necessity in an earlier age, it serves as an excuse for every kind of political cruelty now.

It is one task of ideology to identify victims and victimizers on any given occasion. Its clients adhere to it in order to receive instant guidance. People who do not choose to abandon their own judgment may, in contrast, face the most devastating uncertainties. There is an unforgettable scene in Nadine Gordimer's *Burger's Daughter* in which Rosa is confronted by a black drunk who is beating an agonized, heaving donkey. She cannot bring herself to stop him, because he is the real victim in her eyes. He is "black, poor and brutalized," and as a white South African she is "accountable for him, to him," as he is for the beast. Rosa Burger is not the sort of woman who cares more for animals than for black people. Nevertheless she recognizes in that cruel raised arm *every* torturer throughout the ages. At that moment, she decides she cannot stay any longer in her country. This is not, as it might seem at first, an assumption of collective guilt. Rosa is torn between putting cruelty or political oppression first. If the victim were a woman or a child, would she still go away? According to her own principles, she would have to abandon them, too. In contrast, if she were to put cruelty first, she would recognize the immediately suffering, abused being as the primary victim and would interfere in either case. But as she has put oppression first, it is not illogical for her to say that it inflicts injuries deeper than those of physical cruelty and to refuse to call the white police. To choose between these two evils is simply too difficult, and Rosa can bear no more. When she eventually returns to South Africa, she does so for reasons of loyalty and courage that reveal her to be the heroine of a classical tragedy. And though she is very self-deprecating, we can see her strength of character especially in her refusal to pretend that either decision would have been obvious or flawless. Putting cruelty first might help one to decide who the victim at any moment is, but not without some very real doubts and uncertainties, of just the sort that ideologies disperse so readily. To have standards is not a way of avoiding doubt; only faith can offer us that, and then only at vast intellectual and moral cost.

For all our wealth of historical experience, we do not know how to think about victimhood. Almost everything one might say would be unfair, self-serving, undignified, untrue, self-deluding, contradictory, or dangerous. Perhaps the best intellectual response is simply to write the history of the victims and victimizers as truthfully and accurately as possible. That may well be the most useful and enduring accomplishment. But no history, however attentive to the evidence and however discriminating, can tell us how to think about victimhood. Putting cruelty first is only an incentive to do so; it also leaves us in a state of indecision and doubt. How are we to begin?

Courage: Physical and Moral

Montaigne thought that one should measure the courage and cowardice of the victims and agents of cruelty at the very moment of violence. When he said of himself "it is fear that I stand most in fear of," he was thinking of both the victims and the victimizers.[17] Fear makes the latter cruel and increases the suffering of the former. If we could learn not to fear the void after death, killing would lose both its appeal and its apprehension. The infliction of pain would remain; but Montaigne insisted, in spite of the explicit objections of the ecclesiastical censors, that any punishment beyond mere killing was cruel. However, he seems to have thought that a more rational view of death would do much to discourage cruelty generally. Montesquieu already knew better. Much as he admired the stoic temper he did not think that a dispassionate attitude to death would in any way decrease our cruelty. He thought it might be better if we thought of men as sentient rather than as rational beings. Uzbek, his tyrant, is indeed a model of enlightened rationality and free from any fears of the afterlife, but he is as cruel as the next despot. Valor in the face of death might be admirable, but it did not seem to Montesquieu to lessen mankind's murderous propensities. In either case, learning how to die is hardly a social virtue. Isolation may in fact be one of the costs of putting cruelty first. It leads to an ethic for the isolated, which is the condition of victims.

If victims have more to fear than fear, then there is more

to cruelty than cowardice, in spite of Montaigne and so many others before and since his time. Because cowards are so often cruel, one begins to think of courage as the very opposite of cruelty. But this is simply not the case. One need think only of the cruelty of Machiavelli's leonine princes, who are ruthless and yet admired because they are so brave. Nevertheless, courage does in some way improve cruel actions. Why is it that wanton pain inflicted upon helpless beings, especially children and animals, is so revolting? Why does the defenselessness of these victims move even quite harsh people? There is a cluster of reactions at work here, among which contempt for cowardice must surely be one. Compassion certainly plays its part. If pity is an instant identification with a weak suffering being, then the fact that we all were children once, and remember our vulnerability, readily accounts for the normal response to the torturing of children. However, we pity all sufferers, not only the pain of the weak victims of cruelty. The object of compassion could be simply ill or even a patient undergoing a painful but necessary treatment. Pity does not seem to be the only element in our response to cruelty to the helpless; a sense of injustice must be added. No child can deserve brutality. Punishment is justifiably inflicted in the service of retribution, education, or public security; but if it goes away from, or beyond, these ends we call it "cruel and unusual" and forbid its use. Montesquieu's impartial state had no other end than "to protect the security of the innocent."

The injustice of cruelty obviously does arouse outrage, but that does not completely account for one's horror at the brutalization of children. Only those who put injustice absolutely as the first of evils might even think so. Such people would also say that in wartime one should spare defenseless civilians because they have not consented to the war to the same degree as have soldiers armed for battle. Consent is assumed to create a mutual right to take military action, and civilians cannot be said to have agreed to that, since they are unarmed. But common sense simply rebels against this legalistic distortion of experience. Surely it is the helplessness of civilians that exempts them from attack, not the absence of such consent as might be imputed to a conscript who is shooting at another draftee. It is thought to be crueler to sack a town than to kill armed men, but not because civilians suffer more pain or are more innocent. It is not only pity or a sense of justice that moves us. The sheer absence of courage also makes a cruel act naked, as it were. Without the courage required to overcome the fear of genuine dangers such as those that men face in battle, cruelty is unmitigated by any compensating virtue. There are no extenuations and no veils. It is pure, unalloyed cruelty. The character of those who loot and ravage and who destroy women and children is one of enraged cruelty and nothing else. A brave soldier is simply a less repulsive character than a cowardly one. An armed foe at least has a chance to assert himself, to force his opponent to an effort of courage. He is, in short, neither as helpless nor as pitiable as an unarmed civilian. Conquerors in battle also display courage, and that alters the entire situation. Long before the Christian era, Thucydides brought that out very vividly in his account of the sack of the town of Myclanus. "The Thracian race, like the bloodiest of the barbarians, being ever most so *when it has nothing to fear*, killed every living thing in the town, children, old people, even animals." In particular, they attacked a boys' school and massacred all the children in it. Nothing, according to Thucydides, during that whole long war came near this sack "in suddenness and horror."[18] Thucydides had recounted all the cruelties of protracted war, and there were many; but this barbarism was the most contemptible because it was so cowardly. There was nothing to fear. Courage did not clothe this brutality.

War was to convince Montaigne that valor was not enough. Without pity to restrain us and justice to instruct princes, there were no ramparts against mutual destruction. He had, in fact, begun his essays with reflections on pity and valor in the face of cruelty in war. With little trust in justice, there was nothing to stem his misanthropy other than a belief in the heroism of victims and in the moral modesty of the peasants—socially, the least of the least.

Valor, in any case, has a better private than a public face. That was why Montesquieu abandoned it, even if not entirely without regret. Commerce does not promote those highest aristocratic virtues. It does not make good men or valiant patriots, but it does cure our public life of some of its worst ills. It reduces Machiavellianism, instability, and war. By exchanging valor for greed, we significantly reduce large-scale cruelty. The best modern state, in Montesquieu's view, had no more use for valor than for pity or for any other private virtue. It sticks to one and only one virtue: justice. Implicitly, moreover, moral fortitude had replaced physical valor, for it is not at all clear that a nation of complete cowards could be just. The security and liberty of the citizen depend, if one is to accept Montesquieu's portrait of the English, on conduct that might be zany, but also vigorous and morally brave.

Even at its misanthropic worst, Montesquieu's political theory was less intensely negative than Montaigne's immense *no* to the world of cruelty and pretense. A confidence in trade and law seems quite reassuring, even if it is based on the sacrifice of the higher virtues. However, the mental worlds of those who put cruelty first, in spite of such deep differences as this, retain some deep similarities, especially an easy acceptance of cultural variety and a negative egalitarianism. Since the most spectacular public brutalities are usually visited upon alien peoples, Montaigne and Montesquieu were both bound to investigate the justifications offered for the slaughter and enslavement of barbarians. The oldest and most common argument has been that barbarians are naturally inferior. Since nature was taken to issue rules of conduct, it was clear that she intended Europeans to enslave those lesser peoples whom she had marked out by color for that very purpose. Montaigne entirely agreed that nature was indeed our best guide to good conduct. It was therefore a matter of some importance to him whether or not the differences between cultures were indeed natural, and which, if any, were inferior and superior, when judged in terms of their habitual cruelty. Barbarism, he soon discovered, was anything that "does not fit in with our usages."

Every people seems barbaric to some other tribe. Moreover, the endless multiplicity of customs and opinions which he loved to list proved that not one of them stood out as natural. All were human contrivances. There is nothing that is not decent or indecent somewhere. All are departures from nature's original simplicity, and their variety proves only how insignificant they are, for "nature puts to shame our vain and trivial efforts."[19] Customs as such are all equidistant from nature, and the differences are therefore unimportant in themselves. What does matter is who is cruel. Cannibals eat the flesh of dead people and we recoil in horror, but it is we who torture and persecute the living. Our pride is unwarranted. There are no naturally superior or inferior peoples; but arrogance and cruelty mark Europeans, not those whom they disdain as barbarians. There was, in fact, a vein of primitivism in Montaigne, but that is not necessary to his purpose. Montesquieu did not share it, and he no longer looked to nature for human standards at all. He nevertheless also used the variety of customs to undermine the pride of European civilization. It was simply a matter of exposing the triviality of the excuses offered for the enormous harms inflicted on primitive peoples. "Because the negroes prefer a glass necklace to gold . . . it is proven that they have no common sense." American Indians trimmed their beards in an unfamiliar manner, so they were legally enslaved by the Spaniards. Unlike Montaigne, Montesquieu knew enough not to dwell on any fancied superiority of the native peoples. It was enough to show that no difference could ever justify cruelty. Montesquieu had, moreover, another reason for wanting his readers to know and understand all the cultures: he really believed that "knowledge makes men gentle," just as ignorance hardens us. Not the primitive but the supracivilized may recover from cruelty after all.

For Montesquieu, all inferiority and superiority were the creations of policy. Once we enslave aliens, whom in our ignorance we despise, we reduce them to inferiority. Slavery makes imbeciles, not the other way around. "Nothing makes one more like a beast than always to see free men without being oneself free."[20] Once men have been reduced by enslavement, cruelty acts to make the distance between owner and slave even greater. In Asia, Montesquieu claimed, black slaves were castrated for that reason. And in *The Persian Letters*, black eunuchs are employed to maintain a steady flow of submission and dominance in the harem. They are the tools of their common owner, who rules all by remote control. As one of the speakers in Euripides' *Hecuba* comments, "This is what it means to be a slave: to be abused and bear it, compelled by violence to suffer wrong." The meaning of extreme inequality has never really been defined better. If such social distances create the climate for cruelty, then less inequality may be a remedy. Even Machiavelli knew that one cannot rule one's equals with cruelty, but only one's inferior subjects. Montesquieu occasionally praised those ancient democracies whose frugality and equality made the citizens unable or unwilling to lord it over one another. And Montaigne came to admire the simplicity of the peasantry, whose relations to one another, he thought, were better regulated than those of the nobility. But this was just a rejection of aristocratic competitiveness, not a reflection on inequality as a social situation. And indeed, neither Montaigne nor Montesquieu was at all disposed to treat social equality as a positive good. Inequality mattered inasmuch as it encouraged and created opportunities for cruelty. Theirs was a purely negative egalitarianism rooted in a suspicion of the paltry reasons offered to justify not merely inequality, but its worst consequences.

Inequality, moreover, generates illusions. Montaigne thought that it dims our common sense so badly that we forget that "the pedestal is no part of the statue."[21] This was more than the usual complaint that we fail to value real merit because we are easily taken in by mere finery and trappings. What Montaigne feared was the pure glamour of power, the show of valor that accompanies it, and the cruelty that both encourage. And Montesquieu was, thanks to Versailles and all it stood for, obsessed by the destructive power of courtly show. The court creates around the despot a vacuum that separates him from his subjects, and this is the prerequisite for the maximum both of inequality and of potential and actual cruelty. Nothing, then, could be more dangerous than the deification of political superiors. The desacralization of politics was, in fact, one of Montesquieu's chief objects. Equality was not required for that, and he preferred a hierarchical pluralism, tempered by such egalitarian institutions as the jury chosen by lot. For juries determine the outcome of those occasions when the ordinary citizen is confronted by the criminal law and its physical impact. Negative egalitarianism is really a fear of the consequences of inequality, and especially of the dazzling effect of power, which frees its holders from all restraints. It is an obvious corollary of putting cruelty first.

Not equality but modesty is the cure for arrogance. And no form of arrogance is more obnoxious than the claim that some of us are God's agents, his deputies on earth charged with punishing God's enemies. It was, after all, in defense of the divine honor that all those heretics had been tortured and burned. Montaigne saw that torture had infected the entire official world, both secular and ecclesiastical. It had become the ubiquitous evil. Montesquieu, living in a relatively milder age, was still outraged by the judicial prosecution of sins and minor faults. That was partly because neither one cared about these sins any longer, but also because they put cruelty first. The crimes so brutally punished were not themselves acts of cruelty. They therefore appeared particularly unimportant precisely when put in contrast to the horrors of official torture. Montesquieu advised the courts to leave belief and sexual habits alone and to concentrate on the serious business of protecting the security of life and property. Montaigne had no faith in even this kind of legal reform. He thought most laws useless, because general rules never really fit the actual diversity of individual cases and because most judicial procedures are so cruel that they terrify law-abiding citizens without achieving much else. He and Montesquieu were at one, however, in insisting that the discretion of judges must be as limited as possible. That expressed a considerable distrust of the judiciary in general. This should not surprise us; both were, after all, experienced magistrates, who had spent years on the bench at Bordeaux. They did not trust any ruling class, certainly not their own.

Skeptical Politics

The wisdom of experience only enhances the skepticism of those who put cruelty first. How could it be otherwise? The usual excuse for our most unspeakable public acts is that they are necessary. How genuine are these necessities, in fact? Neither Montaigne nor Montesquieu was blind to the imperatives of law and of reason of state, but they knew that much of what passed under these names was merely princely willfulness. To respond to danger is one thing, but "necessity" in the Machiavellian vocabulary means far more than that. It expresses a great confidence in controlling events once they have been intelligently analyzed. To master necessity is to rule. It is, together with the subduing of Fortune, quite within the power of an astute ruler. Once necessity has been mapped and grasped, it is just a matter of plotting and executing. This is the utopianism of efficiency, with all the cruelty and treachery that it invites. Montaigne thought that politics were far too chaotic and uncertain to be managed according to any plan. He dismissed Machiavelli as being no more plausible than any other political schemer, and just as short-sighted as most. In sum, Montaigne did not think these amoral arguments conclusive. They did not really amount to rational responses to any necessities. But when one doubts necessity, one doubts everything. If princes must commit atrocities, let them at least regret it and let them make some effort to avoid going to war in order to indulge some personal whim, Montaigne concluded.

In this Montaigne was not original. Euripides had recognized the cowardice behind political cruelty long ago. The abominations justified by necessity are rarely more than princely fear, not only of foreign enemies, but, as in Agamemnon's case, for the ruler's own prestige. Who could be both morally and physically more craven than Agamemnon, ready to sacrifice his daughter to the superstitions of an army and to his rivals for power? Iphigenia's courage and selflessness make his instability stand out all the more clearly. In Euripides' Trojan plays, only the crushed and tormented women have either dignity or valor; the heroes are a pack of cowards. After Troy has been utterly destroyed, Polynestor kills Hecuba's last son, even though he himself raised the boy. His action, he explains, "was dictated, as you shall see," by a policy of wise precaution. "My primary motive was fear, fear that if this boy, your enemy, survived, he might some day found a second and insurgent Troy" (*Hecuba*, 1136–39).[22] When in *The Trojan Women* the Greeks with the same political caution hurl Hector's little boy from a wall, Hecuba cries as she cradles the broken body of the child,

> Now when this city is fallen, and the Phrygians slain,
> this baby terrified you? I despise the fear
> which is pure terror in a mind unreasoning.
> (*The Trojan Women*, 1164–65)

The heroic ethos has never taken a worse beating than it received from Euripides' noble women. In all these plays the Machiavellian fox, Odysseus, makes the cruel calculations of politics—calculations that barely hide the personal ambitions and, above all, the fears of these military heroes. If we really prize valor highly, we may have to reject its military expressions and cease to be impressed by the claims of its necessities. Montaigne did, and soon his skepticism grew until it embraced every convention of the public order and all the accepted usages of private life. The passion for fame and glory appeared to be only another vain and fear-ridden ambition to overcome death. The very contemplation of any life—or just renown—beyond the grave seemed to create the psychic terrain for cruelty. Montaigne preferred to enjoy life, and to think of death without fear or hope.

There is no temper that is less utopian than this sort of skepticism. "The world is incapable of curing itself; it is so impatient of the weight that oppresses it that it only aims at getting rid of it, without considering the cost," Montaigne wrote.[23] Montesquieu had more faith in legislation and social change, but he was not an enthusiast. In *The Persian Letters* he wrote an account of a little utopian community. But even in this imaginary world, utopia appears to prove only that it must quickly end. Age and continuity are the best recommendations for institutions, not because they are anything but "barbarous" and "monstrous," Montaigne argued, but because "we wonderfully incline to the worst."[24] Most of our laws and customs are beneath contempt, but if we alter them we fall into instability and direct destruction, which might well be worse. A decent but not excessive loyalty to the existing order without excuses seemed to him the only way. To that extent he had chosen sides in the civil war, since it could not be avoided. But he remained fair to the opposition. As an admiring Emerson was to write of him, he found himself "equally at odds with the evils of society and with the projects that are offered to relieve them"; Montaigne "denies out of honesty."[25] Honesty in this case meant that Montaigne saw no reason to suppose that changes in belief altered human behavior significantly. Those who have attempted to correct the world by new beliefs, he noted wearily, have removed only the surface vices; the essential ones have not been touched. The best religion, therefore, with peace in view, is the one into which one is born—the one most established in one's country and the one which one is most used to. This is not an attempt to disregard the enormous faults of existing ideologies and institutions. It is, rather, the recognition that the alternatives are no better. It is the conservatism of universal disgust, if it is conservatism at all. For in what sense can one be said to support an existing order of affairs if one cannot think of anything to say on its behalf except that it is there? It is an act of perfect dissociation, but not necessarily a retreat from the public world.

When one begins with cruelty, as Montaigne did, an enormous gap between private and public life seems to open up. It begins with the exposure of the feebleness and pettiness of the reasons offered for public enormities, and goes on to a sense that governments are unreal and remote from the actualities about which they appear to talk. It is not that private life is better than public: both are equally cruel. It is, rather, that one has a sense of the incoherence and discontinuity of private and public experience. Montesquieu thought that it was impossible that the good man and the good citizen should ever be the same. The two were inherently incompatible. The demands of social life and those of personal morality are simply different. This may cause us much unhappiness, but it cannot be altered. "It is one of the misfortunes of the *human condition*," he wrote, using Montaigne's celebrated phrase, "that legislators must act upon society more than upon the citizen and more upon the citizen than upon man."[26] He did not despair, because he believed that on the whole we could control our public life more effectively than our personal characters. The climate works directly upon us; and although its effects can be modified by forcing us into specific social directions, we do not as individuals really change. The English, said Montesquieu, have an excellent constitution and are solid citizens, but are perfectly awful people. They also suffer from incurable melancholia and suicidal tendencies. Laws can make collective life better or worse, but each of us is fundamentally unalterable, and morality is, at some point, a personal matter. He was in fact moved to optimism by believing that politics and morality were wholly dissimilar. One could attempt social reforms without demanding a moral revolution, which is both impossible and tyrannical in the extreme.

To separate morals and politics in this way is to open the door to a potential Machiavellianism that was impossible and intolerable for Montaigne. He thought, unlike Montesquieu, that our ability to control our personal life, even if only in isolation, was greater than our ability to manage our collective existence where Fortune ruled. Human volition was simply reduced in politics, and public men were forced to perform abominations as if out of necessity. For Montaigne did not deny that there was much that was unavoidable in politics, but he would not call it right and he wanted no part of it. And even when he was resigned to public cruelties, he could not quite accept them as inevitable. There had always been generous and great men who had avoided them. His mind was self-divided, a picture of distraction. Of his public career he said that "the Mayor and Montaigne have always been two, very distinctly separated."[27] Montaigne the mayor had played a part on a stage as a matter of duty and had fulfilled its demands as best he could. He was not one of those fastidious souls who preserve their inner purity by shunning politics altogether. As mayor, he tells us, he did as little as possible—a policy that he defended as the least harmful course of action available to him. He obviously felt more helpless in public offices than in his library, but there was for him no moral difference. Loyalty remained the same under all circumstances. He would not betray his prince for a private individual, but neither would he betray the latter for the sake of the prince. Epaminondas seemed to Montaigne particularly admirable because he would not kill in battle an enemy who had once been his guest. Nevertheless, the irrelevance of goodness in politics did impress him deeply. Let princes be just; if they tried to be magnanimous, they would only be arbitrary. Moreover, society did not depend on personal virtue for its survival. A society of complete villains would be glued together just as well as any in existence, and would be no worse in general. Not morality, but physical need and laws, even the most ferocious, keep us together. After years of religious strife, Montaigne's mind was a miniature civil war, mirroring the perpetual confusion of the world. But his jumble of political perceptions reflected not intellectual failure, but a refusal to accept either the comforts of political passivity or of Machiavelli's platitudes. He did choose sides in the civil war, did his duty, and kept a sharp eye on the mayor.

Montesquieu's vision of a free society was grounded on assumptions no less grim and just as unflattering to mankind as Montaigne's. It is only that he added to his hatred of cruelty the belief that public justice and political freedom could limit our worst propensities. He was, however, very remote from that active and positive humanitarianism that was about to become extremely popular, especially in England. The age of reform that began in the eighteenth century was fueled by an increasing revulsion against cruelty. It may not have been put first, but enough people hated cruelty so intensely that the mores and institutions of the Anglo-American world were significantly altered. As A. V. Dicey, the eulogist of that age, reminds us, it was not the inalienable rights of the Declaration of Independence but a new sense of the suffering of slaves that brought about the abolition of slavery in the South.[28] The effect attributed to *Uncle Tom's Cabin* speaks of the same power of pity. This is but a half-truth in both cases, no doubt, but not wholly misleading. From Hogarth's horrifying cartoons to the protection of animals, and from moralizing fiction to prison reform, something was being said and done that was quite new, and known to be so. Outrage against cruelty had much to do with practical reform for well over a hundred years, and it still does, even in the midst of the bloodbaths of our age. Of its origin, as indeed of social reform generally, it is often, if not wholly accurately said, that it belongs to the age of Jeremy Bentham.

Moral Cruelty and Misanthropy

It is among the more grotesque intellectual misinterpretations that Bentham should now occasionally be regarded as in some way a contributor to the terrors of contemporary dictatorship. His plan for improved prisons is now scorned as the model for future gulags and camps. This libel, designed to discredit all critics of the traditional order, need not detain us. A moral theory that begins by identifying evil with pain will obviously take cruelty seriously; and indeed Bentham did hate it, as did his many disciples who did so much to reform prisons and hospitals and to diminish the brutality of everyday life in England and the United States. The difference between the Benthamites and Montaigne or Montesquieu was not one of sensibility, but of expectations.

Bentham was entirely untouched by misanthropy and he really thought that benevolent activity was a primary pleasure: pity is a painful emotion, and relieving the suffering of others is a relief for oneself as well. We may, moreover, all expect to enjoy benevolence even more, as we learn to reject religion and to plan our lives more rationally. Calculating our own future pleasures, we would move from private prudence and benevolence to responsible and helpful government. Looking into himself, Bentham thought that he was ideally fitted to act as a planner for people who were already on the verge of learning accurate moral and political accounting. Among his many projects was one for the government of the indigent, which in retrospect is a model of moral cruelty. Pauper management, as Bentham saw it, would certainly eliminate the most severe physical pain of poverty and do so efficiently and economically. It would also prescribe in the most minute detail how every moment of the day of the institutionalized poor was to be managed by their omnipotent governors. That the poor might want a few choices or a little freedom did not figure in this piece of practical philanthropy. Indeed, it does not seem to have occurred to Bentham how much he was constraining his future charges, because he was so overwhelmed by their present physical misery.[29] The mixture of benevolence and moral oppression is, however, not an encouraging one and can readily ignite every sort of bossy and unfeeling private and public officiousness. Bentham's greatest error was, perhaps, to have believed in the likelihood of a benevolent ruling class, as humanitarian as himself in its concern for ending physical cruelty to slaves, criminals, animals, the poor, and the weak.

Bentham was not among those revolutionaries whose pity moved them to a violent public zeal. He was no Robespierre. Indeed, ever since Mandeville and Montesquieu, there had been a general recognition that pity was not a good guide to any public policy. It was a necessary restraint upon all of us as individuals, who would otherwise be given to cruelty. The stoic contempt for pity as just another emotional disturbance was abandoned, but the limits of pity were widely recognized and discussed.[30] That did not, however, imply a mistrust either of personal benevolence or of all public reform. There were, to be sure, challenges all along to the humanitarian transformation of Europe's and America's manners and feelings. The Marquis de Sade had his admirers, the more orthodox Christians did not forget sin, and the hypocrisy of much humanitarian cant could not go unnoticed. There was an army of social critics who were contemptuous of a sentimental, self-satisfied, and quasi-humane culture. There were always people who detected a certain moral cruelty in the ministrations of philanthropy. Hawthorne and Nietzsche were, in fact, only the most interesting and articulate among those who were repelled by a humanitarianism unshaken by skepticism and unmindful of its own limitations. Some people even came to prefer physical cruelty to the monstrous moral cruelty they saw.

What is moral cruelty? It is not just a matter of hurting someone's feelings. It is deliberate and persistent humiliation, so that the victim can eventually trust neither himself nor anyone else. Sooner or later it may involve physical hurt, but that is not inherent in it. Painful as humiliation is, it does no bodily damage. Montaigne was well aware of moral cruelty, and saw it as a personal danger, but he never confused it with physical brutality. He took care not to humiliate or to betray others and to avoid being insulted. His entire case for personal autonomy and for careful self-examination was a plan for moral self-defense. He did not look into himself, as did such later athletes of introspection as Rousseau, in order to redeem himself by posing as a universal model of moral victimhood. He knew himself and liked himself far too well for that. He was therefore saved from moral cruelty. Like him in this respect also, Montesquieu avoided any schemes that might recreate the moral cruelties and humiliations that he associated with revealed religion. Nevertheless, it was left to Protestant writers to dwell not only on the petty cruelties of Christian practices, but on the self-torment of its internalized morality. Of the anguish of a cruel conscience, Montaigne and Montesquieu knew relatively little. They were not New Englanders, after all.

To appreciate the anguish of a morally cruel private conscience one need only look at Hawthorne's *Scarlet Letter.* Arthur Dimmesdale kills himself with self-hatred and guilt. He is, to be sure, a weak and self-absorbed creature, but his self-inflicted suffering is terrible, far worse than anything that is done to Hester by her Puritan persecutors. She is, moreover, protected by pride and courage against their pious viciousness. Dimmesdale the minister has none of her decidedly unchristian resources; he merely tortures himself and does nothing for her or their child. When he wrote his true nightmares about Puritan Boston, Hawthorne had reached the same point on the road away from Christianity as had Montaigne and Montesquieu. He could still use the most traditional and orthodox rebuke to religious practice: that it had abandoned the religion of love and the purity of the original faith. But he also wondered, as they did, whether there was not something inherently cruel about Christianity. For someone who puts cruelty first, that cannot be a trivial question.

The Scarlet Letter is not an unmitigated attack on Puritan Boston, but the virtues that Hawthorne ascribed to his ancestors were civic rather than religious. The cruelest of his stories is not *The Scarlet Letter* but "The Gentle Boy," in which a whole town unites to persecute an unresisting Quaker child. The children are especially fiendish, and even the boy's one friend, a cripple, lifts his little crutch to strike him. While the boy suffers, his mother is away—too busy promoting her brand of religion to care for her child. The truth about Christianity, as Hawthorne saw it, was that it feeds and thrives on our natural propensity toward cruelty. And when it can find no external object, it turns inward upon the self to yield misanthropes like "Young Goodman Brown," who sees sin everywhere. But Hawthorne was characteristically sustained by a belief in the virtues of the victims. Common sense, competence, and above all a very unchristian pride save some of the women in his novels, and indeed make them altogether admirable. When they do not possess these tough virtues, they are destroyed by the zealots around them; this happens to poor Zenobia in *A Blithedale Romance.* There is, however, no hope and no redemption for the self-haters, the sin-haunted males, like Dimmesdale.

No one would have understood the fate of Dimmesdale better than Nietzsche, who had also emerged from Protestant religiosity. He, no less than Hawthorne or Montaigne, spent his life contemplating the spectacle of Christian cruelty, but he could not imagine victims who like Hester Prynne were worthy of one's admiration. His misanthropy was far too deep for that. The horror of cruelty turned against oneself seemed to him so overwhelming and he hated it so cruelly that he finally looked to physical violence for relief. In this he was not unlike Machiavelli. Both saw the religion of meekness as a vast engine of such cultural dishonesty and humiliation that only an outburst of pagan energy could suffice to obliterate its effects.

There is a world of difference between Hawthorne's grim belief that the quantity of evil is constant, though its quality alters, and Nietzsche's view of history as a perpetual decline. While Hawthorne knew that a certain dignity and probity had been lost with Puritanism, he did not regret it. He pursued the psychological logic of putting cruelty first and embraced America's mediocrity, rejoicing in its simplicity of manners and the modest aspirations of its people. Nothing but cruelty comes from those who seek perfection and forget the little good that lies directly within their powers. That is what made him so wary of crusading philanthropists like the prison reformer Hollingsworth, who ultimately destroys himself and those who love him. Of such single-minded reformers, Hawthorne wrote: "The besetting sin of a philanthropist, it appears to me, is apt to be a moral obliquity. His sense of honor ceases to be the sense of other honorable men. At some point in his course—I know not exactly when or where—he is tempted to palter with the right, and can scarcely forbear persuading himself that the importance of his public ends renders it allowable to throw aside his private conscience."

The abstractness of Hollingsworth's prison reforms makes him not merely intolerant, but blind to the actual emotions and sufferings of the people closest to him. They exist for him only as aids or hindrances to his project. He is not even conscious of sacrificing them, since he cannot acknowledge any personal claims. When it is finally brought home to him that his cold indifference has driven Zenobia to her death, he loses his convictions and is reduced to a helpless imbecility. Hollingsworth would convince anyone of the primacy of the private man, even in public places, for private feelings are our true character. If we have none at all—only public "causes"—we are insane, as Hollingsworth soon becomes.

For Nietzsche, Hawthorne's placid resignation was an unthinkable, mediocre sham, and cruelty became for him an obsessive and unmanageable preoccupation. He sometimes thought of it as a vice of immaturity that men would outgrow. At other times, recalling the horrors of the Inquisition, he feared that political sects were still quite capable of such cruelties. But however often he shuddered at physical cruelty, he detested moral cruelty far more. Pity and hypocrisy seemed to him veritable plagues, the diseases of a decadent and putrid culture. Pity is not natural for us—it is learned; and Nietzsche thought Europe had learned it far too well. It was all sheep and no wolves now. The physical discharge of cruelty had been blocked by Christianity and turned inward against the self. Such a psyche was made to suffer cruelly from sin, guilt, and bad conscience. Toward others one felt only pity, because thanks to a humiliating religion everyone could identify instantly with suffering and victimhood. Self-made victims, Europeans were now not only a mass of self-mortified Dimmesdales; they were mean-spirited weaklings who squelched every spirit stronger than their own by concentrated social force. In its long career, Christianity and its secularized offspring had made Europeans sick, crippled, tame, weak, awkward, mediocre, bored, timid herd animals. It had castrated and vivisected and turned each one of them into a "hideous old woman."[31] This is quite a list, and Nietzsche added to it from time to time. Europe had been tamed permanently, but cruelty had not been overcome. It had merely been re-directed inward, and covered with a thick hypocritical layer. Moral cruelty, the priestly weapon, and pity, the ideology of the weak, had reduced even the most noble spirits to impo-tence, as would an infectious disease. Even at our highest intellectual levels, only repression and spiritual torture rule. Kant's categorical imperative reeks of cruelty. It is a hanging judge seated within our minds. The great minotaur was no longer a symbol of animal cruelty, in Nietzsche's view, but its opposite; our own self-devouring cruel conscience.

As we turn our cruelty inward, we also transform physi-cal cruelty into the moral tormenting of other people. It was not always so. Cruelty used to have a purpose. No religion and no art are possible without it, according to Nietzsche. The God of the Old Testament, with his demand for sacri-fices, his plagues, and his rages, was cruel enough, yet self-justified. Who can forget the unspeakable cruelties enacted in Greek drama? Nietzsche claimed that it was meant to en-tertain the gods, who enjoyed the spectacle of human suf-fering. There can be no festivals, no celebrations, no health, no art, no genuine culture, and no great, god-like men without open, healthy cruelty. Mankind in fact has only two possibilities: a cruel self-mutilating conscience ruling the empire of the weak, or ruthless egotism in which the strong cruelly dominate their inferiors. We are reduced to a choice between physical and moral cruelty. In such a vision the world is turned upside down. The weak are the powerful, thanks to their guile and numbers, while the genuinely strong individuals are really the victims. That is how Nietzsche managed to teach the socially powerful classes and the various megalomaniacs of interwar Europe to fear the weak. Indeed, not only were poverty and physical weakness to be hated; the poor and weak became justifiable targets of cruelty. Europe's most flourishing ideologies of those years were not violent attacks on socialism. Fascism really hated the weak. That may not have been Nietzsche's intent, but the cruel hatred of moral cruelty underwrote physical brutality. In this as in many other respects,

Machiavelli and Nietzsche were much alike. Both found their revenge against religion, philanthropy, and compassion in a glorious cruelty. The First World War was bound to put life into these notions. Humanitarian cant joined to unimagined physical suffering created a generation that truly loathed hypocrisy as Machiavelli and Nietzsche had loathed it. These men "elevated cruelty to a major virtue because it contradicted society's humanitarian and liberal hypocrisy."[32] The revolt against hypocrisy was an affirmation of joy through cruelty.

When Montaigne spoke of his cruel hatred of cruelty, he had physical brutality in mind.[33] If one, however, puts moral cruelty first, whether it be injustice as revolutionaries sometimes do, or self-torment and hypocrisy as Nietzsche did, one can readily adopt every one of Machiavelli's cruelest maxims. For those who put physical cruelty first, dishonesty and hypocrisy will also be reprehensible. Montaigne thought these vices ugly, cowardly, Machiavellian, and conducive to cruelty. They are a danger to the ties of society that depend on mutual trust. He did not, however, as Nietzsche did, put them first. Hypocrisy was too conventional a fault to do more than arouse his contempt. Even betrayal has a place in politics, but not cruelty. To put cruelty first demands a different and altogether more dislocating reordering of moral rules. It becomes a radical spirit of denial. When Montaigne compared "us" to animals he revealed an acute sense of his moral distance from his own or from any historical society. Montesquieu's Persian visitors to Europe achieve the same effect—a loss of the habitual acceptance of one's own world. After reviewing all the actions that men esteem as honorable and useful, Montaigne decided that there was really only one "action which is most necessary and useful for human society, which will surely be marriage. And yet the council of the saints has concluded the contrary."[34] That is a rejection of both misanthropy and of a world whose fantasies and aspirations sooner or later lead us to cruelty, but it also meant that Montaigne had turned away from the world in which he lived.

That putting cruelty first should have such drastic consequences for Montaigne was quite probably due to his sense
of the futility of public action. In this, Montesquieu differed
from his master, as we have seen. Montesquieu put cruelty
first, but in such a way that he was able to devise a theory of
constitutional government—a theory that had its greatest
impact upon America. It enriched the native tradition of
natural rights by enshrining a certain grim realism and a
fear of unified political power in its constitutional law. Here
misanthropy had found its place at last. Indeed, hating cruelty, and putting it first, remain a powerful part of the liberal consciousness. It is not, however, as simple a position
as those who just intuitively say "I hate cruelty most" may
think. Such an ordering of the vices has consequences that
perhaps only Montaigne faced fully. It makes political action difficult beyond endurance, may cloud our judgment,
and may reduce us to a debilitating misanthropy and even
to a resort to moral cruelty. These pitfalls can be avoided by
skepticism and an isolating aloofness. This is open to few of
us and may even be beneath our dignity, as Montaigne
thought when he became mayor of his city. Misanthropy,
especially, is something we may dread as much as he did.
We have learned to shrug at massacres, especially among
peoples whom we cruelly disdain as our racial or cultural
inferiors, but we still react to those that occur in our own
cultural orbit. Like the religious wars of early modern Europe, they reveal not only our capacity for cruelty, but also
an infinity of illusion and hypocrisy. And it is the latter,
rather than the cruelty they seek to mask, that appear to
arouse the greatest public censure.

Montaigne's concentration on cruelty is, of course, difficult to endure. That is why we are just as evasive when we
talk about cruelty as were our philosophical ancestors.
When cruelty is mentioned we immediately say "sadism,"
which is a pathological condition, just as Aristotle chose to
discuss brutishness.[35] Even more often we dodge cruelty by
gravely arguing about whether human aggression is innate
and hereditary, or learned and conditioned by the environment. Presumably one of these alternatives gives us some

hope that cruelty might abate eventually, though why this should be the case is far from clear. I suspect that we talk around cruelty because we do not want to talk about it. That might merely be intellectual cowardice, but I do not think so. It seems to me that liberal and humane people, of whom there are many among us, would, if they were asked to rank the vices, put cruelty first. Intuitively they would choose cruelty as the worst thing we do. They would then quickly find themselves faced with all the paradoxes and puzzles that Montaigne encountered. These will not go away. They are there waiting for us; we simply do not choose to recognize them as we would have to if we spoke about what we know. What we do seem to talk about incessantly is hypocrisy, and not because it hides cowardice, cruelty, or other horrors, but because failures of honesty and of sincerity upset us enormously, and they are vices which we can attack directly and easily. They are easier to bear, and seem less intractable. Nevertheless, to make hypocrisy the worst of all the vices is an invitation to a Nietzschean misanthropy and to self-righteous cruelty as well. That is why hypocrisy and those who hate it are of compelling concern to anyone who puts cruelty first.

*L*et us not be hypocritical

Becket. The world is certainly tending
toward butchery, Baron. The lesson
of this battle, which cost us far too
much, is that we will have to form
platoons of cutthroats, that is all.

Baron. And a soldier's honor, my
Lord Chancellor, what of that?

Becket. A soldier's honor, Baron, is
to win victories. Let us not be hypocritical . . .

Baron. What a mentality!

—Jean Anouilh, *Becket*

2

WHAT IS THE MENTALITY of those who put hypocrisy first?
The question is not trivial. Hypocrisy remains the only un-
forgivable sin, perhaps especially among those who can
overlook and explain away almost every other vice, even
cruelty. However much suffering it may cause, and however
many social and religious rules it may violate, evil can be
understood after due analysis. But not hypocrisy, which
alone is now inexcusable. Not that the hypocrite was ever
popular. Every age, every form of literature, and every public stage has held him up for contempt and ridicule. Even if
in the past the hypocrite was joined by a far greater number
of other kinds of wicked people in the rogues' gallery, he
was never anything less than utterly despised. We therefore

know a great deal about various types of hypocrites. Our literature is infinitely rich in portraits of them. But we have been told far less about those who, like Becket, cannot abide hypocrisy and who see it everywhere. What is the professional antihypocrite like? Can he escape the web of pretense he sees all around him? Or are he and his adversaries locked into a mutually enhancing rather than destructive conflict? What sort of figure is he?

Putting Hypocrisy First

When Becket mocks the barons he is not yet a saintly cleric, but still a worldly courtier. Clearly he regards hypocrisy as far worse than cruelty, which he can accept with aplomb. Dishonor does not trouble him much either, apparently. But honesty is for him an aesthetic necessity, a compelling need for inner purity. As might be expected, he tends toward a sardonic misanthropy, but not without uneasiness. His lack of feeling worries him. Eventually we also discover that his personal honor means much to him, but it is a sense of dignity that has nothing to do with the feudal code of the barons. His contempt for their brutish stupidity is so deep and their cultural distance from him is so great that he does not try to explain his and the king's policies to them. He merely abuses them. Their talk about honor is doubly hypocritical, in his view. They use it to hide from themselves the fact that soldiers are merely butchers, and to justify their social complacency. Like all traditional ruling classes they pretend that all is for the best as long as their hoary customs prevail, even when these are demonstrably absurd. The Thomas à Becket of Anouilh's play is not part of their world at all. He is not a medieval intellectual, but our contemporary. The barons, not surprisingly, find him totally incomprehensible, and they dislike this stranger. When the king suggests that they kill him, they are delighted to comply. The king, however, has learned much from his former friend. He accuses the martyred Becket of hypocrisy, of having feigned to defend the honor of God when he was actually only asserting his own. There is much truth in this royal observation, but could anyone escape being a hypocrite if we see hypocrisy through such eyes? Is every self-deception, insincerity, and inauthenticity hypocritical, even when these are states of mind and not acts designed to deceive others? For those who put hypocrisy first, that is indeed the case, and their horror of hypocrisy is enhanced precisely because they see it everywhere.

If Becket strikes us as extreme, we should remember that he is not unusual, but part of an old moral tradition. Hypocrisy has always been odious. What is less obvious is just what hypocrisy is and why it should be so intensely resented. The *Oxford English Dictionary* is always helpful. Originally hypocrisy meant acting a part on the stage. For practical purposes the definition that counts is: "assuming a false appearance of virtue or goodness, with dissimulation of real character or inclination, especially in respect of religious life or belief." Especially in respect of religion! There are many kinds of hypocrites, but the religious hypocrite is the first and most enduring of all. Glossing over his errors to himself and inventing endless shifts, he actually tries "to hoodwink the Almighty."[1] The moral hypocrite is similar. He pretends that his motives and intentions and character are irreproachable when he knows that they are blameworthy. Then there are complacency and self-satisfaction, the hypocrisies of the wealthy and powerful who are so well able "to bear the misery of others without a murmur." Whatever is in their interest somehow is always also for the public good, in this best of all possible social worlds. There is, finally, a cluster of attitudes which taken together we call insincerity and inauthenticity. These need not express themselves in conduct that injures others directly, but they are said to deform one's personality. Any attempt to hide one's feelings, every social formality, role, or ritual, even failures to recognize one's character and possibilities are called acts of hypocrisy or self-betrayal. Here the very act of playing a part at all is utterly condemned.

Our levels of moral exigency clearly determine what we do or do not regard as hypocritical. Ideological conflict, however, contributes as much as moral rigor to making it the chief of the vices. When political actors disagree about right and wrong, and everything else, they can only undermine each other with the revelation that their opponent is not living up to his own professed ideal. It is not difficult to show that politicians are often more interested in power than in any of the causes they so ardently proclaim. It is, therefore, easier to dispose of an opponent's character by exposing his hypocrisy than to show that his political convictions are wrong. That is how Becket dealt with the barons. Eventually, ideological discourse puts hypocrisy into the forefront of political sins. Liberals are particularly liable to be charged with it, because they are given to compromise. The paradox of liberal democracy is that it encourages hypocrisy because the politics of persuasion require, as any reader of Aristotle's *Rhetoric* knows, a certain amount of dissimulation on the part of all speakers. On the other hand, the structure of open political competition exaggerates the importance and the prevalence of hypocrisy because it is the vice of which all parties can and do accuse each other. It is not at all clear that zealous candor would serve liberal politics particularly well. Nevertheless, the distance between the demand for sincerity and the actualities of politics can become a great distraction, especially in time of social stress such as during an unpopular war.

These habits of ideological combat were inherited from religious controversy. The art of unmasking one's opponents has always been a favorite weapon in religious warfare. All sects accuse one another of hypocrisy, and the anticlerical can never see anything but hypocrisy in a preacher. Those who put hypocrisy first see not merely a personal weakness or an inclination to profess beliefs one does not hold, but an entire character, a whole personality. As an Elizabethan book of characters put it, the hypocrite is "the worse kind of player, by so much as he acts the better part, which hath also two faces, ofttimes two hearts . . . He is the stranger's saint, the neighbor's disease, the blot of goodness, a rotten stick in a dark night, a poppy in a corn field, an ill-tempered candle with a great snuff that in going out smells ill, an angel abroad, a devil at home, and worse when an angel than a devil."[2] The writer of this unmincing passage, Bishop Hall, was evidently a devout Christian expressing the most traditional sentiments. The intensity of his loathing cannot be missed. Here is a sin that everyone must fear, not only in others, but within oneself as well. Compared to hypocrisy, misanthropy, contempt, malice, and ridicule seem almost insignificant.

The *Oxford English Dictionary*, in fact, refers us to two very revealing passages in the New Testament which show how enormously troubling hypocrisy was even in the earliest days of Christianity. Sham faith is a haunting shadow for a genuinely religious mind. The striving for religious perfection is interminable, and the demand for greater fidelity is ever more exigent. The stricter these requirements of faith are, however, the more likely real or imputable pretense becomes. But the only weapon against it is to insist on even greater efforts, which in turn encourages the very vice that is to be extirpated. Exigency creates hypocrisy as one of its inevitable by-products and Puritanism is invariably accompanied by hypocrisy and duly ridiculed for it. Here, too, there is a great deal of mutual spiritual aggression. The devout, on principle self-critical, are not likely to spare the errant neighbor. That is why in Matthew 6 and 7 we read of Jesus' excoriating not only the hypocrisy of the ostentatious almsgiver but also those people who dwell on the minor faults of others while remaining oblivious to their own enormities. It is almost as if Jesus recognized the tension in his own message. Genuine secret charity and a constant and severe self-scrutiny are psychologically unthinkable without the moral pride that is all but inseparable from spiritual energy. That is what was to anger Paul so intensely, because he also perceived the will to lord it over others in every show of excessive zeal (1 Timothy 4–6). It is hypocritical to "command" people to abstain from meat, because food is one of God's many natural gifts to mankind. The hypocrisy here is in pretending to a piety that is greater than God requires, and therefore, in fact, a covert form of pride, of which fake humility is indeed the most common expression.

The difficulty for Paul is that in calling for even greater, more genuine humility, he is probably stimulating the pretense. There is here a very clear recognition of just what is wrong with hypocrisy per se: it is a form of coercion. As Pascal was to say, it is the sheer unfairness of being forced to esteem someone more highly than he deserves that is so infuriating. Nevertheless, for all their insight, neither the Apostles nor others who have sought seriously to raise the standards of moral purity can escape the spiraling escalation of hypocrisy, unwittingly set in motion by the very hatred of hypocrisy. That is especially so when Christian charity and humility, which are matters of motive and of inner disposition, are at stake. Puritanism came to acquire its awful reputation because it was difficult not to suspect that its excessive show of godliness did not hide a sinister character. As an old English couplet puts it, "Pure in show, an upright holy man / Corrupt within—and called a Puritan."

Puritans are inherently prone to hypocrisy and to antihypocrisy because they are exigent and fearful. They suffer from an inner tug of war as intense as the perpetual accusations they thrust at others, because they are terrified of their own weaknesses and suspicious of their neighbors' lapses. Fear of the real self is added to fear of God. This is the kind of religiosity Hazlitt had in mind when he spoke of a "man afraid of looking into the state of his soul, lest at the same time he should reveal it to Heaven; and who tries to persuade himself that by shutting his eyes to his true character and feelings, they will remain a profound secret, both here and hereafter. This is a strong engine and irresistible inducement to self-deception." Such a man is not merely suspected of hypocrisy; he suspects himself and especially others of fraudulent piety. Fear of failure, of being crushed by an overpowering God, induces in him anxiety about his own faith and provokes doubts about that of others. An inability to face himself only encourages censoriousness, as a form of self-protection and self-reassurance. If, by raising the standards of piety, he adds to his fear for his own soul, he also finds comfort in the righteousness of his public zeal.

The upshot is a whole culture of fear in which hypocrisy and antihypocrisy flourish in all their manifestations.

Tartuffe is the matchless black comedy of the Puritan culture of fear and of the opportunities it offers hypocrisy.[3] The unctuous Tartuffe, by posing as a model of faith and humility, persuades his rich and pious host, Orgon, to love and trust him. Orgon is already inclined to see sin in everything around him; soon he has quarreled with his family and, subtly manipulated by Tartuffe, he disinherits them and leaves his fortune to him. Tartuffe, fortunately, has a weakness: he is not a pure hypocrite. He tries to seduce Orgon's wife and loses the confidence of this disabused husband. Tartuffe then tries to blackmail Orgon with a politically damaging letter; but the authorities know all about him, and he is, finally, sent off to jail. The play is not only about Tartuffe, the almost-complete hypocrite. It is also about Orgon and his equally zealous mother, who create the credulous and overscrupulous atmosphere in which Tartuffe can flourish. Tartuffe could never have done his mischief without Orgon. The latter is predisposed to inquisitorial and tyrannical behavior. The puritanical hypermoralism of the *devots* and Jansenists had already aroused the irritability and credulity of this aging enthusiast. Tartuffe is able to part him from his family and his property because he is ripe for it. This virtuoso of hypocrisy is, unlike his victim, not undone by self-delusion. He is in it strictly for profit, and we learn at the end that he is an experienced crook with a long criminal record. Orgon was not the first to be fingered by this versatile con man, but he provided Tartuffe with splendid opportunities. He offered an ideal environment for fraud. Molière, moreover, knew perfectly well that there is a political aspect to this moral climate. An oppressive regime is very likely to have many uses for a man like Tartuffe, who professes as deep a devotion to his king as to God. In fact, he thinks that he is doing quite well as an informer. So does the audience—until the last moment, when Tartuffe is confronted by a wise and just monarch (Molière's patron), who sends him back to jail and returns Orgon's property. We are, however, given an anxious moment to remember that Tartuffe's scheme to entrap Orgon might well have succeeded under a more persecutive or less intelligent government. And we are made to remember that the character of government may have much to do with the incidence of hypocrisy.

Tartuffe is political in an even more profound way. Orgon's family lives in the kind of fear that tyranny always spreads. His children and servants suffer, and so does the insecure tyrant. His fear is more consuming than theirs is, because it has no focus. Above all else, Orgon fears reality. He cannot bear evidence that would shake his trust in the con man or in his own righteous fury. He is subject to all the illusions that accompany domination. Even less cruel and oppressive people are like that. All of us wrap ourselves in unreality to protect ourselves against people whom we are certainly not crushing, but whom we do not choose to see or to help. No one, in fact, can bear all the facts all the time. That is what Molière's Alceste will not accept, in *The Misanthrope*. He and those who, like him, are antihypocrites first and foremost are not infuriated just by Tartuffe and his kind, but by all the casual artificialities of daily life. Alceste is not outraged merely by the injustices that complacency endorses, but by every pretense, however slight and however harmless. And he is determined to let nothing interfere with his pursuit of perfect purity. He has no use for the good sense of his best friend, who tells him,

> In certain cases it would be uncouth
> And most absurd to speak the naked truth.
> With all respect for your exalted notions
> It is often best to veil one's true emotions.
> Wouldn't the social fabric come undone
> If we were wholly frank with everyone?
> (*The Misanthrope* I, 1)

Alceste is, of course, not interested in "the social fabric," but only in personal openness: "By God, I say it's base and scandalous, / To falsify the heart's affections thus" (I, 1). Not for him "those soft speeches and that sugary grin," and no decorum or politeness either: "We should condemn with all our force / Such false and artificial intercourse" (I, 1).

Why is Alceste so single-minded in his contempt? He not only cruelly hurts the feelings of an untalented poet, but also quarrels with his friend, and finally loses Célimène, the woman he loves, all because of his antihypocritical stance. Alceste is afraid of being fooled. His terror of being deceived is such that it makes him a bully and, in the end, the dupe of his own suspicions. The reason for his mortal fear of being taken in by pretense is that it might threaten his domination over those around him. That is why he is so susceptible to the schemes of the spiteful spinster, Arsinoé, who is an exaggerated version of himself. She uses the cant of perfect frankness to make innocent behavior seem guilty. She brings out that hypocrisy implicit in Alceste's harsh candor which we merely suspect in it, especially in his refusal to be anything but "himself" on all occasions. That, he claims, is his mark of honesty, but Célimène does not agree: she can see quite clearly that such conduct is merely domineering, and she mocks his love, which "Would find its perfect consummation / In ecstasies of rage and reprobation" (2.5). Since he cannot force her to renounce the company of all other people for his sake, he gives her up and decides upon a solitary existence in which he will not find any occasion for his self-righteous anger. His friends pity him because they are kind, but no one should marry this archetype of the moral oppressor.

It is not difficult to recognize the flaw in Alceste's antihypocrisy: it is too undiscriminating. The misanthrope does not single out those like Tartuffe or any other spiritual and social con men. He spreads his hatred evenly over injustice and politeness. His friends are decent people who do not deserve his scolding. They even admit that they are not blameless, because they do not bother to protest at all, as if all were well in their world. Theirs is perhaps a too stylized rather than a too complacent culture. To really see a society wholly mired in hypocritical complacency, one must turn from Molière to Victorian Britain and the "Podsnappery" that Dickens saw everywhere there.

The Hypocrisy of the Complacent

A good look at the new middle classes showed Dickens that theirs "was not a very large world, morally," and when they were faced with "disagreeables," they said "I don't want to know about it; I don't choose to discuss it; I don't admit it!" In *Our Mutual Friend* we meet Podsnap, who "had a good inheritance and married another." Podsnap turned his eyes away from destitution, from social cruelty, and above all from sex. He was a "representative man," determined to preserve his own dignity as one who had "thrived exceedingly well." "The question about everything was, would it bring a blush to the cheek of a young person." This was "the voice of society" at its worst, but Dickens was not alone in his disdain. He was joined by Carlyle, Mill, Huxley, Clough, and many others, in a chorus of biblical thunder against hypocrisy. Some feared that science would be stifled by the conventions of an ostentatious religiosity. Others saw the death of individuality in an enervating timidity that seemed incapable of sustaining any sort of positive character. And not a few simply felt an enormous nausea at such a mass of insincerity, dishonesty, sentimentality, and willful self-deception. Failure to face the facts and religious and moral pretense were blended in their eyes to form a single mass of hypocrisy.

Since these challengers won the day, one now asks what the fuss was all about. Certainly the Victorian middle classes were self-protective, and their critics frightened them into an even deeper defensiveness. Insecure in their lately acquired position, and in the midst of a religious revival, they were not morally expansive, not daring. Were they, however, hypocritical? Did they not wish to be what they proclaimed everyone ought to be? To fail in one's own aspirations is not hypocrisy. In fact, they really believed in chastity, monogamy, thrift, charity, and work. If many did not achieve these, many others did, at considerable psychic cost. Self-repression is not hypocrisy. Only their refusal to admit that the endless slums of Mayhew's London even existed—that is, only their complacency—was hypocritical.

They were hypocrites because they hid something evil when it was in their interest to do so. Sexual repression and emotional silence, however, are self-inflicted wounds, not social crimes or hypocrisy. They were part of the self-imposed discipline of a massively self-distrusting, newly arrived, religiously unsettled middle class, which could feel the contempt from above and the rage from below, while it had to endure the torments of ideological, scientific, and literary upheavals. Theirs was the self-hatred that marks all puritanism. Self-scrutiny and fear of illusion are essential parts of the puritan mind. That is why its defensive system, whether personal or cultural, is brittle. There is a bias against hypocrisy there also. Podsnap read Dickens week after week and, in time, it wore him down. His heirs were no less hypocritical than he had been, but the "condition of England" improved. The shrill antihypocritical chatter of post-Victorian writers may have had some political effect, but the real social transformation was the work of liberal democracy which has its own hypocrisies. Politicians eventually reacted to injustice and misery, but not because they had no protective veils.

There is, after all, a great difference between attacking the evils that complacency may hide and concentrating one's resentment on its hypocrisy. Dickens, for one, could see, even within the culture of hypocrisy, the difference between extortion, theft, or cruelty and mere hypocrisy. Hypocrisy is made very profitable in such a society, but it did not blind him to the moral distance between crime and pretense. There is a stunning scene in *David Copperfield* in which Dickens's immortal hypocrite, Uriah Heep, explains why his always being "umble" pays. David may not care for professions of humility or any other exhibitions of that sort, but he does, in spite of his general obtuseness, begin to see that Uriah was brought up to be a hypocrite. Uriah was, as his parents before him had been, one of the deserving poor.

"There now," said Uriah, looking flabby and lead-colored in the moonlight. "Didn't I know it! But how little you think of the rightful umbleness of a person in my station, Master Copperfield! Father and me was both brought up at a foundation school for boys, and Mother, she was likewise brought up at a public, sort of charitable establishment. They taught us all a deal of umbleness—not much else that I know of, from morning to night. We was to be umble to this person, and umble to that, and to pull off our caps here, and to make bows there, and always to know our place, and abase ourselves before our betters. And we had such a lot of betters! Father got the monitor-medal by being umble. So did I. Father got made a sexton by being umble. He had the character, among the gentlefolks, of being such a well-behaved man, that they were determined to bring him in. 'Be umble, Uriah,' says Father to me, and you'll get on. It was what was always being dinned into you and me at school; it's what goes down best. Be umble, says Father and you'll do! And really it ain't done bad! ... When I was quite a young boy," said Uriah, "I got to know what umbleness did, and I took to it. I ate umble pie with an appetite. I stopped at the umble point of my learning, and says I, 'Hold hard!' When you offered to teach me Latin, I knew better. 'People like to be above you,' says Father, 'keep yourself down.' I am very umble to the present moment, Master Copperfield, but I've got a little power!"

Dickens did not excuse Uriah's numerous villainies. Indeed, he made him both morally and sexually as unattractive as possible. Uriah is also a con man, and deserves to land in jail, as he eventually does. It is not his crimes, but only one of his hypocrisies, his all-purpose, serviceable humility, that Dickens wants us to understand. For hypocrisy, whatever its specific function, is socially learned behavior, and Dickens reminds us of it. In the absence of friendship and spontaneous generosity, we must have charity as an office and as a public obligation organized by church or state. In either case its beneficiaries, the poor, must prove themselves worthy. That means showing that they have reached a psychological bottom of utter humility that will also guarantee their gratitude for whatever they may receive. Otherwise, there would be no rewards for the distributors of alms, and they would have no sense of their own worth.

56

Dickens knew as well as anyone that hypocrisy makes cruelty especially easy, but he does not leave us in doubt about the difference between refusing to feed a starving child and pretending that this is a righteous act. And we may well ask whether we would be improved by being openly and honestly vicious. It may be that we shall never learn to be charitable without being mean, dishonest, and humiliating. Does that imply that we should quit trying— even at the cost of hypocrisy?

To be sure, one does not have to rejoice as one listens to "philanthropic" politicians speak ever more loudly of their compassion. In return, one may expect a sullen abjectness among its recipients. Few have the resources to become self-aware, scheming, accomplished hypocrites like Uriah Heep. Perhaps this is the best we can do, and one ought not to scoff at an inadequate charity; it is better than none at all. Dickens merely noticed its costs. Without a drop of pity for the clammy-handed Uriah and his crimes, Dickens makes us see at least that an early exposure to public benevolence had helped him to become so ostentatiously "umble." His misdeeds are not to be pitied away, but we do see Uriah Heep in his social setting, and we recognize that hypocrisy was not the worst of his faults.

Dickens was a great connoisseur of hypocrisy, yet he was not obsessive about it. He could see the playacting of all his characters, even the most agreeable ones, who are as outspoken as David's wonderful Aunt Betsey. He hated the humbug that sugarcoats meanness, just as he loved the eccentric gruffness of real generosity, but he never forgot the difference between wickedness and mere pretension. Why has his sense of humanity been so rare? Why are people so overwhelmed by loathing for hypocrisy? Hegel thought that there had been a change in the quality of hypocrisy that made it peculiarly repulsive. In this he may have been mistaken, but he did uncover aspects of the psychology of conscience that render the perpetual wrangling among all kinds of hypocrites and antihypocrites comprehensible in his age as well as in our own.

The New Hypocrisy: Sincerity

The new conscience that Hegel contemplated with a baleful eye was, in his words, "lacking in objective content" but full of "the infinite certainty of itself."[4] What happens to a conscience that is uninformed by God and social mores? What does the inner self do when it is left unwatched and bereft of those commonsense rules of natural and divinely sanctioned conduct? Saint Paul relied on them, and a conscience tutored in public and revealed knowledge was for a long time after considered the best protection against all temptations, including hypocrisy. Nevertheless, as we know, the hyperactive conscience has always been treacherous. If even the trained conscience can be a false guide, what of one abandoned to its own devices? Can such a conscience cope with the hypocrisy and reactive antihypocrisy to which it is always liable? To Hegel it seemed clear that it could not, and that the new subjectivity had given rise to a hideous reign of hypocrisy of a peculiarly assertive kind, quite unlike the old "naive" sort. The "naive" hypocrite hides acts and beliefs that he knows to be wrong. His conscience may even trouble him. That is why he resorts to subterfuge to quell his own guilt as well as to escape censure from other people. The new hypocrite simply adjusts his conscience by ascribing noble, disinterested, and altruistic intentions to all his behavior. He is the sole instructor of his own conscience. If everyone were to accept these self-evaluations, there would be such a moral chaos that even accusations of hypocrisy would lose all their force. That is what one would expect from those who are accepted at their self-declared worth by others of like mind. At most, these sincere folk might from time to time confess to their only possible moral failure: the betrayal of their real inner self. Rousseau's *Confessions* is the acknowledged masterpiece of this technique. Hegel apparently expected these habits to become universal, and he saw before him an unchecked anarchy of puffed-up hypocrites.

The assertive hypocrisy Hegel saw all around him was

certainly spreading, but it was not new. Hegel saw its beginnings in Jesuit casuistry. The Jesuits had, in Hegel's view,
authorized adjustments of one's conscience to circumstance.
Now there was no need to ask for their permission to do so,
as conscience was left to the free discretion of every individual. Good intentions were the excuse in both cases. There is,
however, a difference that Hegel did not want to recognize.
The Jesuits did not make a fetish of sincerity, but the new
hypocrisy did make sincerity its central virtue. In this it
does not depart wholly from impulses that were always
present in a Christian conscience, which demands both obedience to God's rules and inner sincerity. It was never
enough to do the right thing. One must, as in almsgiving, do
it in the right spirit. When conscience lost its "objective
content," as Hegel put it, sincerity came to rule all alone.

Alceste, the self-centered misanthrope, was already in the
moral state Hegel described, just as Tartuffe was the perfect
representative of naive hypocrisy, but even he already knew
how to manipulate sincerity to his own advantage. He went
in for self-abasement and verbal self-flagellation when he
was in danger of being exposed. The difference between
naive and assertive hypocrisy, however, was not as clear
and real at the time when Pascal and Molière were dealing
with the hypocrites they faced. According to Pascal, Jesuit
"probabilism" taught that if any authority can be cited to
justify an action, then it is permissible to perform it. Authority could be used to clear the conscience of the actor
and free him from the fear of sin, whatever he did. Conscience had clerical masters, and anything they considered
"probably" good *was* good. Tartuffe, the prince of hypocrites, immediately used these convenient doctrines in his
armory of pious deceits:

> Heaven is not averse to compromise.
> There is a science, lately formulated,
> Whereby one's conscience may be liberated
> And any wrongful act you care to mention
> May be redeemed by purity of intention.
>
> (*Tartuffe* IV, 5)

Tartuffe is relying on Jesuit science to help him in a seduction.

Unlike Hegel, both Pascal and Molière were convinced that conscience had reserves of fortitude with which it could defend itself against the appeal of these deceptions. Thus, one of Molière's characters in *Tartuffe* says with quiet confidence, "Let's strive to live by conscience's clear decrees / And let the gossips gossip as they please" (I, 1). Pascal's solution was the same: an appeal to a resolute conscience to remember the path of true morality and to reject the temptation to accept Jesuit excuses and laxity. Conscience was perceived as quite capable of dealing with the threat of hypocrisy. Hypocrisy was obviously no joke, but it was not taken as the primary evil. After all, naive hypocrisy *is* an attempt to hide a truly serious crime against God or man, not just dissimulation for its own sake.

Pascal was quite clear that when the Jesuits manipulated the consciences of their pliant clients, this hypocrisy was designed to give the former the greatest empire of all: over the human mind. The real evil was not the hypocrisy, but the abuse of power by the Jesuits. The doctrine of "probabilism," with its concentration on intentions and its easy supply of "good" ones, had terrible objectives and consequences. Men were induced to sin and so led to their perdition. The crime itself, not the hypocrisy, was for Pascal the real horror. Conscience could, however, defend itself effectively against this danger. It was the best cure for its diseases.

But when conscience is reduced to sincerity, it is futile to appeal to it against its own deceptions. The more Alceste insists on being true to himself, the more egotistical and misanthropic he becomes. To call upon the sincere to become even more so, only compounds their difficulties. What can sincerity do for Alceste, the professional antihypocrite, when he rails,

> Let men behave like men, let them display
> Their inmost hearts in everything they say.

Let the heart speak, and let our sentiments
Not mask themselves in silly compliments.
                                    (*The Misanthrope* I, 1)

Sincerity could not possibly cure Alceste's *libido domi-
nandi* or his moral cruelty; it would only aggravate them. His
real self would merely assert itself more insistently, but in
the same antihypocritical vein. At least Alceste had friends
who still believed in their own consciences. Hegel saw a
world in which individual conscience was no longer supported or checked by others of its own kind, identical or at
least similar in content and structure. The sincere have no
moral rules to share with one another, and would therefore
only urge Alceste on in his solitary vices instead of rescuing
him from them.

Although Hegel expected the anarchy of the sincere to
bring about a general indifference to hypocrisy, he was, in
fact, the herald of a veritable army of ferocious antihypocrites. The uncertainty and suspicion felt by those who are
confronted not merely by the affectations of the sincere, but
also by the undiminished vigor of naive hypocrisy, are
overwhelming. The world is not made up exclusively of
sincere, authentic anarchists, bent solely on expressing their
given heart or ego. Personal conviction is, to be sure, "the
sole measuring rod of duty" for many people, just as Hegel
foresaw; but there are many other moral types around. An
anarchy of the self-expressive does not prevail, although
there are people who entertain with longing this psychological fantasy. The actual state of affairs is one of conflicting
moral attitudes, among which rule-bound, conventional,
and traditional ethics continue to hold their own. This mixture of anarchy and convention makes the interplay between hypocrisy and antihypocrisy extremely intense. For
each one, to some extent, shares as much as he detests the
inclinations of the other. They live together, affect each
other, and must repeatedly accuse and justify themselves to
each other. As Hegel noted, the pure in heart do not keep
quiet, or just insist on their sincerity, but proclaim that

whatever they do springs from the most noble motives, such as patriotism, pity, or creative genius. Others may see no trace of these traditional virtues in conduct that looks rebellious, boorish, and egotistical. They will say, as Hegel did, that this is just assertive hypocrisy; to which the sincere will reply that nothing is more so than the "sugary grin" of the conventionally polite and just. What we have to live with is a morally pluralistic world in which hypocrisy and antihypocrisy are joined to form a discrete system.

Hegel was, in fact, confronted by several moral phenomena, which he did not quite sort out. First of all, there was the new primacy of sincerity and the silence of conscience as a source of shared public moral knowledge. These changes were only too clear to Hegel. So was the inherent hostility of sincerity to all conventional rules, because these are the most powerful of all external threats to the unalloyed inner self. To respond to any appeal other than personal conviction is perceived as a betrayal. It is false, inauthentic, and hypocritical to abide by set rules, to seek public approval, to meet expectations, or simply to please others. The first voice to cry "hypocrite" in a pluralistic world is that of the sincere. The second voice is the response of the conventional, who are, as conscience has always been, also committed to sincerity, but not to the exclusion of other considerations. They do know enough about intentions to distrust the professions of the sincere, and they accuse them not merely of simple wrongdoing, but also of hypocrisy. Both sides measure the distance between assertion and performance and then both say, "Hypocrisy." They are determined to undermine the confidence of those whose moral style offends them, because they can neither wholly accept nor reject each other. The charge of hypocrisy is the weapon of choice in a war between those who cannot do without public values which they must distrust, and those who rely on convention but also insist on sincerity. Finally, to these opponents must be added those who, wearied by these wrangles, treat morality as a matter of taste. They see dogmatism, imposition, and aggressive hypocrisy everywhere. These perpetual fulminations against hypocrisy are, in short, an expression of massive moral confusion, and not the fault of any one of the participating dealers in moral goods. The hypocrisy Hegel already knew is systematic, not occasional. The hypocrite as an identifiable and hated character has been replaced by hypocrisy as a universally available insult. All this is part of the language of distrust that uses threats rather than arguments.

Accusations of hypocrisy under these circumstances are not expressions of self-confidence. They are signs, rather, of a real moral insecurity, which can be seen readily by anyone who looks at the kaleidoscope of our sexual mores. Many people still believe, as did the Victorians, that chastity and monogamy are not just morally right, but the very essence of all morality. At the other end of the spectrum are those who think that sexual behavior is subject to no special rules. There are only preferences. The liberated see nothing but hypocrisy in the words of the staid. Even if the latter practiced what they preach, which it is said they rarely do, they would still be hypocritical, because monogamy is not sincere. It is a pretense which does not yield the constant love and pleasure that must mark the marriage of true minds. The monogamist may be peculiarly vulnerable to these charges because he also believes in sincerity, and he may well pretend to feelings he cannot summon up. He might, in addition, be self-repressing and complacent. He therefore half agrees with his tormentors, who have done everything to undermine his self-confidence and nothing to show that he has injured or wronged anyone. In response, he will accuse the liberated of unfeeling and joyless promiscuity and of threatening the familial order. The liberated do not care about the latter complaint, so they are not disturbed and may not even answer it. The indirect charge of hypocrisy is the only one that can touch them, for they do insist on the sincerity of their affections, even if they be fleeting, or at the very least claim to be having a very good time. In principle, a funless hedonist and an unfeeling experimenter are hypocritical, at least if they advertise the happy emotional openness of their style of life. Such extremes of sexual attitude are too remote from each other to be touched by direct moral attack; but to insinuate that someone is hypocritical is to collapse his self-image, and that has an effect. That is why the rigid and the liberated can so easily wound without altering one another. Each one feels threatened by sexual opinions that he can neither share nor completely reject. The liberated do not view Victorian sexual mores with the detached tolerance that they would bring to the habits of a distant primitive tribe. The Victorian shudders in unconcealed disgust at the liberated, not only because he disapproves of them, but because he is not indifferent to the primacy of the sexual honesty they so loudly proclaim. If he cannot satisfy this demand within his code, he is exposed to self-doubt as much as to ridicule. The liberated are in the same boat, for they are still haunted by the possibility of enduring love. The conflict within stimulates a moral dispute in which the urge to exercise psychic dominion is hardly disguised.

The quarrels among people who choose different sexual lives are clearly contests for moral supremacy, and charges of hypocrisy tend to erupt in such conflicts. We need only return to the ostentatious almsgiver, so reviled for his hypocrisy in the New Testament. He may well have been the unknowing victim of an imperial conscience. He was, after all, not doing anything wrong. On the contrary, he was helping the poor. If he did so in order to earn the approval of his fellow citizens, he may simply have been living up to the highest values of the pagan world. He may have been a Greek, not a Christian, and his generosity may have been deeply ethical. It did not, however, meet the standards of Christian charity. The established practices of his society were being challenged by conscience in revolt. The demand for secret charity might not have made any sense to this citizen, at home in his public culture. To call him hypocritical is something of a dodge. It does not indict what he was doing, but spurns the spirit in which he was going about his almsgiving. He is being undercut, rather than condemned for doing something reprehensible. He is also the butt of a political attack. Private conscience, when it is very expansive, as Christianity is, is bound to assert itself against cus-

tom and the established order as well as against the unre-
flective, habitual acceptance of a given social environment.
Every evil ignored, conscience says, is an evil endorsed,
which is why all conventionality is so hypocritical. That is
why it is often the function of conscience, and always of
sincerity, to be on poor terms with the laws and manners of
actual societies. The plurality of moral accusers has only
proliferated the verbal arms which conscience has always
been ready to use against public mores that failed to meet
its demands.

As private conscience expanded politically, it was inevitable that those whom conscience accosted should see aggression in a public display of sincerity and should attribute
hypocrisy to its claims to perfection. The best defense is a
counterattack, but it is not enough. There is an element of
political Podsnappery in all conventional hypocrisy that refuses to face the distance between established moral profession and practice. It is the hypocrisy that sustains
established institutions and the self-satisfied people who
run them and live for and off them. Such are the barons,
with their talk about their honor. Such are all ruling classes.
They must studiously ignore actuality, employing a self-
protective rhetoric that supports their world. It is precisely
people like Becket—outsiders—who are most likely to expose conventional hypocrisy such as this to contempt. In
turn, these scourges of the insiders are very apt to resort to
ideological causes, which may serve as counterhypocrisies
and perform highly integrative functions for them. When
this cycle becomes an accepted form of politics, the habitual
seesaw between competitive unmaskings and remaskings
has set in. This is the pattern of ideological politics in which
charges of hypocrisy are exchanged with unbroken regu-
larity.

The shape of these politics was sensed even before they
were realized. To Hegel, with his usual prescience, it
seemed evident that ideological exchanges, in which each
protagonist stands for a "cause," were the public equivalent
of the new morally assertive hypocrisy. "Causes" act just
like good intentions, since they can be used to purify any

sort of conduct. As long as the "cause," however remote, is "moral," the actors who claim to promote it can do whatever they choose, if only they can claim that their acts serve it. This is extremely easy.

In the world of political "good intentions," "causes" are the untestable promises of a good future that serves to liberate adherents from the responsibilities and constraints of the present ethical and legal order. This is often a very naive sort of hypocrisy in which political con men clothe their crimes. On a large scale, it is how terrorist regimes and ideologists behave, and it is also how Tartuffe reigned over Orgon's distraught family. All opponents are traitors, the agents of dangerous religious, class, and national enemies against whom virtuous rulers are protecting a happy people. Even the most ardent antihypocrite may be more impressed by the cruelties than by the lies of these regimes. The hypocrisy is naive, for it is secondary to their crimes. On a lesser scale, that is also true of those noble causes that pursue improbable and distant goals. The purity of their aims, and the wickedness of actuality, combine to absolve their followers not only from their normal duties, but from looking at any facts that disturb their beliefs. One might suppose that once this game of giving mischief fine names had been understood, its opponents would concentrate on the actual misdeeds. That is not likely, however, once a system of hypocrisy and counterhypocrisy has become established. The glamour of good ends is too great for that; and here, too, contestants are reduced to seeking the "psychic annihilation" of their opponents by exposing their hypocrisy.

For the observer of the play of ideologies, it is clear that the basic hypocrisy affecting all of them is the pretense that the ideological needs of the few correspond to the moral and material interests of the many. It is a hypocrisy to which all politically active intellectuals, who generally are also extreme antihypocrites, are especially given. More impressive than these antics, however, is the endemic and systematic character of public hypocrisy and its maze-like inescapability. For the defenders of convention, who attack the self-righteous fraudulence of the political parties of new "causes," only sink into the swamp of their own hypocrisy in disguising the enormous gap between profession and behavior. That gap marks all established orders, and the counterhypocrisy of the rebellious invariably feeds on it. The public stage, in short, collectively replays the struggles of the politics of daily life, and vice versa. In the unending game of mutual unmasking, the general level of sham rises. As each side tries to destroy the credibility of its rivals, politics becomes a treadmill of dissimulation and unmasking. To call an opponent evil might boomerang, but he need only be unarmed by charges of hypocrisy.

Hypocrisy and Liberalism

The contribution of personal conscience, when it expresses itself on the public stage, does nothing to mitigate systematic hypocrisy. It sees hypocrisy everywhere, among politicians who habitually promise more than they can deliver, who profess beliefs they do not hold, and whose moral pretensions are intolerable. That is particularly so in liberal states, which are, in any case, the only open testing grounds for conscience and all possible ideologies. The revolt of private conscience against liberal governments is not, in fact, due to their exceptional depravity, but to the extraordinary hopes that liberalism once inspired and still sustains. Because its moral achievements have fallen short of these expectations, liberalism is accused of hypocrisy more frequently by its adherents than by its enemies. The latter in fact are often disappointed liberals.

To recapture some of the intensity of the moral aspiration of liberalism in the years before the First World War, one need only read John Morley's celebrated essay "On Compromise."[5] The author was a learned, influential, experienced, and excruciatingly high-minded Victorian. His earnest expectation was that freedom would shrink the purely political realm of compromise, caution, and calculation to minimal proportions. Free in liberal England to ignore oppression, Morley concentrated on the deviousness of politicians, in and out of office. They were a real danger to the dauntless pursuit of truth, the highest of human obligations, upon which all human improvement depended. The end of striving was progress, and it was the nonpolitical intellect that would achieve it, if it was not fettered by the temptations of politics. Hypocrisy was the very greatest of dangers, not only to truth, but even to politics. Morley could endure the compromises that liberty itself imposed on politicians, who could not force improvements on those who were unready for them or who could not accept them. But the art of the possible must not be artful. It must not be hypocritical, as the political spirit, with its eye ever on "the immediately feasible," was apt to be. That is why liberalism, the faith in progress through freedom, must reduce the scope of the political until it is replaced by something less dangerous to freedom. A dramatic decline in hypocrisy was bound to come when people engaged in vigorous and free discussion. There would be less irresponsible "pharisaical censoriousness" when everyone came to recognize the difference between disagreement, disapproval, and punishment. Morley's intellectual puritanism was clearly as single-minded as the sexual obsessions of his fellow Victorians. In any event, the free competition of moral ideas did not reduce censoriousness, politics, or hypocrisy. On the contrary, it enhanced them, because freedom does not screen off the political spirit but liberates it to grow unchecked. The hopes that liberalism aroused have not been realized, and its adherents feel defrauded because they can no longer be as confident as Morley was so long ago.

American representative democracy has fared no better than English liberalism. As soon as democracy became a working political system, it was damned as a sham. For it soon became obvious that it, too, had a government whose agents were far from perfect and that its laws yielded less than complete justice. Democracy was just hypocrisy at large, to those who had suffered an intense erosion of faith when the actual republic replaced the city of their hopes. American representative democracy was meant to be unlike other governments in all ways, not only in some. The difference proved to be insufficiently great and the actuality was perceived as fraudulent. In fact, representative democracy must, like any form of government, maintain its legitimacy by reinforcing the ideological values upon which it is based. Not only must these be invoked on all possible occasions, but they must serve as the justification for specific policies. These norms go well beyond the sources of legal authority, especially when derived from a document, however revered, like the United States Constitution. The Constitution itself is embedded in less explicit, but no less binding, principles and sentiments. No one can hope to govern without reference to these values. It is neither psychologically feasible nor politically possible to evade them when every utterance is sure to receive close public scrutiny. That means that those engaged in governing must assume at the very least two roles, one of pursuing policies and another of edifying the governed in order to legitimize these plans. The more widely shared a political language and other traditions are, the easier this is. There is nevertheless a built-in tension; for the disparity between what is said and what is done remains great, and the better the speaker the larger that distance is likely to be. The gap exists in every association, not only in political units. No one lives up to a collective ideal. This is the fatality on which Machiavelli capitalized, and on which his political honesty thrived. And those, of whom there are many, who do not accept the legitimizing norms at all will use hypocrisy as their most telling accusation.

One cannot, however, govern with overt antihypocrisy as one's only rule of conduct. Antihypocrisy is a splendid weapon of psychic warfare, but not a principle of government. Nevertheless, it does point its finger at a perpetual difficulty. The best politicians are those who can both reinforce the ideology upon which their authority is based and devise adequate policies. But very few are equally adept at both. Even those who are are peculiarly subject to charges of hypocrisy and to debunking. Such was the fate of both Lincoln and Franklin D. Roosevelt. Each one was able to use rhetoric and showmanship to give a new vigor to flagging political principles and loyalties. With that, they also raised the level of moral and political expectations. They failed to fulfill the standards they had themselves revived. Other presidents were not expected to achieve so much, but they had also made fewer claims for the political order with which they were identified. Hence the endless accusations of hypocrisy that pursue the most capable statesmen. Without ancestor worship or divine providence to rely on, modern liberal democracy has little but its moral promise to sustain it. That is why it generates both political exigency and the interplay of hypocrisy and vocal antihypocrisy.

The basic norm of liberal democracy is the consent of the governed, and consent is not easily won or preserved. The means to achieve it are bound to heighten governmental hypocrisy. Parties organize campaigns, and leaders make up the reality, if not the promise, of electoral regimes. In the back-and-forth of competing charges and countercharges which is both the action as well as the specific end of any election, there certainly is a fund of hypocrisy. Elections are rituals in function and in form, and the choice of parts is fairly limited. The pretenses therefore are standardized, and the conventions of exposing them are equally predictable. The voters' expectations are not, as a rule, particularly great, and their tolerance for eccentricities and departures from the script is low. That is why some Americans, as soon as they discovered that their government was not as unique as they had expected, tended to see hypocrisy everywhere. Hawthorne was not the first Jacksonian to see that America was not as different as had been expected, but he was the most literate. He was also more intensely preoccupied by a sense of ubiquitous hypocrisy. He spared no one—not his friends, or himself, or those whom he disliked. He was the greatest artist since Molière to make hypocrisy his main theme. The pretension was simple: the people ruled. In fact, they did not—they only played a role in elections, and the claims for post-Revolutionary republican government were exaggerated. It was in some ways superior, and in others inferior, to the Puritan authoritarianism of an earlier age. Hawthorne felt no great regrets and no enthusiasm for either one. In both times hypocrisy flourished, not to mention the vices to which all men are prone, especially greed and cruelty. That much cannot be helped, only recognized. However, styles in guile change, and electioneering has its own kind. Consider Judge Pyncheon in *The House of the Seven Gables.* He is privately as wicked as can be, but in public a pillar of the community. He expects to be elected governor of the state. "As is customary with the rich, when they aim at the honors of a republic, he apologized, as it were, to the people, for his wealth, prosperity, and elevated station, by a free and hearty manner towards those who knew him; putting off the more of his dignity in due proportion with the humbleness of the man whom he saluted, and thereby proving a haughty consciousness of his advantages as infrangibly as if he had marched forth preceded by a troupe of lackeys to clear the way."

"Proving" it, in any case, to a man as sensitive to sham as Hawthorne. Pyncheon, like Tartuffe, is utterly wicked, and his outward demeanor hides the immense wrong he did in sending his innocent cousin to jail. Hawthorne, moreover, hints that the qualities acquired in lifelong domestic and family brutality and meanness are just those most likely to make a successful republican politician, for neither the voters nor those who know the candidate for what he really is can act effectively. "A little knot of subtle schemers will control the convention and, through it, dictate to the parties." In fact, their measures will "steal from the people, without its knowledge, the power of choosing its own rulers." What they like is a safe man of visible public irreproachability and "spotless private character." To suit them, one would have to be a hypocrite; though, to be sure, Judge Pyncheon is in a class by himself. Hawthorne's Jacksonian friends, however, were not without their own hypocrisies. They, too, wanted to rule. Their censoriousness was very much a claim to govern.

The current quarrel between those who see democracy as a system of citizen participation and those who are content with it as a system of leadership selection is just the latest rerun of the Jacksonian script. And it is as evident now as then that "the people" so ardently championed is not an actual but an invented entity. Hawthorne was able to express the immense disappointments that representative democracy must inspire when it becomes an ongoing system of government. Its workings force participants to promise a moral order that nobody can create. Elections must be prepared, and candidates, especially rich and clever ones, are bound to pretend to a common touch, youthful poverty, and inordinate virtue. That is the bleak side of the picture, and Hawthorne, like all the great American novelists, had an eye for darkness. It was only to be expected that he would soon see it among the reformers of his age as well.

The advantages of a system that seems to produce hypocrisy as a kettle gives off steam also were recognized very early. Hawthorne concentrated on hypocrisy because it had destroyed the specifically democratic hope. But how much frankness does democracy actually require? No one can accuse even the most democratic of the founders of the republic, Benjamin Franklin, of political enthusiasm. He was a shrewd calculator who took it for granted that the politics of persuasion required hypocrisy, but that did not discourage him. Franklin did not for a moment underrate the political changes he had worked for in Pennsylvania. He had done much to create a wholly new political society based on a civic consciousness in which self-improvement and practical philanthropy were joined. This transformation did not require zeal, only guile and persistence. And Franklin was capable of both. He was also tolerant and easygoing, as a matter of principle; and in this he very much resembled David Hume, who could say quite simply of hypocrisy that "the common duties of society usually require it" and that it was "impossible to pass through the world without it." Both were glad enough to have escaped from the rigors of the congregation and of the kirk, and not inclined to torment themselves or others with the fears they had so recently left behind them. That a public man should try to make himself acceptable to his fellow citizens did not strike Franklin as despicable; on the contrary, he carefully taught himself to hide much of his native character.

72

Franklin was, by any standards, a great man. He always knew that about himself. In his *Autobiography*, which is itself a very artful work, he tells us he realized that he would have to play a very difficult part if he was to succeed in Pennsylvania politics. To get his many projects through, he had to acquire a new vocabulary and new personality.

> I even forbid myself . . . the Use of every Word or Expression in the Language that imported a fix'd Opinion; such as *certainly, undoubtedly*, etc. and I adopted instead of them, *I conceive, I apprehend*, or *I imagine* a thing to be so or so . . . The modest way in which I propos'd my Opinions, procur'd them a readier Reception and less Contradiction . . . This Mode, which I at first put on, with some violence to natural Inclination, became at length . . . easy . . . to me . . . And to this Habit I think it principally owing, that I had . . . so much Influence in public Councils.[6]

This was done in a spirit of cool calculation without any claim to humility. As Franklin noted, humility was quite beyond him; he would only be proud of it if he were to try it. Here is hypocrisy as a conscious act in response to a situation that demands it. Persuasion is not natural; it requires a great deal of effort, and in a man as superior to his fellows as Franklin was, it takes exactly what he described. It was a mark of Franklin's intelligence that he always knew what was called for and could do what he thought right. He was at all times, Jefferson wrote to his grandson, "the most amiable of men," because his rule was "never to contradict anybody." What strikes one about the *Autobiography* is its complete lack of sentimentality. Franklin had a pronounced character which he presented very acutely, but he did not think of himself as primarily a unique inner self. He was all his many roles, although he put the first one above all others, as he wrote in his testament: "I, Benjamin Franklin, of Philadelphia, printer, late Minister Plenipotentiary of the United States of America to the court of France, now President of Pennsylvania." There is much pride of achievement in this, but no vanity at all. It is also a wholly social ego. Franklin was still of Molière's mind.

The distance between Franklin and Hawthorne is immense. Franklin was the sum of his actions, while Hawthorne and we have romantic egos that cannot bear the notion that one's manner of acting one's roles measures true character. For Hawthorne there was a private self that was one's true, supreme, and only honest part. That is why he thought it important to take "the private and domestic view of public men," and why the discrepancy between the two made him so bitter. For Franklin the domestic self was one among several. No remnants of an immortal soul bothered him, and he needed no replacement for it. His private affections were not politically relevant. Perhaps Pascal's Jesuit adversaries had a point when they argued that they simply did not want to make men desperate, that each condition had its peculiar vices, and that life, and religion as well, could be made more tolerable for priests, gentlemen, commercial people, and the poor by easing their consciences as they went about their appointed tasks. The necessity of assuming social roles is not only inevitable; it does not merit, apart from the notion of a supreme inner self, the charge of hypocrisy, for it does not hide a public crime. Franklin was not a con man; he disguised his enormously superior intelligence, not some secret vice. To be sure, he did mean to dominate, but it was within the confines of the political stage, where the question isn't to rule or not to rule, but the manner in which one shall rule. If it is to be by persuasion, then Franklin had to find the right tone, which was extremely hard for a man so much better informed and so much more intelligent than his colleagues. His example is so important because it has both political and psychological meaning. He saw with perfect clarity what the demands of democratic assemblies were, even in their infancy. He also recognized what personal behavior it imposed upon him before the new morality of the supreme inner self had insinuated itself into every mind. He could therefore describe his pretenses with perfect self-confidence and good humor, knowing that he was contributing to a new and better political order. That also accounts for the charges of hypocrisy and calculation that Melville, D. H. Lawrence, and lesser romantics were to hurl at him in a later age. Did they, then, possess moral and political knowledge he lacked?

In one respect, Franklin's example is highly misleading, because he was a man of extraordinary strength of character as well as of immense intelligence. It was easy for him to be one man among his peers in the Royal Society, another in the small, provincial world of Philadelphia politics, and a third at Versailles. Always aware of the huge social distance he had covered since his impoverished childhood in Boston, he was simply pleased, and not at all upset, by the changes he had experienced, or, to be exact, created for himself. Others have found social mobility more difficult to absorb. The result is that democratic regimes are beset by two forms of the antihypocritical mentality. One is inherent in any openly competitive political system. The other arises from the psychological difficulties of social mobility, up or down. Because political hypocrisy is part of the rhetoric of legitimization and of the politics of persuasion, there is an uneasy fear of fraud and dissimulation in liberal democracies. Democracy generates disappointment, and a sense of always being deceived. Franklin was already a participant in this system, but it did not dismay him. His was not the mentality of the later consumers and beneficiaries of this extremely complex polity. We, however, who still share Hawthorne's political sensibility, are utterly remote from Franklin. We cannot let up on hypocrisy. It bothers us all the time.

One reason for the fear of hypocrisy is also a necessary by-product of liberalism: social mobility. It had not yet revealed all its possibilities in Franklin's age. It brought with it an added sense of universal hypocrisy. Franklin's extraordinary rise in society was as unique socially as was his psychological ability to cope with it. It is, however, likely that the romantic obsession with the true inner self and with the hypocrisy of playing social roles is related to the personal experience of large numbers of less hardy persons. Social mobility became less rare in the nineteenth century, especially among the intellectually gifted. Romantic morality may reflect much of the anguish of people who leave the social world of their childhood behind them and adopt new manners and roles. The true inner self is identified with one's childhood and family, and regret as well as guilt for having left them behind may render new ways artificial, false, and in some way a betrayal of that original self. This personal self is seen as having a primacy that no later social role can claim; and indeed the latter may be despised as demeaning, "stereotyped," or simply "fake"—in any case less genuine than the primordial self. Snobbery becomes a troubling fact of life, as does the sense of self-betrayal.

The malaise of the socially mobile may be more severe in more rigidly caste-like societies than among the sons of newly enriched fathers in America, but it was not unknown here. The pain may have been less acute, but it has been more common. There is, consequently, another source of antihypocritical feeling generated by a liberal social environment: the morality of those who regard the assumption of diverse and contradictory roles—the necessity of playing many parts and taking directions from a variety of social circles—as hypocritical dissimulation, even though no particular evil is done. It would be entirely erroneous to see the psychological uneasiness of the mobile as the sole, or even the chief, source of romantic morality. The pure inner self has many, far earlier antecedents. We need only recall its source in the religious conscience and its display by Alceste. The spread of romanticism, however, occurring as it does from the nineteenth century onward, is not unrelated to it and to the anger against all sham and social show. The mentality of this kind of antihypocrite surely has some relation to the plurality of groups that individuals must move into and out of in liberal societies.

In addition to romanticism, there is the egalitarian component of liberalism, which harbors a strong aversion to the hypocrisy implicit in established social roles. If men accept themselves as the sum of their roles, it is said, then they are doomed to inequality. Only if we assume that there is a self, apart from all social definition, which is capable of morality and therefore deserves respect, can we justify the claims of equality on which not only social justice but liberty itself depends. Hypocrisy is seen in the denial of that inner self, of the source of sincerity and common humanity, and therefore it appears to be the weapon of the beneficiaries of a hierarchical class- and role-obsessed society. And indeed it is hypocritical to claim that class servility suits anyone in our world. These feelings of revulsion against artificiality and pretense as the handmaidens of an unjust inequality are not implausible; but are they always reasonable? Is this sort of antihypocrisy well considered, even from an egalitarian point of view? Does equality not have more to gain from a flexible attitude to all roles, to easy transitions from role to role, and to a multiplicity of roles for each citizen? Why not consider a possibly hypocritical appreciation of all legitimate roles, types, and conditions? Hypocrisy can do as much for equality as it does for inequality. It may be indispensable if we are ever going to fully accept human diversity in all its individual manifestations.

The democracy of everyday life, which is rightly admired by egalitarian visitors to America, does not arise from sincerity. It is based on the pretense that we must speak to each other as if social standings were a matter of indifference in our views of each other. That is, of course, not true. Not all of us are even convinced that all men are entitled to a certain minimum of social respect. Only some of us think so. But most of us always act as if we really did believe it, and that is what counts. Our manners are just as artificial as those seen at Versailles in Molière's day, but they are infinitely more democratic. Snobbery is hardly unknown in America, but it is not what it was in the *Ancien Régime* either. It certainly is not the official order of state and society.

Would frankness, conceived as the display of a primary inner self, really do anything for democracy? Only if one assumes that each individual does and must invariably play only one role and that roles must be ordered in rigid hierarchies. That is by no means the case; and if we had a greater parity among various roles and esteem for unfamiliar values, then the extrasocial self as the primary moral agent would lose all egalitarian ideological force. That also makes it all the more worth asking whether public and private roles call for identical degrees of sincerity, given that manners are part of both.[7]

In fact, we assume that our public roles carry greater moral responsibilities than our private ones. We expect to behave better as citizens and public officials than as actors in the private sphere. The whole concern about corruption in government turns on that, and it does yield immense hypocrisy; but pretended virtue may curtail graft and similar vices as well. It is, far more significantly, no longer acceptable in the United States to make racist and anti-Semitic remarks in public; yet in private conversation racism and anti-Semitism are expressed freely and frequently. Southerners used to sneer at this as a display of Northern hypocrisy. In public now, Southerners and Northerners alike are down to a few code words at election time. Would any egalitarian prefer more public frankness? Should our public conduct really mirror our private, inner selves? Often our public manners are better than our personal laxities. That "sugary grin" is, in any case, not a serious issue. On the contrary, it is a very necessary pretense, a witness to our moral efforts no less than to our failures.

Indeed, one might well argue that liberal democracy cannot afford public sincerity. Honesties that humiliate and a stiff-necked refusal to compromise would ruin democratic civility in a political society in which people have many serious differences of belief and interest. Our sense of public ends is so wavering and elusive because we often do not even see the same social scene before us. We do not agree on the facts or figures of social life, and we heartily dislike one another's religious, sexual, intellectual, and political commitments—not to mention one another's ethnic, racial, and class character.

Ideology and Mutual Unmasking

No occasion reveals the incoherence of our public values more than war. War is of course a very commonplace situation, but it is an extreme one. It disrupts the delicate balance of pluralistic societies and radicalizes everyone, as hard-won restraints and inhibitions give way under unendurable pressures. That is why war is psychologically and morally so revealing, as all readers of Thucydides know. In our age it is also the occasion on which charges of hypocrisy may be exchanged with unmatched virulence. That this spectacle should morally reassure anyone is surely astonishing, yet Michael Walzer in his book *Just and Unjust Wars* finds comfort both in the efforts of soldiers and politicians to conceal their misdeeds and in their relentless unmaskers. Indeed the whole interplay between the hypocrite and his pursuers is seen as a sign of shared moral knowledge. "The exposure of hypocrisy," Walzer writes, "is certainly the most ordinary and it may also be the most important form of moral criticism," for it shows that both the critic and his target share at least some "commitment that goes deeper than partisan allegiance and the emergencies of the battle." When these "deeper" engagements are broken, moral indignation should be expressed, and when lame excuses are offered, the cry of "hypocrite" should be heard loud and clear.[8] It should, in Walzer's view, be heard when war is declared unjustly and when in the course of wars the rules of warfare are disregarded by soldiers and statesmen, who then offer false justifications for their actions. This is surely a historically doubtful view, for while charges of hypocrisy may occur in a context of such moral consensus, there is no reason whatsoever to suppose that liberal societies in wartime and postwartime differ from those in peacetime in this respect. The conditions of moral confusion and ideological conflict remain the same. Those who must unmask their opponents are reduced to exposing hypocrisy and attacking their moral and political prestige because, having no shared commitments, they cannot reach them directly. That is clear during the course of unpopular wars, and even after those wars that were generally accepted. For wherever there is political freedom there are recriminations, and accusations of deceit.

The very notion of wars as either just or unjust is by no means universally accepted among the citizens of liberal democracies. Just-war theory places war at the end of a continuum that has the harmonious consensual community at its other extreme. War is not outside the rules of law and morality, but is their extension into a disastrous extremity. As such it remains a normal, rule-governed collective activity. But if one puts cruelty first, one will follow some version of Kant's doctrine and see war as beyond the rules of good and evil, just and unjust. It falls in the realm of pure necessity, where the impulse to self-preservation extinguishes the very possibility of justice. It is the world of kill or be killed. In war the moral law as a set of binding rules is as silent as all other laws. *Salus populi suprema lex*, and the only remaining imperative is to end war as soon as possible, and in such a way as to avoid its recurrence. War, in this view, is not an extreme moral situation; it is wholly devoid of any moral compensation save personal courage. Even wars of survival are not just—merely inevitable. The Kantian is very likely to accuse the just-war theorist of gross hypocrisy, encouraging people to enter upon wars recklessly and then baptizing his own side with the holy water of justice. Every enemy can easily be made to look the aggressor. The just-war theorist will not hesitate long before he in turn accuses the Kantian of vile hypocrisy, because those who declare wars to be hell fight them with unrestrained savagery. Both charges are quite justified in that they point to the characteristic temptation that is most likely to undo each one. But in neither case is the theory of the other shown to be erroneous. These charges of hypocrisy about war become systematic precisely because each side must justify itself to the other in terms of its sincerity, since neither can shake the other's convictions about the substance of their disagreement—the status of war as such.

There is nothing new about such quarrels. Becket and the barons were already engaged in that sort of conflict. Becket no longer had any use for the notion of war as the noblest sport of gentlemen, while the barons were repelled by the idea of war as the pursuit of royal profit and power. What they lacked in that moment of confrontation was shared moral knowledge of any kind whatever. Each side looked for the psychological soft spot of the other and aimed at that. Then each was accused of hypocrisy, which was merely a failure to live up to its own standards, not a failure to meet mutually recognized obligations.

This is the normal character of political discourse between irreconcilable ideological opponents within societies that are so free that wars can be discussed openly even while they are being waged. In times of such stress, the intensity of recriminations is naturally great. One need only consider what "hawks" and "doves" say to each other. The "dove" routinely accuses the hawk of appealing to military necessity when in fact his party's economic and political fortunes are his only concern. The "hawk" in turn will work over the dove's psyche and will expose a moral show-off who covers up a private weakness with fanatic public displays. Since "hawk" and "dove" do not see the same moral scene, they can charitably blame each other for blindness or imbecility, which seems hardly adequate in times of extraordinary tension such as war. Therefore, each one tries to dismiss and devalue the other by calling him a hypocrite, which is more offensive. Obviously this imputation does not imply shared knowledge, but mutual inaccessibility. In fact, the contempt for hypocrisy is the only common ground that remains, and that is what renders these accusations so effective.

When Walzer levels accusations of hypocrisy directly, it is not surprisingly at soldiers, whose military ideology he finds unacceptable. Some military men, he notes, proclaim strategic military necessity when in actuality they are merely promoting their own careers. From the point of view of a pure strategist, who judges military actions only in terms of their cost and effectiveness, this is a completely meaningless observation. Who cares about an officer's motives as long as he fights intelligently and successfully? That is Becket's stance when we first meet him. Motives mean nothing, and performance is all that counts. Only the consequences of strategies and tactics matter, and in principle we should be able to calculate these correctly. In practice it is, of course, no easier to make exact calculations about matters of fact than to attain a knowledge of the good and beautiful. It is not hypocritical to fail, however—merely inept, which, to the strategist, is the supreme evil. Becket is telling those barons to go out and win intelligently and cruelly, and not to lose expensively in a gentlemanly sort of way. Moreover, he recognizes that he could easily avoid hypocrisy by eschewing moral pretensions altogether and getting the business over with as quickly and effectively as possible. The reason Walzer is so anxious to see hypocrisy among these hard-boiled types is not because he finds them deeply committed to his values, but because they so chillingly reject them.

Becket did not have to defend his sanguinary plans to a liberal democratic public. Walzer can accuse the military strategist of hypocrisy only because the latter often does have to face accusers who differ from him in every relevant respect. Faced with publics that do not share his approach to war or political combat, the strategist pleads necessity and takes other measures to evade criticisms. That hardly implies that he accepts the validity of these reproofs, especially as they usually come after the event. The fact that the sense of military necessity is more urgent during war than when it is all over renders these exchanges peculiarly artificial. The strategist sees hypocrisy in the retrospective moralist who never had to bear the burdens of instant choice, and who now feels safe to charge him with gross brutality and hypocrisy. These arguments, however, easily become an integral part of normal ideological discourse in free societies. What was and was not a military necessity is as much subject to differences of interpretation as any other policy in dispute, and it is readily absorbed by the system until it is replaced by some more immediately striking subject of controversy and new charges of hypocrisy.

When the normal situation of pluralism is upset and some degree of moral unity prevails, the cry of hypocrisy is no longer heard, because no one is out to "psychically annihilate" or unmask the opposition. One need only remember the Second World War to understand that. There were few cries of hypocrisy on the English-speaking side, even from the left, after Hitler invaded Russia during the years of struggle. It was a unique period of moral certainty and assurance. Hitler was so awful, so obviously a *summum malum*, that his effect was to act as a temporarily unifying, shared *summum bonum*. The brief moral knowledge shared was that Hitler had to be defeated. Within the circumference of this ideological unity the talk was entirely strategic: how to win. As for Hitler, his sincerity was hardly an issue. When one really knows that someone is evil, one has no time for his possible hypocrisy. One also does not accuse people with whom one shares an overriding aim. Lord Cherwell's critics challenged only his estimates, not his motives, when during the war they objected to the massive bombing of working-class neighborhoods in German cities. Other disagreements were also couched in similarly neutral terms. The memory of those five years has had its effect on hypocrisy and counterhypocrisy. Among those too young to recall them, there is a longing to relive what seems like a heroic moral condition. The young see a complacent hypocrisy in that older generation that cannot or will not recognize anything quite resembling that battle in all the many conflicts that have followed it. The old see only a callow hypocrisy among the young, who demand their adherence to causes that do not even reawaken the memory of that earlier war.

When the Second World War was over, the normal process of recriminations naturally resumed its course. It had always been more than one war. In Britain it had been a war of imperial survival and a war against fascism. The intelligent and enlightened members of the traditional ruling class assumed the leadership of Britain at war, and the antifascists, overwhelmingly intellectuals of the left, fell into line. Even during the war there were strains—over an early second front, for instance. However, it was only after the war that Labour's Lord Snow questioned Tory Lord Cherwell's character. It was then also that Evelyn Waugh wrote *The End of the Battle*, that masterpiece of outrage against every hypocrisy and every betrayal during the war. Among these the adulation of Stalin was, to Waugh, the most reprehensible and revolting, but it was scarcely the only hypocritical folly.

In retrospect it also seemed to other, more ardent antifascist warriors that they had lost their moral purity, while those who had fought to save their country felt that they had lost their honor to their military allies. What had and had not been necessary became the subject of dispute, and each side accused the other of bad faith and a revolting hypocrisy. Americans have habitually traded charges of hypocrisy during and after most of their military ventures, as befits the oldest democracy. Let us not forget that archetype of American political antihypocrites, Henry Thoreau, surely one of Alceste's most legitimate heirs. Even in his relatively homogeneous America there was already more ideological unmasking than shared moral knowledge in the acrimonious arguments about the Mexican War.

Charges of hypocrisy, of course, also are made when people *do* agree about the ultimate purposes of politics. When that happens the hypocrite is, however, not said to be just feigning virtue; he is also accused of covering up a crime. In the classical age of *raison d'état*, matters were exactly as Walzer describes them. Jansenists and *dévots* might well have called Cardinal Richelieu a hypocrite when he defended his alliance with Protestant powers on religious and moral grounds. How, after all, can anyone claim to defend the true faith by encouraging and arming heretics? The paid apologists of the cardinal were political con men and their master was a very wicked man. They were condemned not only by the views of zealots, but by their own; for they were all religious men holding the same beliefs. Here the traditional sanction of moral outrage is indeed a proof of shared moral knowledge. Reason of state covered much for Richelieu, but it was not above his religion. As we have seen, the *dévots*, like all puritans, suffered from hypocrisies of their own, but that is not the point here. When they accused Richelieu of hypocrisy, he and they knew exactly what was at stake: a betrayal of the faith for merely political ends, thinly veiled by the excuses churned out by paid scribblers.[9] When everyone really knows a policy to be absolutely wrong, disguises can be ripped off to reveal the intolerable, and so may bring the errant soldier and politician back to a state of rectitude. It is not at all surprising that "naive" hypocrisy became such a great issue in the age of the nascent modern state. This is the world of Pascal and Molière, and events do much to explain the intensity of their interest in hypocrisy. Neither then nor now, however, is there any reason to rejoice in these acrimonious outbursts. That is what Molière appreciated so fully. His fear of Tartuffe did not mellow his contempt for Alceste. One can condemn the ruthless strategist without embracing the righteous warrior.

Within our situation of systematic hypocrisy, Alceste and Tartuffe are still around. They continue to flourish. Con men still meet their match. Alceste and his followers, all devoted to perfect candor, are still unhappy with every "social fabric." Anarchists in feeling if not in fact, they are no threat to any historical society, because they must either try solitude, like Alceste, or join in the accepted pattern of antihypocritical political behavior that sustains a liberal order. In other societies their prospects are too poor to bear description. There are also cynics, driven by contempt for ideological politics to reject all public standards as mere sham. They also seek purity. A small, cerebral group, they have been driven by an excessive honesty out of politics and even out of current moral life. A hard but honest "realism" will inevitably appeal to such people, unable to bear the pseudo-sincerity of all visible politicians. Christopher Marlowe's stage Machiavelli, who held that "there is no sin but ignorance," and Nietzsche with his vision of "honest liars" appeal profoundly to these disappointed idealists. Honesty was indeed Machiavelli's great claim for his enterprise. He and he alone had dared to see things as they are and had put before us a model of an "honest" prince, who is not ignorant because he is not self-deceived. Although he lies and cheats and betrays, he does so in full awareness of his acts. Such a figure is, of course, more likely to appear on the stage than in history. Anouilh's Becket tries this stance, but he cannot keep it up. Most Machiavellian princes soon fall prey to their own deceptions. Nevertheless, in a world of cloying sentimentality, of cheap compassion and verbose charity, Nietzsche's call for a pure, steely honesty for its own sake cannot but attract. This was the moral climate that drove him to misanthropy, and it has gained him a following that, in due course, has turned its disdainful back upon liberal democracy.

The only voice that damns hypocrisy to some purpose is one that laments that the society in which we live does not live up to its declared principles, promises, and possibilities. This outraged jeremiad is the mark of a moralistic rather than a moral society, perhaps; but it is not without effect, because this type of antihypocrite does at least have a sense of what is wrong, rather than only an urge to spread the blame. He may well frighten politicians enough to inhibit them to a significant degree. Even the participants in the system of hypocrisy and counterhypocrisy perform unintended services to liberal societies. Each fears the other enough to restrain himself. Their discourse conveys little moral urgency, but it does maintain some standards of decency. The politics of unreconciled political neighbors are not as liberating as earlier liberals had hoped, not as edifying as had been expected, and certainly far less democratic; but they make for a society far less dishonest and far less cruel than its known alternatives. It could hardly survive without hypocrisy.

To put hypocrisy first entangles us finally in too much moral cruelty, exposes us too easily to misanthropy, and unbalances our politics. These considerations are not to be taken as an endorsement of hypocrisy, least of all the naive kind. They merely point to the difficulties we encounter if we make more of hypocrisy than of cruelty, for example. There are, to be sure, hypocrisies that are morally exceptionally cruel because they humiliate and embitter people, and that also are not in keeping with the mores of liberal democracy. This is the feigning that is called snobbery. And although not all forms of snobbery are hypocritical, some indeed are. It is to snobbery that one might, therefore, look to find a vice one might despise without running the risks posed by a too ardent loathing for hypocrisy in general.

What is wrong with snobbery?

It is impossible, in our condition of society, not to be sometimes a snob.

—Thackeray

3

THE WORD "SNOB" has had many meanings since it surfaced in the late Middle Ages, none of them good. It began as an all-purpose insult, used to express contempt.[1] By now it has certainly earned its evil reputation. For us, snobbery means the habit of making inequality hurt. The snob fawns on his superiors and rejects his inferiors. And while he annoys and insults those who have to live with him, he injures himself as well, because he has lost the very possibility of self-respect. To be afraid of the taint of associations from below is to court ignorance of the world. And to yearn for those above one is to be always ashamed not only of one's actual situation, but of one's family, one's available friends, and oneself. Snobbery is simply a very destructive vice.

Awful as it is, snobbery may, however, be quite ineradicable, flourishing in both aristocratic and democratic societies. In the hierarchical order of the Old Régime, the characteristic exchange of snobberies occurred between the aristocratic nobleman and the bourgeois pretender to rank. This was always recognized as a violation of both the aristocratic and the Christian codes, but it outlasted these. Played out in any number of variations, this archetypal encounter was repeated long after most other traces of its original time and place had disappeared. Snobbery is, in fact, also impervious to the rules of democracy, although these condemn it as an obnoxious violation of the public ethos. Indeed, while the oldest forms of snobbery survived, a new and less deliberate kind was to be added. Even without obsequiousness or arrogance, we may often become snobs in spite of ourselves, if we live in freedom. As we join a multiplicity of groups that include some people, we also exclude most others. These little societies are by no means equal in social standing and neither are their individual members. Inevitably some outsiders will be rebuffed and hurt, and this would be the case even if there were no groups that make social exclusion their chief business. Given any degree of inequality and any kind of choice of intimacies and interests, there is bound to be snobbery in effect, some of it inadvertent and some intentional. The snub that wounds and the aspiration that demeans flourished in the Old Régime, and they are still conspicuously among us. In this snobbery resembles hypocrisy, except that its practical consequences are far greater.

The link between hypocrisy and snobbery is obvious enough: both are false claims to merit; both are expressions of utter insincerity. That is why the first and most respected and quoted authority on the subject, Thackeray, thought of snobbery as a particularly obnoxious form of hypocrisy: social pretension. He was, however, never quite satisfied with his own definition of a snob—one "who meanly admires mean things."[2] It is vague; and after describing every kind of snob, he still could not explain these creatures. He even thought that he might be one himself, which was distressing, since Thackeray really disliked people who boasted of their wealth and pedigree or were ashamed of their calling and poverty. His most distinguished successor, Harold Nicolson, himself a compulsive snob, had the same difficulty. He could not pin down or describe the snob's character, even though he could point to his unyielding presence. The snob, in fact, seems to lack a personality , so that he is revealed only in his rituals of repulsion. As Nicolson observed him, he is always out "to enhance his own position by avoiding the society of his social inferiors and by cultivating the society of the rich and powerful."[3] He lives in constant fear of being seen with undistinguished people, which means that he may reject his family and old friends to seek out the company of those who appear to have more prestige. In action, that is how we see him; he emerges as self-destroying and dishonorable, and in his public manners thoroughly undemocratic. Because he is such a poseur, he is often hard to know or to define.

The defenders of snobbery have not been numerous. Indeed, the only claim on its behalf is that it can be useful. At best it is forgiven as a side effect of more noble ambitions. Aldous Huxley warned us that without culture snobs, such as the tone-deaf patrons who pretend to elevated musical taste, artists could not survive and real music lovers would be without operas and symphonies. Snobbery does much to support such unproductive and nonutilitarian pursuits as the arts and humanities. Indeed, Huxley went on to say, "a society with plenty of snobberies is like a dog with plenty of fleas: it is not likely to become comatose." Every snobbery demands of its devotees unceasing efforts, a succession of social sacrifices.[4] While this unflattering praise does remind us of the ritualistic character of snobbery, it sees only the upward striving and forgets the kick aimed downward. There are at least as many snobs who look down upon the poor scholar and artist as there are patrons. If anything favorable can be said about snobbery, it is entirely in the realm of the literary imagination, not in action. Our memories of the ways of the old gentry and aristocracy are woven into our dreams of the past, and they can still enchant us. Whether in laughter or tears, the greatest novels, from Jane Austen to Marcel Proust, have been nourished by them. Snobbery may well be a private and a social menace, but like misanthropy it does nourish the creative imagination. That is a feeble recommendation perhaps, but it is the only possible one.

The most consoling view of snobbery is that it is utterly trivial. There are historical optimists who see it as something that occurs in the brief interval between the Old Regime and the classless future. Even as such, it is, they say, a mere bubble on the sea of bourgeois society and a minor manifestation of its class system. A revolutionary ought to attend to the latter and even a radical democrat should keep his eye on the "power elite" rather than on "the pretentious monkey business" of the upper crust.[5] The idea is that we ought to worry only about the "deeper levels" of bourgeois society. To call three centuries "a mere phase" is in fact silly, and the so-called "mere surface" of society is where we all live all of the time. Here and now, snobbery is no trifle. Contemporary Americans clearly resent any claim to superiority other than that of a higher standard of living. Just as they admire achievement and wealth, they hate snobbery, the snub that insults. It is not the mere fact of unequal wealth that arouses their deepest social anger, but unearned, and therefore unmerited, displays of status. As Tocqueville already noted, "the people do not want the rich to sacrifice their money, but their pride."[6] Not only is snobbery an important vice in the eyes of most people; it is also not just a passing interlude in our history. It was known to monarchical Europe, and it has survived in a democratic polity which had never even known Thackeray's "brutal, unchristian, blundering feudal system." It was generally expected that snobbery would eventually simply die out in America. But while the democracy of everyday life was and is one of its great glories, America still has its snobs; so, too, have all the now democratic countries of Europe. Snobs have been around for a very long time and are not likely to vanish, and neither will the pain and rage they habitually cause.

Primary Snobbery: Birth versus Achievement

The durability of snobbery has suggested to some observers that it may be the price one pays for social mobility and that it must be treated as one of the many costs of the revolutions of the eighteenth century which opened all careers to talent. Some sociologists even claim that there is more snobbery in democratic America than in Europe.[7] Status anxiety is said to drive some Americans to it occasionally. It is hard to imagine how snobbery can be measured. It is surely not a matter of quantity but of degrees of incongruity. In a society of orders and well-defined status lines such as the France of Louis XIV, snobbery is quite functional. It is expected, and it keeps the various levels of society apart. Nevertheless, snobbery was known and roundly condemned even in the old monarchies. In a democratic society, snobbery is far more conspicuous because it is wholly out of place and a violation of its patriotic values. Here it is a public vice in its own right, a primary wrong. That is why snobbery in America is far more interesting, though probably less common, than in Europe.

Snobbery is evidently not only a very old vice; it is also very adaptable. It moves with the rules that govern social inequality. The reasons for detesting it alter as well. In the Old Regime, snobbery was seen as a reprehensible expression of social mobility, upward and down, which was itself a direct threat to the system of authorized orders. Molière, the voice of humanism, ridiculed it as a form of personal degradation and blindness. Not least, Christians could not abide snobbery because it was a manifestation of deep sins, such as pride or inordinate selfishness. Molière's laughter has survived best, because he put the most enduring of all snobbish encounters on the comic stage and, in the person of Monsieur Jourdain, revealed to all that the snob is a man without "quality" in all senses of that term. To understand snobs one should observe them, as Molière did, in a succession of typical scenarios, each with its own meanness.

The pedigree of snobbery is amply illustrated in the literature of the seventeenth century because the age was rich in caricatures of social types of every kind, chief among them the courtier and the would-be gentleman. Both were recognized pretenders to unmerited places. The ruthlessly climbing courtier sneering at everyone below him and fawning upon his betters was a fixture on the Jacobean stage. Bosola, the murderous villain of *The Duchess of Malfi,* put it nicely:

91

"Places in the court are but like beds in the hospital, when this man's head lies at that man's foot and so lower and lower" (I, 1).

Later in the century, Samuel Butler spoke of the courtier as "a cipher, that has no value but from the place he stands in. All his happiness consists in the opinion he believes others have of it."[8] But our most elegant authority is La Bruyère. His *Characters* shows us courtiers who are always pretending to be what they are not, quickly forsaking candor, generosity, equity, good nature, and delicacy, as they advance at the court of Louis XIV. Such especially is his finest portrait of a snob, Pamphile, who is afraid to be seen with a clever man who is of a low order. He may shun you one day; but if he sees you in the company of someone important on the next, he will be very friendly. And he will leave you at once to join a nobleman. He acts always as if he were on a stage, never naturally.[9]

La Bruyère's portrait of the snob-as-courtier is quite charitable. It was the social climber who really provoked his sharpest wit. Molière's incomparable Célimène had already mocked a man who "Fawns on dukes and princes and is bored / With anyone who is not a lord." La Bruyère had even less use for such people than she. If the courtier had false social values, the climber had no sense of social order at all. As far as La Bruyère was concerned, there was far too much movement in society. There were far too many new noblemen whose fathers could not even have been pages in the families whose sons-in-law they now were. Even without these changes in status, there was an unseemly scramble for gain. Such people were not parents, or friends, or citizens, or Christians, or really men; they were just money. Yet these appalling people claimed noble standing and often succeeded in their quest. What we see in La Bruyère is the violent clash between the actuality and the orthodoxy of the *Ancien Régime*. The fact was that especially in the city, poor nobles married rich commoners, and the king ennobled commoners as a reward for a variety of services to the Crown. The orthodoxy was that noble blood could only be inherited and that only heredity could bestow the charisma required for genuine honor. Warfare and high office were the only honorable occupations, everything else was base. To work with one's hands was utterly defiling and so was trade. Nobility, moreover, could not be earned. The principle of heredity stood in direct opposition to that of achievement. Because the Crown and even some of the nobility did honor personal wealth, especially as a title to honor, there was a disruptive creedal tension. The mystique of an unalterable hierarchy with the pure of blood at one end and the impure laboring at the other was incompatible with the notion of individually earned wealth as a claim to honor. Even royal favor was not enough to interrupt, especially, the provincial nobility's sense of its unique and closed place. This is evidently not a struggle between ideas of equality and hierarchy, but between individual achievement and inherited honor. No one was interested in equality. La Bruyère thought that too much inequality was the work of sinful man, but the inequality necessary for order and decency was God's law. It was generally held that society should resemble the Great Chain of Being. This cosmic hierarchy was as pleasing to aristocratic as to Christian sensibilities, and both feared disruptions. When La Bruyère noted that most families touched the people at one end and princes of the blood at the other, neither he nor his contemporaries thought that this was a pleasing spectacle. It merely proved that some people had failed to keep their assigned places.

To keep that great chain intact meant that ranks must be separated clearly. The necessity of keeping the city and the court apart is what made snobbery such a real danger. In Massinger's Jacobean play *The City-Madam*, it is neither the wealth of the newly knighted merchant nor his wife's fancy finery that is objectionable. These in fact are a source of pride to the city. But when this wife aspires to the manners of the court and forgets that "a fit decorum must be kept, the court distinguished from the city" (III, 2), then she becomes a threat to the social order. She shows this plainly by defying her husband and encouraging her daughters to ignore paternal authority. She has forgotten her "sphere," and this is an invitation to villainy and corruption and domestic disorder. There is nothing amiss in a poor noble's marrying the daughter of a merchant in Massinger's England. The young lord does accuse his mere gentry rival of being "the first of his dung-heap created a gentleman," but their quarrel is soon patched up. Indeed, the rich commoner does not fail to return the insult by scorning the nobleman's shabby clothes and unpaid bills. The tension is tolerable, though the basic difference between being born a noble and being made a noble is there. The new gentleman is not, however, a danger to the patriarchal order here. The threat comes from the court-imitating city-madam, because she tries to break through the barriers that keep the established orders apart, each confined to its own sphere.

In her place, the city-madam was respected, and that made her ambitions appear unreasonable and illegitimate. Her contempt for her set place was an aberrant act of snobbery, which her husband was bound to punish. Not all snobbery is provoked by such overt assertions. In France there had been a lively tradition of antibourgeois satire since the later Middle Ages. Much of it expressed a simple loathing for the bourgeoisie as such. To be bourgeois was to be out of one's place and unwanted. The occupations of such people were neither noble nor menial, so there was something unfitting about their very presence. This is not the only root of European snobbery, but it is the oldest. From the very first, the ennoblement of commoners had been a subject of ridicule and resentment. Molière's George Dandin, the rich peasant who marries a noblewoman so that his sons might be gentlemen, was a stock figure. That he was cuckolded and put down by his awful in-laws was to be expected. He says so himself.[10] In fact, long before there was much social mobility, marriages between commoners and noblemen created a veritable inferno of snobbery. This is where the "primary" form, the archetype of all other snobberies, occurs.[11] An arrogant nobleman is driven by poverty to desert his honor, while the rich commoner cringes before him. Each hates himself and the other. Contempt and rage, self-loathing and greed, glare at each other, so that in the last version of the would-be gentleman's comedy, Lesage's *Turcaret*, everyone corrupts everyone else in a sea of shared knavery. Forty years after Molière's *Bourgeois Gentilhomme*, the confusion of wealth and rank was complete. Turcaret, a rich financier, not only has blotted out his family and his past; he hopes to commit bigamy with a noblewoman. The aristocrats are just as unscrupulous, grasping, and dishonest as he is. There is no effort here to flatter the nobility or to excuse anyone. All the social distinctions have wholly given way to greed, and snobbery is just incidental to the general decay. Such is the effect of La Bruyère's men who are "just money."

Not one of its imitators, however, was ever to come close to Molière's *Bourgeois Gentilhomme* in exposing all the subtleties of primary snobbery. That is because Molière did not judge his characters as parts of a sanctified social order, but as individuals. The count who exploits M. Jourdain is a clever crook: snobbery pays. M. Jourdain's faults are personal: obtuseness and a lack of personal pride. He cannot appreciate himself, his family, and his considerable fortune but must grovel before a disreputable nobleman who robs him and a marquise who mocks him. Mme. Jourdain, in sharp contrast to her fatuous spouse, does not forget that both their parents were cloth merchants, and her plain honesty and self-assurance compare very favorably with his pathetic efforts at refinement. She may be a little blunt, but she is very intelligent; for she does not want her daughter to marry a gentleman. Such marriages do not prosper, she tells us, especially as the children look down on one pair of grandparents. The real hero of the play, however, is Cléonte, her prospective son-in-law. When M. Jourdain asks him whether he is a nobleman, Cléonte honestly denies it, even though he knows that this will not promote his suit. Proudly, and in language far more refined than Jourdain's plebeian speech, he admits that although his parents have served the state and he has been an officer in the army for some years, he is not a nobleman. He obviously belongs to the highest reaches of the official bourgeoisie and could easily claim a higher standing, but he is too proud to make a false claim. What Cléonte stands for is personal honor divorced from any social status. He does not make a case for his social standing, but for his own probity. Certainly he has not even heard of an egalitarian dignity of man. Cléonte defiantly and courageously chooses to be what his situation has made him. He could pretend to be something else, but he prefers to remain loyal to his parents and himself. That is a personal ideal, and it is an obvious and enduring threat to every kind of snobbery, both the cowardly and the arrogant kind. That it owes something to the traditional ideal of social honor is clear, to be sure. That is why both the count and the marquise like Cléonte and do their best to help him with his courtship. Nevertheless, his pride is not theirs. His honor is an achievement, an act of will; theirs is merely a matter of birth and arrogance. Subversively, Molière was telling Jourdain to show some pride in himself, his family, and his wealth and to stop abasing himself before courtiers.

However absurd M. Jourdain's conduct may be, it is the nobleman who is greedy, not the bourgeois. And indeed the land hunger of both peasants and aristocrats expressed degrees of greed and rapacity that might well make a modern businessman blush. Greed is no more peculiar to traders and manufacturers in practice, nor to laissez-faire liberalism in theory, than to the habits of military conquest and to its expansive ideologies. Only the objects have changed. The charge that "middle-class" liberalism as a doctrine is exceptionally favorable to greed is merely one more expression of "primary" snobbery, which was once common among the nobility and is now shared by nostalgic intellectuals. Molière was more realistic and less solemn than these types usually are.

Molière's laughter exposes the moral dodges of both parties in the game of "primary" snobbery, and it does so in a wholly secular way. These people are not judged according to the standards of Christian morality. In Molière's comedy of ideas, the ethics of self-esteem collide with the false pride and the follies of snobbery in a purely human world. If any religion appears at all here, it is the myth of noble blood. It would, however, be completely mistaken to think that the mythology and rituals of heredity were the real religion of the *Ancien Régime*. It might move both M. Jourdain and his tormentors, but Christianity was both the official and the genuine faith of their society. What troubled a Christian like La Bruyère about snobbery was not its dishonesty and vulgarity, but its indifference to real merit—that is, to Christian virtues. Some of the great were so proud, he wrote, that they could not bring themselves to share a God or a religion with the people. And the aspiring bourgeois sins in his unchristian greed, envy, and avarice. Since the late Middle Ages, in fact, the ambitious bourgeois and especially the lawyers among them had been reviled as bad Christians. Now both the would-be gentleman and the hustling impoverished nobleman became equally sinful. Neither one of them practiced the Christian virtues, or appreciated them in others. Their snobbish struggle was an unholy expression of pure egotism. Pride was at the root of all "primary" snobbery, and there was nothing more unbecoming to a Christian gentleman. All this social rising and falling was, for La Bruyère, above all else a sign that true virtue, personal merit, and Christian morality were being neglected. If they were observed, people would be satisfied with moderate degrees of wealth and honor. In this he was entirely traditional, far more so than Molière. So also in Massinger's very conventional *City-Madam*, it is quite typically the Machiavellian villain who sneers that there is "no vice but want," which is a dangerous sentiment, unwelcome to the decorous men of both the city and the court. Nevertheless, these moral platitudes could only enhance the uneasy self-contempt of the commoner as he continued to yearn for honors which he knew to be available to men who had claims other than "true merit." Preaching also did nothing to soften the arrogance of the poor aristocrat, who was not prepared to humble himself before his commoner creditors. He preferred to cheat and to insult them, even though he knew that this was indecent for a Christian gentleman.

La Bruyère's distress at the fate of true merit throws some light on Montesquieu's later remark that in Europe men received three educations, "a thing unknown in antiquity."[12] The first education was that of their fathers, the second was that of religion, and the third was that of the world. In the end, only the last was effective. Although Montesquieu did not go into details, we may assume that honor was taught by noble parents, Christian virtue by the Church, and the means of getting ahead socially by the world. It is the awareness of the tug-of-war among these three teachings that brings snobbery into relief, as an avoidable fault; but it also indicates its psychological depths. Montesquieu's cure, so unlike La Bruyère's, was to lessen the impact of honor and religion. The result would be the commercially successful, enterprising, independent, and utterly self-centered gentleman, as he appears in Montesquieu's idealized England. There, though the ranks of society were separated by the constitution, the nobility and the people were close to each other because personal relations were free and easy. An English gentleman might well be educated according to Locke's instructions. No snobbery for him; he is affable to everyone. And though he is well-born and Locke made some faint concessions to prevailing prejudices, this gentlemanly youth is to be taught a manual trade and bookkeeping. All this will make him a rational, prosperous, and successful landlord, as well as a sound local magistrate. The martial skills are not part of his upbringing. This commercial gentleman is certainly no democrat, but he is no "bourgeois gentilhomme," like M. Jourdain. He is also remote from the French nobility that was so suicidally incapable of abandoning its faith in blood, honor, and idleness. This new man would not pay for a fabricated family tree, and he need neither expect nor tolerate the condescension of aristocrats. In Montesquieu's idealized England, snobbery was a personal flaw, not a systemic vice.

Although they were so much more rigid than the ideal Lockean gentleman, the French nobility did occasionally embrace intellectually and artistically gifted commoners. There were, as Jourdain's music and dancing masters tell us, real connoisseurs of the arts among the nobility, and some were intellectuals in their own right. Often they went even beyond patronage in their relations to men of letters. It did little for the independence of the latter. On the contrary, it led to their enduring self-identification with the aristocracy, to snobbery, and to a diffuse resentment. A gentleman raised by Locke would avoid all that. He would be neither a patron of the arts, nor an intellectual of any sort. Independence of mind, sound habits, and practical skills would and did do very well for the ruling class Locke had in mind.[13] It would invite neither imitation nor rage. Montesquieu evidently also preferred the outcome of a Lockean education to the experiences and example of a young bourgeois, Arouet, who chose to go under the name of M. de Voltaire and to live *noblement* at Ferney. But then Montesquieu had never been insulted by the servants of noblemen as Voltaire had been.

Montesquieu was clearly concerned with the political costs of snobbery. He had every reason to be appalled by a decadent ruling class, and his contempt for courtiers was aroused not by their failure to sustain the old social hierarchies and Christian morals, but by their political ineptitude. La Bruyère's attitudes, however, had by no means lost their vigor, in spite of Locke's and Montesquieu's challenges. In Jane Austen's novels, the Christian gentleman is still the very opposite of the snob. Her many-tiered local world is a veritable zoo of snobs. A very great lady such as Lady Catherine de Bourgh; a vicar's wife, Mrs. Elton; and a country gentleman, Sir Walter Elliot, are three perfect snobs, but in each case something morally more serious is the matter with them. Sir Walter Elliot is vain, we are told, and stupid as well. He truckles to his titled relations and brushes off a kind teacher who had helped his daughter, but that is only a fraction of his vanity, foppery, and foolishness. Mrs. Elton, a vicar's wife, is so silly, selfish, and vain that one would dislike her even without her vulgarity, but this socially insecure snob is one of Jane Austen's least harmful. Lady Catherine de Bourgh, who is very grand, is far worse. She is proud, selfish, inconsiderate, ill-mannered, boastful, and domineering. She insults not only Elizabeth Bennet, but all her family as well, in order to prevent Elizabeth from marrying her nephew Darcy (who is not unlike his aunt). That is why Elizabeth, in refusing his first proposal, tells him that she would not have accepted him even if he had been more gentleman-like. She means that he has been too proud and that his manners were too snobbish for a gentleman. He is mortified, but in time accepts her judgment and soon reforms. When he marries her he is as gentlemanly as a rich and well-born man should be. He has come to love some of Elizabeth's relations who are in trade, because they are kind and well-mannered people. Neither he nor his wife cares for those members of their respective families who lack the social and the Christian virtues. Jane Austen approved of people rising in society through their own efforts, and often laughed at the prejudices of the gentry against trade; but she just as obviously believed that the prevailing hierarchy was entirely acceptable, as long as true merit was honored and unchristian conduct censured everywhere. No genuine gentleman would ever be a snob in such a world.

For Jane Austen, a gentleman did not have to inherit his honor. In this she differed from the more traditional Burke and Dr. Johnson. In Burke's view, inherited attitudes made the English gentleman a bulwark of civilization, but Dr. Johnson, always robust, wrote in his *Dictionary:* "Gentleman: a man of ancestry. All other derivations seem to be whimsical." It was surely her finer eye for snobbery that led Jane Austen to separate the Christian gentleman so completely from the merely well-born but possibly proud or vain men and women. The distinction had existed since the Renaissance, but birth had been a necessary quality of gentlemen then and it remained so. Jane Austen and Thackeray tried to establish an essentially nonhereditary gentlemanly ideal. Their new gentleman is not without means; otherwise he could not behave generously to his inferiors. Brave, wise, and decent, he is free of Thackeray's most hated vice, "lordolatry." Nothing of the detested feudal past clings to his "graceful outward manner." He is loyal to his parents and he pays his debts. This paragon appears in many of Thackeray's novels, but he does not bear the burden of the case against snobbery. Jane Austen's gentleman was really both the last and most perfect response to "primary" snobbery seen as an offense against Christian morality.

Thackeray's *Book of Snobs* is, in fact, a great turning point in the history of snobbery. It is no longer merely an ungentlemanly vice, a political danger, or part of an unbecoming social scramble. It is now a vice in its own right. Snobbery is a direct attack against equality. The snob no longer violates true Christian merit, but the rights of men "created equal." Snobbery itself had, moreover, changed. It had proliferated. To the "primary" encounter of snobbery, the old interplay of climbing commoner and haughty nobleman, were now added literary, military, university, and radical snobs, each with a special circle. Anyone who closes himself off from his fellow men and who lacks a sense of his own and other people's equal rights is now a potential snob. That is why Thackeray noted that snobbery had spread in his own lifetime as quickly as the railway lines in Britain. He suddenly saw it everywhere, because it stood out so vividly in contrast to a spreading democratic outlook. Snobbery became, as it still is, a public as well as a private vice of the first order, rather than just a symptom of a deeper flaw.

Secondary Snobbery: Bad Political Manners in a Democracy

What equality meant to Thackeray is not altogether clear, but it resembled the then prevailing ethos of Jacksonian America, with its slavery included. Nothing that he said would have been very new to contemporary American readers. In fact, because they had had so much more experience with democratic government than he, they had a far more acute sense of the political and not just the social impact of snobbery. The boundaries between acceptable and intolerable inequalities were a burning issue for Americans from the first. Somewhere there had to be a line that marked off legitimate differences of wealth and talent from unacceptably undemocratic and unrepublican political manners and activities. The traditional solution of educating gentlemen who would rise above all social differences, except those of true moral merit, could not serve in the United States, because it was not genuinely democratic. It did not imply political equality, only self-restraint. Egalitarian conduct requires something more spontaneous, in keeping with the natural order among people. What that was to be could not be settled, except negatively as a continuing and necessary protest against aristocratic pretensions. Inequality became snobbery when it rose above its always uncertain but intuitively well-recognized limits in the daily relationships between citizens, especially on the political stage.

If there was to be any place at all for a gentleman in a democratic society, then he would have to be a completely new character. One need only look at James Fenimore Cooper's *American Democrat* to see how far from Europe this gentleman had come. He is genuinely democratic. Naturally he admires General Jackson and his views, for he knows that the poor have just as much of "a stake in their country" as the rich and that universal manhood suffrage is to be taken for granted. Cooper's hero is a political agent first and foremost, and because he is better educated than his fellow citizens, he has special political tasks. He must have a great deal of civil courage; he is candid in opposing public opinion and those popular measures that he knows to be wrong. His speech is manly and very simple, in order to maintain high standards of public discourse and to protect the purity of language. Puritan religion, with its authoritarian work ethic, does not appeal to him, for it is too limiting. As befits a democrat, he is no slave to tradition, least of all to the English past. Sir Walter Scott he regards as unsuitable fare for a democratic nation. Above all, Cooper's gentleman is seen entirely politically. That is all that matters. His contribution to the polity is his moral courage, as befits a republic of majority rule and minority rights. Such a man is obviously not a snob, especially since snobbery in a democracy has an added political dimension: fear of the people and aloofness from one's fellow citizens. Snobbery was now a political menace, not merely a personal infirmity or a sign of such sins as pride and vanity. It was an offense against the spirit of the Declaration of Independence, and as such it was far more significant. But it did not go away, not even in the democratic United States. The old habits of primary snobbery survived in the New World.

Americans were not unaware of this anomaly, and it was much discussed long before Thackeray composed his sketches. They did not use the word "snob" during these years so much as "aristocrat," which has a sharper political edge. It was not that they feared a return of the exiled Tories or the sudden emergence of feudalism. Rather, they suspected that inequalities of wealth might interfere with daily democratic manners and diminish their political rights and liberty. This was thought especially likely if governments became powerful and an object of the ambition of the rich. "The few" feared the power of the people, who had, after all, never consented to such unequal wealth. As debtors, especially, the people often asserted themselves politically in state legislatures, and this was troubling to men of property. Their enduring uneasiness, however, had no such specific cause. It was simply that their wealth, even though quite safe in fact, could not buy them perfect immunity from the psychological insecurities created by democratic government and an officially egalitarian ideology. The possibility of losing one's social place by public demotion through majority votes was always there. Most citizens were far from rich. That is why John Adams feared both "the many" and "the few." That "the few" would use their advantages to corrupt "the many" seemed to him a simple fact of human nature. He dreaded "the few," he glumly wrote to his old friend Thomas Jefferson; and since in Adams's mind anyone who could control more than one vote was an "aristocrat," there really was much to fear. In his view, a man who had such an unjust share of power was sure to become domineering. Moreover, anything could engender enough prestige for such electoral domination. Good looks, money, birth, even a Harvard education—all these could give one an undue political advantage. He had no confidence at all in Jefferson's educational scheme that would train a "natural" aristocracy of the academically gifted to rule America in place of all "artificial" aristocracies. Social ambition has the same mischievous results whether it drives natural aristocrats or "pseudo-aristoi." At his gloomiest, Adams predicted that his and Jefferson's efforts to keep hereditary offices and honors out of America would fail.[14] Exaggerated as they were, Adams's worries were not without substance. He could see that the problem of inequality in an open representative electoral system, in which majorities ruled, could not be abated by political careers open to talent only. Prestige had politically dangerous possibilities and, given the intensity of social ambitions, he did not see how one could contain "the few." This had made him, conservative though he was, the openly acknowledged precursor of modern radical democrats, especially of anti-elitists.[15] His real intellectual interest, however, is that he formulated the American idea of aristocracy or elite, as a group that somehow usurps an unfair share of political influence and power, and that misuses the prestige of wealth for undemocratic political ends. Snobbery becomes an instrument of political manipulation in the hands of such men. It is therefore profoundly subversive of representative democracy. Yet, as Adams so despairingly recognized, it seemed unavoidable to some degree, even if it did not always have fatal results. He certainly had no confidence in the "many," whose rapacity and gullibility he dreaded.

Jefferson's most ardent admirers eventually came to share Adams's suspicions, and they were just as uninterested as the latter had been in natural aristocrats. What puzzled Jacksonian democrats was why there was so much "aristocracy," so much unrepublican snobbery, in their country. That it existed could not be doubted. The opposition to universal suffrage was merely the tip of an iceberg of fear of the people. We catch a sense of it in some of the interviews that Tocqueville wrote down in preparing his book. It was not his main interest, but he did notice the insecurity and fearfulness of this moneyed aristocracy, and he was not surprised. An inherited title of nobility cannot be taken away—one *is* a count; but money comes and goes. Anyone can, in principle, make money and lose it. Tocqueville thought that their fears of popular confiscations and general rapacity were quite false. The American people respected property rights profoundly. Debtors would not, and indeed did not, ruin their creditors, and the fears of the latter were vastly exaggerated. In fact, he did not like this commercial aristocracy, but he did not think it was a threat either. Individualism kept Americans so much on the move that they forgot their localities and ancestors, so a settled aristocracy was unlikely. Tocqueville's American disciple Grimké agreed with him. The third estate was too large and the professional classes were too well integrated into it for differences of wealth to harden into castes.[16] Nevertheless, there were grounds for concern.

To understand the perpetual irritation of the Jacksonian democrat, one must turn from Tocqueville and Grimké to another visitor from Europe, the liberal German Francis Grund, whose *Aristocracy in America* is an encyclopedia of our native snobberies, arranged by a wholly unsympathetic observer.[17] Grund was completely baffled by what he discovered. Why, in the absence of both a hereditary aristocracy and a feudal past, were the rich in America so addicted to "primary" snobbery and so hostile to the excellent institutions of their country? To a European liberal, it seemed incredible in the years 1828–1840 that there should be so much disaffection in America. What Thackeray had called "lordolatry" lived on even without his despised monarchy and court-gazettes. In a country built on the denial of the principle of heredity, the rich continued to yearn for, indeed to worship, English peers. Grund understood that slave-holding encouraged pride in birth, but he failed to see that inherited wealth also invigorates the value of heredity and its associated ideas, so that they could easily survive the challenge of republicanism. He was therefore not prepared for what he found in New York, Boston, and Philadelphia. What confronted him and outraged his Jacksonian friends was a commercial upper class trying to imitate the English nobility. Since they did not in fact possess the manners of the latter, their Europhilia was doomed to frustration.

When they actually met an aristocrat, they instantly became the ridiculous victims of classical "primary" snobbery. Grotesque as it might seem in the context of America, they managed to put themselves into M. Jourdain's position whenever the opportunity of meeting a real English lord occurred. They were therefore doubly humiliated. Their fellow citizens refused to defer to them; the Europeans mocked them. They expressed their unsatisfied ambitions by an intense, unabating, and open hatred for their own country and its free institutions. Having gained all the wealth that their society could yield, they craved something more—honor; but the democratic beliefs of their countrymen put stringent limits on the deference they could expect. The prospect of being Cooper's democratic gentlemen did not appeal to them. They were unreconciled to Jackson's presidency and contemptuous of the people. Electoral politics was beneath them, since "any blackguard meddles with it." The one political activity that did engage them was to demoralize the elected representatives of the people, whom they "took up" with bribery and flattery. The new immigrants, they claimed, should be denied the vote, because otherwise these newcomers thought they were "just as good as our first people." These "aristocrat's" manners were, as one might expect, just awful, since they never showed any consideration for the feelings of others; putting people in their place was their obsession. Nor were these people well educated, preferring common sense to culture. Thus, none of them contributed directly to the advancement of higher learning. Neither as politicians nor as teachers were they prepared to do anything for their country. Indeed, they were so afraid of the people that they shut themselves up in tight little cliques, which enforced a deadly conformity upon their members. Here they spoke a rabid private language, unlike their public speech, which was less contemptuous. In this self-imposed isolation they felt increasingly oppressed, unable to be free in an environment that they distrusted. The only people who wanted political change in America, Grund noticed, were the rich men. They had expected to rule the people and had been thwarted.

Their fear of equality was translated into a fear of being polluted. In response, they refused to participate openly in public, emerging at most to engage in grudging philanthropies that only underlined their snobbery. Theirs was a life of multiple frustrations, scorned by the English upper classes and angrily disdained by their own people. Grund found these pseudoaristocrats vulgar, incomprehensible, and politically dangerous because they were so obtusely unwilling to appreciate America's institutions.

The chief burden of Grund's tale, apart from its account of a revolting group of plutocrats, is that snobbery has political implications in a democracy. His Jacksonian friends certainly shared that view. The democratic nationalism of the Jacksonians was a direct response to the Anglophilia and exclusiveness of this commercial aristocracy. In fact, both the patterns of snobbery and antisnobbery—or "antielitism," as it came to be called eventually—were set in that period. There have been adaptations and alterations, but it was in the decades preceding the Civil War that this dispute acquired most of its enduring characteristic features.

The response of a Jacksonian democrat when he was confronted by Grund's snobs was to suspect sinister conspiracies and European influences. In either case, there was a threat to America's integrity as a democratic nation. A Jacksonian democrat did not see the Bank of the United States as just a bad economic policy, but as a sinister political incursion upon popular government. The entire bearing of these "aristocrats" showed that they aspired to what Walt Whitman called "the old moth-eaten system of Europe." Worst of all were the idle rich. A Jacksonian found inequalities of wealth quite acceptable, but a refusal to work was a deep cultural offense. It was not just a failure to contribute to the production of useful goods, but a defiance of the national ethos. "Wealth independent of merit and industry" was an English corruption and a pretense at aristocracy. It was an unacceptable snobbery. For it was an expression of that ancient contempt for human labor which had no place in America or in any democracy. The Revolution was supposed to have wiped away the old odium at-

tached to honest labor. In fact, the dignity of labor and tech-
nology were part of a developing new ideology. It noted that
workers and inventors had contributed more to the progress
of mankind than had all the aristocrats and the snobs of
centuries. The men who worked with their hands, not the
knights of romance, were the real heroes of civilization. It
was a very generous vision of what America was meant to
be, but had not yet become. Honor and prestige had not
followed the flag in the most democratic way, and as long as
that remains our actuality, the Jacksonian case against
snobbery will survive in full vigor.[18]

At the very end of the last century America's greatest
student of snobbery, Thorstein Veblen, had relatively little
to add to Grund and to the Jacksonian democrat's com-
plaints. To be sure, America was very different, but the
forms of snobbery had not altered very much. In Edith
Wharton's New York novels, the idle rich are as walled off
and as futile as ever, their passion for Europe's surviving
aristocrats just as ardent. The enormous wealth of some
now made them more welcome in those quarters. Indeed,
Veblen's account of the elaborate rituals of "leisure-class"
conduct testifies to their transatlantic assimilation.[19] In
some cases it seems to have required something close to
human sacrifice. Certainly the brutality with which Mrs.
Vanderbilt forced her daughter to marry the duke of Marl-
borough came close to it. Veblen was, in fact, at his ironic
best when he described the self-mortifications of America's
idle rich. Decorum, ceremonial clothing, and fear of un-
cleanliness and of contact with production all played as
much a part as the pleasures of conspicuous consumption in
the lives of these people. The suffering caused by those
transatlantic marriages and by a life without purpose was
substantial. Here was a quasi-ritualistic worship of heredity
and the aura of honor it might confer. Never had prestige
been purchased more irrationally, expensively, or incon-
gruously, especially when one considers what the rest of
America was doing in 1899. But then, Grund had already
been amazed by conduct so completely out of keeping with
the customs of the country. This was not altered when the

children of Veblen's super-rich decided that simplicity of dress and good works were more suitable modes of distinction. What mattered is that they had thoroughly absorbed the old, European notion that it is disgraceful to participate in production or commerce, and that honor cannot be achieved—that it can come only through inherited wealth and through demonstratively useless activities like sports and display. One can marry honor, but one cannot earn it; indeed, one must not seem to work productively at all.

Veblen was even more astonished by all these atavistic ways than Grund had been. Why were manners and beliefs so much more enduring than artifacts and statutes? To account for it, he resorted to the discredited notion of the heredity of acquired characteristics and "inertia." He also invented an implausible theory of the stages of social development, from savagery to industry, to point out when specific attitudes were acquired. All this pure speculation only made his story more confusing. Like many lesser social theorists of his era, he believed in holistic social change. When a "stage" of development is outgrown, an entire society must be transformed. This leaves unexplained the survival of former ruling classes and ideas, of the rituals of old religions—indeed, of traditions handed down by families. Montesquieu's three educations were not synchronized. Subsequent generations have each been subjected to a similar educational multiplicity. Indeed, Locke had already found it necessary to explain the unfortunate persistence of irrational religions and political habits. He offered the association of ideas as a more convincing account of how our ideas are either put into a correct order, or dislocated to form plausible but false sequences. The pressure of convention and our complex inheritances are the main sources of false associations of ideas. The oldest of such superstitions, as Locke no less than Veblen knew, were those of the impurity of labor and the charisma of birth. Both stand outside the world of commercial and industrial enterprise, and belie the evidence of scientific knowledge. To these they are unyielding strangers. In spite of Locke's convincing explanation, the survival of "atavistic" beliefs caused some consternation even in Europe. Joseph Schumpeter, a decade after Veblen, noted how much these habits of mind contributed to imperialism. He then discovered that the old feudal classes had managed to hang on to their political and ideological power, thanks to a middle class that was still pure Monsieur Jourdain, though a lot richer and better educated. Max Weber, who observed more calmly that the status system was still intact in Europe, nevertheless thought that in democratic America members of the same tax bracket danced together.[20] Veblen could have told him that it was not so. Eastern "old money," the kind that Edith Wharton described, was too absorbed by surviving European notions to dance with anyone but its cousins. That also should occasion no surprise, apart from implausible theories of history.

The avenues for "false" associations of ideas were always wide open. America has always shared a language and a culture with Britain. Political conflict was never as deep as those transatlantic ties, and those Americans who resented democracy would naturally be drawn to that older home, even at the cost of real humiliation there. The lure of "primary" snobbery is so great that it simply survives. The primordial notion that labor is coarse and impure was readily reinforced by its association with the cheapness and physical hardship of manual work, whereas the honor of good birth has always been buttressed by the experience of family continuity, by marrying upward, and eventually by self-serving and gross misinterpretations of Darwin. All this is far more readily explained by Lockean psychology than by Veblen's grandiose theory of history. Those critics of Veblen who say that more was happening in the United States than snobbery are also not altogether unfair. Theodore Roosevelt did manage to get Edith Wharton's bloodless gentry back into public life with his ideal of *noblesse oblige* in the form of "progressive" reform. He also presided over a United States that was mired in ideologies far too sinister to pass for mere idle snobbery. Social Darwinism and Anglo-Saxonism were versions of the hereditary principle that underwrote imperialism, racism, nativism, and anti-Semitism. Democratic theorists did challenge this pseudobiology and its dreams of a white, Protestant "manifest destiny." And ultimately they did so successfully. However, these power fantasies were in their day new and far more serious politically than the old sneering withdrawal from public life, which had been only occasionally broken by corruption. Here indeed was a post-commercial aristocracy. It might lead to a mixture of medievalism and racism or to a call for a military cure for the decadent effects of commerce. The brothers Adams, shut out and self-exiled from industrial and democratic America, could blame everyone but themselves for being insufficiently honored. Most of their kind of hostility as well as their "primary" snobbery has abated, but it has left its traces. Americans appreciate achievement, but some of them also feel proud to belong to the same gene pool as all kinds of distinguished people. Finally, the most important kind of pride in birth, and by no means only in America, is racism, which is far more significant than snobbery. It is not, however, irrelevant to recall that two of Europe's main racist theorists, Gobineau and Lapouge, were bogus counts. Snobbery and racism, in fact, belong to the same family: cousins.

Democratic Responses

Democratic Americans were never prepared to wait for history to do their political work for them. Ever since Jacksonians thundered against "aristocracy," education was thought to be the best democratic remedy for snobbery. As Locke had thought to break the taboo on labor and commerce by teaching them to young gentlemen, so his American heirs hoped to use the public school to create self-confident democratic citizens assured of the dignity of work. Not humiliating "charity schools" but schooling as a right of citizenship and as the necessary ground of self-respect would once and for all dispel those inherited prejudices that insulted the laboring classes. Education was to raise the worker's social standing and his self-esteem, and

it would also put an end to snobbery. The content of education, however, told another story. Schooling is not un-
ambiguously democratic. History and literature reflect a
class-ridden past, wholly unsuitable for the minds of young
republicans. That was one of the reasons why "the literary,
erudite, intellectual and scientific class" was so given to
snobbish airs. Its mental habits had been formed in "feudal" colleges where young people learned to set up "insuperable barriers between the unlettered mechanic and the
classical dignitary." Not only did they come to think of
themselves as "a virtual nobility," refusing to share their
learning with "the mass of society," but they also maintained the customs, literature, and sciences of America's
defeated enemies, the British. The consequences of education are so unpatriotic in effect that they tend to undo the
principles of the American Revolution. With all this in
mind, John O'Sullivan, Hawthorne's friend and occasional
publisher, called for a new American culture. He even regretted that Americans spoke English, for this meant that
they were "covered by the mind of England," and "enslaved
to the past" by the weight of an old language. O'Sullivan
did not deny that English literature was "a delicious fountain," but he thought that it fed undemocratic sentiments to
the young. He was not prepared to call for a purely techni-
cal education, though that was eventually suggested as a solution. He could only hope that an American literature
would eventually suffice. In reality, O'Sullivan's problem
has no solution. The plays of Shakespeare, the stained-glass
windows of every great cathedral, and all history books stir
the imagination. They make the people of the past our contemporaries and their feelings and beliefs become, at least
occasionally, our own. The trouble with the past is not that
it is an alien reality, but that it is not compatible with the
democratic ethos. O'Sullivan's lament echoes on, but in
vain.[21]

In all these Jacksonian protests against aristocracy, but
especially those directed against the literary and scientific
classes, there is a note of outraged patriotism. Snobbery is
caused by a disloyal Europhilia, which is fundamentally

undemocratic and false to the spirit of America. Even when, by the end of the century, it was clear that this was not the only form of native snobbery, it remained the most objectionable. And "lordolatry," with its variants, did remain conspicuous. That is why, from Mark Twain to Sinclair Lewis and beyond, there is an American tradition of anti-snob literature that is unconsciously but profoundly patriotic in tone. In *The Gilded Age*, Mark Twain pictured Washington, D.C., as having two kinds of aristocracies, "the Antiques" and "the Parvenus," both equally ridiculous. The first were vacuous and elegant; the latter often sported European airs and were vulgar. Between them, pride of precedence and Frenchified pretensions constituted a repertory of social distinction. But in good old corrupt Washington, they did not count for much. The United States is not, after all, Europe; the families of most public officials were modest enough and not given to arrogance. This was one of Twain's milder jabs at the remnants of the European past, which, though it was not the only source of snobbery in America, remained for him and for his contemporaries of special interest. One need only remember Gilbert Osmond in James's *Portrait of a Lady*. Surely he must be one of the nastiest snobs in modern literature, as well as one of the most memorable expatriates. When he meets Isabel Archer he appears to be a solitary gentleman-artist, wholly indifferent to society. His stoic autonomy and devotion to beauty are just what attract Isabel. Once he has married her and her fortune, it becomes clear that rank, appearances, and social standing are his overwhelming obsessions. Snobbery is possibly his only passion, for he is an icily cold misogynist, as his brittle chatter and his cruelty to his wife, mistress, and daughter reveal only too plainly. But both his egotism and destructiveness are incidental to his snobbery, to his pursuit of "tradition," by which he means the remaining European aristocracy. This does not in any way hide his very real intelligence. Osmond even understands himself. He tells us that as the son of wandering Americans he had no place at all in any nook of Italian society. His mother married his sister off to some awful Italian count and Gilbert Osmond was left enough money to buy a few "good" things and to do no work of any kind, as long as he could do some discreet sponging. As soon as he is rich, Osmond gives up his aloof pose and spends his life considering whom he and his wife should and should not see. He also tries to marry his daughter off to an English peer who, as Osmond knows, is in love with Isabel. That Isabel once refused to marry this aristocrat is the only thing about her, except her money, that he likes; it is a great distinction. Generally, however, he hates her and her easy "untraditional" ways. For Osmond is the snob as villain. There is nothing funny in his cruelty, especially to his helpless daughter. His wickedness, as he knows, is not just personal, but social, related to his rejection of his country and its culture in favor of an unreal "tradition" that is not and cannot ever become his own. He has nothing to restrain or direct his conduct—no work, no family, no country, no obligations. He is proud of his uselessness, because he is part of no community and of no culture, a mere connoisseur of an alien one. This is the snob as a detached predator. He is also an extreme Europhile, even if wholly distorted. But it is not expatriation as such that is menacing. Isabel's cousin Ralph is a lovable and honorable transplant to England. We know from James's other novels that Europeanization in itself was not a threat. It was the infection of the already demoralized American aesthete by European snobbery that was so devastating and such an assault on his native land. For Isabel Archer is America despoiled.

Gilbert Osmond is the extreme that illuminates. The persistence of "primary" snobbery among Americans and its association with Europhilia was quite real, especially when Europe could still excite hopes of honor not available in America. Not all longing for tradition is, however, as false and as hollow as Gilbert Osmond's. James's friend William Dean Howells created a variety of snobbish characters, mostly Bostonians, who are not swayed by European illusions. Even though Europe does impinge upon them, they are like Twain's "Antiques"—part of a local hierarchy. For Howells's Bostonians, Europe may be a personal dream, but they are not overwhelmed by it. They are intensely attached to the idea of "family," but not as lineage, only as a set of customs. The most perfect of Boston snobs is Bromfield Corey in *The Rise of Silas Lapham.* Corey has to cope with Silas Lapham, who is a newly rich businessman, because Tom Corey, his son, wants to go into business with Lapham and marry his daughter. Lapham and his family are uneducated, unrefined, rural, and brash. They have also preserved the moral virtues of their native New England village— honesty, family love, simplicity, helpfulness, and decency. Lapham rose to be a colonel in the Civil War and takes care of the family of a fallen comrade. In the end he is ruined because he will not sell his property to dishonest speculators. In Boston he is, however, for all his wealth and virtues, socially unacceptable. He has no idea of etiquette, he is uncouth, and his every sentence betrays an unpolished, unlettered person. We are forced, however, to admire his moral rigor, and in the end so does Bromfield Corey, whose brother-in-law, in fact, does his best to save Lapham. Nevertheless, both Corey and his wife are appalled by their prospective in-laws. Bromfield's father made a fortune in the India trade; he is therefore too close to the world of business to be able to stop his son from joining it. Why not take up mineral paints with Lapham? Corey himself did not fight in the Civil War; he spent his life in Italy, first as an artist, then just as an idler. He is in no way vicious, only slightly bloodless; but he is far too intelligent to give way to his snobbish disdain for the Laphams. They are invited to dinner, and this social disaster is an epitome of its kind. Mrs. Corey is inadvertently rude, the ladies are flustered, Lapham does not know what to do or say, and finally gets drunk. He and his family feel humiliated, and the Coreys embarrassed. The latter did not want things to turn out so badly. But their manners, habits, and shared proprieties are so ingrained that they cannot alter their behavior enough to make the Laphams feel comfortable. The Laphams want to do their social best, but it is beyond them. It is because there is no intentional ill will here that we get a glimpse of real American snobbery, as a sort of inevitability. To be sure, we fault

Corey for his Europhilia, for his weary, idle superiority; but we also know that there is no malice here. This is not Gilbert Osmond. We are also more than a little irritated by Silas's virtuous vulgarity. Must he be so crude, even though he is so good? It is not, however, these people but their situation, forced on them by Tom Corey, that dooms them so painfully to snobbery and its effects. Given the distance between country and city, new rich and declining wealth, the cultivated and the raw, the Europeanized and the local American, nothing but mutual unhappiness was to be expected. It is poor Silas who loses—devastatingly—in the end, but that is in no way Bromfield Corey's fault.

In these scenes from Howells's Boston, we begin to discern a far less aristocratic and very diffuse "secondary" sort of snobbery, the snobbery of cliques. It revolves around family and money. There clearly has to be some of the latter, but it must be a generation old at least and not unstable. Family means simple exclusiveness. One's "own kind" are one's childhood friends, a small circle of individuals of more or less equal wealth and education, who live in the same neighborhood and in similar houses, and who have been taught identical manners and a uniform dread of anything new. Anyone who has read *The Late George Apley* can see at once that without Bromfield Corey's self-mocking intelligence, this sort of snobbery is a mixture of self-satisfaction, conformity, and xenophobia. It does not depend on "blood," but having colonial ancestors helps. To be a white Anglo-Saxon Protestant is essential to the customs that "tradition" has preserved. This sort of family attachment is now something of a regional joke, though it has not disappeared. Everyone now has "roots" and looks for a genealogy. Perhaps these old habits have now proliferated so much that they are less offensive. Contemporary "secondary" snobbery has lost much of its old "primary" aristocratic bite, as everyone acquires instant traditions and a pedigree. Even the will to exclude is no longer the primary object of quite as many social groups as before the Second World War. Only some clubs and fraternities make it their sole purpose. And in these not just snobbery but economic and political monopolization of influence and power is often the real issue. "Secondary" snobbery, however, is the consequence of any sort of pluralism and of the multiplicity of groups that include and exclude people in terms of some common end that seems worthwhile to the members. Almost all groups are selective, and that means they will in effect create insiders and outsiders so that their ways will be felt to be snobbish. Those who do not like to be excluded or resent the character of a given circle will feel offended and will often perceive snobbery. But that is a side effect, often inadvertent and deeply regretted by democratic members. One can easily become a "secondary" snob in spite of oneself. It is one of the unintended outcomes of freedom.

Americans do not like to admit that they socially exclude or grade one another at all. Survey research and more casual observation show that to recognize the prevalence of even "secondary," indirect snobbery is quite difficult for a democratic people. A careful survey of Kansas City and Boston citizens revealed that the majority of them regard standards of living as the only legitimate social classification.[22] This is acceptable because they regard the United States as what is now called an "effortocracy," where one can and does succeed with hard work. Achievement, not standing in some hierarchy, is supposed to count. The most admired people, therefore, are self-made individuals who have become rich even without education or any other advantages. The poor, correspondingly, are blamed for their poverty, which is said to be caused by idleness or drink. The actual behavior of these respondents tells a very different tale, however. They in fact make all kinds of distinctions in their associations and social choices. Styles of consumption, leisure activities, neighborhood, religion, and race all play a very great part, often far greater than a similar standard of living, in determining a family's social circle. This means that, whether they like it or not, they do rate one another subtly, and exclude one another from their social niches. It is unavoidable and yet hard to admit.

The efforts of democratically inclined people to escape snobbery are often, perhaps always, futile. Indeed, the more one struggles against it the more entangling it may become, like an unrolled length of Scotch tape. For neither family "tradition" nor differences in wealth will give way, and to these, even in the absence of Europhilia, snobbery sticks like a burr. Americans are not alone in this. Thackeray had already noticed university and radical snobs, and they are not uncommon in the United States. Even radicalism has its snobberies, which is more surprising than snobbery among the very rich, from whom one has, since Grund's day, come to expect it. The snobbery of cliques, of exclusion, is in fact ubiquitous. In the third grade, little girls frequently form clubs with no other end than to keep the boys out. The boys do it, in retaliation, throughout their adult lives. The habits of cliquishness are acquired early in life, and they persist. How much can be discarded? How much must we endure? What is likely to happen if we try to reform ourselves? Can we do so, actually?

The stranglehold of family tradition was already clear to Hawthorne's Jacksonian hero, Holgrave. He had only to see the wrecks inhabiting *The House of the Seven Gables,* isolated and impoverished by the burdens of the Pyncheon family's pride. When the young man sees what this "tradition" has done, he cries out, "Shall we never, never get rid of this past?" Democratic man lives not in the past of his family but in the present, where he can exercise his own rights. And he does not build houses for posterity. "To plant a family! The idea is at the bottom of most of the wrong and mischief which men do," this perfect example of young democratic manhood tells us. To stand still—or, worse, to fix another human being in one place—is already an invitation to look up and down, as one stands solidly still in one's own patch of social ground. Holgrave has done nothing of the sort. Independent since boyhood, he has supported himself by every means from peddling to dentistry, and is now a daguerreotypist, after having wandered all over Europe and America. He is answerable to no one, only to his own conscience; and he is alert to the slightest threat to his integrity and freedom. His sense of personal dignity is impressive, as is his hope to be "the champion of some practicable cause." We need not doubt that he would do well in reform politics. Hawthorne liked and admired Holgrave and his kind, but he knew that the past and the future would catch up with him. Holgrave falls in love and marries the last of the Pyncheons, who inherits the family property. He, too, will have a house and a family. His wife is quite free from the Pyncheon pride and snobbery, but she is entirely happy to be part of a family and a community, and she will presently reconcile Holgrave to Salem and to the confines of family and local life. Even without either her or his ancestry, Holgrave will change in ways that he would have regretted in his radical days. He will live, as Hawthorne did, in his ancestral town as a matter of fate, not of choice. Like other family men, he will close the door upon his house harboring his own people and will exclude most of his fellow citizens.

The Holgraves were probably a very liberal and unsnobbish family, but like all others it may not have been wholly democratic. The family by its inherent structure, and with every social inducement, teaches us our sense of social place. There we early learn to draw distinctions and to develop personal loyalties. In every family there are, moreover, psychological possibilities for breeding snobs—possibilities deeper even than Holgrave suspects. Most children will, in the course of the Oedipal struggle, daydream what Freud called "the family romance."[23] They will persuade themselves that their father is not their real father, but that they are the offspring of some socially far more exalted or glamourous person. Most children outgrow this fantasy, but many do not. This "romance" may well be what drives so many people into the most self-destructive social pretension and snobbery. Its persistence explains, as well, why in so many plays and novels a low-born hero or heroine turns out in the end to have really been the lost child of some rich or noble family. Even George Eliot could not resist such a denouement in *Felix Holt*, where the bride turns out not to be the daughter of a poor preacher after all. Sometimes even the sons of aristocratic parents seem to feel that they must invent a more superexclusive family and

threateningly proud ancestors for themselves. Harold Nicolson tells of a young marquis who had some literary talent,
but who refused to associate with d'Annunzio and would
not allow himself to appear in an essay by Proust, since the
former was common and the latter "juif, juif, juif." He had
to behave in this way, he said, because his family would be
deeply dishonored if he did not. In fact, they were very liberal and easygoing and thought him quite crazy. His imaginary family and ancestors dominated him so much that his
snobbery became "an active torment, destroying his intellect as those of others have been sapped by drink."[24] Everyone knows Jews who choose to reject their actual parents
and invent imaginary gentile ones, and blacks who try to
"pass" as whites. Their suffering and their very frequent
inner paralysis are not unlike those of Nicolson's demented
marquis. Whereas he lived in terror of being seen with an
inferior, they are terrified of being found out, or of having
to face the reality that their fathers were indeed what they
were. The family "romance" can be staged as a drama of
intense self-destruction. That is why the psychology of personal snobbery has so often attracted novelists, many of
whom were not wholly untouched by this malady. The provincial hero, ashamed of his family and his father's name,
who flees to the big city, wasting his parents' money while
he tries ruthlessly to become part of high society, has Balzac's Lucien de Rubempré as his immortal model and Clyde
Griffiths as his tragic American counterpart. Both are
encouraged by a competitive and heartless society; both
die young in jail. And in both cases we wonder about the
authors' moralism. Social climbing is not really that dangerous. It is not always self-strangling because only few aspi-
rants are such passionate snobs. The unhappiness and then
the punishment visited upon the young heroes of *Lost Illusions* and *An American Tragedy* seem altogether disproportionate. However, even if they had ended their lives later
and less melodramatically, we know that they would have
been miserable people. Disloyalty, their creators told themselves no less than us, does have its costs.

The testimony of psychology as well as of art reveals the

family and its tensions to be a closed society, and to be the most fecund field of snobberies. Holgrave's democratic apprehensions were a proof of his intelligence. That he accepts marriage and all its consequences, however, proves Hawthorne's higher realism, his sense of the inescapable. In any event, the family is not the only universal source of snobbish attitudes. Money is just as generally and insuperably so. No country, however democratic, can escape the social consequences of unequal wealth, and no individual effort to ignore it can wholly succeed. Indeed, it may make matters worse to pretend that these differences do not matter. Who can ignore the snobberies that assert themselves when one refuses to adapt to the fact of inequality? The Holgraves' children might discover that. Even in Jacksonian America, they could have problems with a mother whose name and money spelled prestige and whose father was poor and unknown in Salem. What they might try is now called "inverted" snobbery—that is, they might insist on a class background lower than their actual origins. Who has not heard someone boast of being of "working-class" parents? Such parentage proves either a rugged proletarian character, much admired by radical university snobs, or the achievements of a self-made man, admired by everyone else. How often does one, however, find a solid suburban respectability rather than a mining town behind these inverted snobs? The Holgraves' imaginary progeny would be charged by Salem's citizens with gross hypocrisy and also with being inordinately uppity. For to reject one's colonial ancestors, even awful ones like the Pyncheons, and even worse, to pretend that money means nothing, is to display a wounding contempt for neighborhood values. Trying to liberate oneself from one's family history and wealth may not be worthwhile. It may express a deeply felt psychological impulse, but it is socially self-defeating. To free oneself from one's family's manners and one's ancestors' money does not gratify one's neighbors.

Consider Zenith, the midwestern, far-from-European city of Sinclair Lewis's *Babbitt*. In Zenith, good business requires that egalitarian manners prevail in the marketplace. The state-university reunions are nostalgically classless. Politics are meant to be probusiness Republican, as befits a city that has no use for alien, snobbish, uppity, overintellectual reformers. There are, however, rich and poor, and standards of living do differ enormously. Instead of the one ghastly dinner party in *Silas Lapham*, *Babbitt* features two, and they reveal subtle snobberies at the very heart of a supposedly standardized culture. There really are no "Antiques" in Zenith. The descendant of its oldest family does enjoy some extra prestige, but he is also an important banker, and that is what counts. All the real divisions depend upon current wealth. There is only very sporadic "primary" snobbery, and little if any anti-Semitism—and this, at most, as part of a joking inverted snobbery. There are few opportunities for real exclusiveness. These, however, are not ignored. Zenith boasts two clubs, one open and large (the Athletic), the other closed and small (the Union). The members of the Athletic say that the Union Club is a "rotten, snobbish, dull, expensive old hole," which they would never join, but in fact always do if they are asked. Business and casual relations between the members of the two clubs remain cordial for political and commercial reasons, and because there is a shared culture. Nevertheless when the merely comfortable Babbitts invite the reluctant very rich McKelveys to dinner, everyone is uncomfortable. The following has to pass for conversation: "I suppose you see a lot of pictures and music and curios and everything there," Babbitt says to Mrs. McKelvey, who often goes to Italy. "No," she answers, "what I really go for is: there is a little *trattoria* on the Via della Scioffa where you get the best *fettuccine* in the world." Babbitt is crushed, which was just what she had wanted to avoid. Not long after, the Babbitts find that unwillingly they must have dinner with a poor classmate. That dinner is also a miserable failure. His hostess says to Babbitt, who often has to go to Chicago, "It must be awfully interesting. I suppose you take in all the theaters." To which Babbitt replies, "Thing that hits me best is a great big beefsteak at a Dutch restaurant in the Loop." He is being perfectly truthful, and we know that he really does look forward to his steak, because he treats his son to it at once, when they go to Chicago together. The parties are not repeated; the richer couples do not return the invitation of the poorer ones. Nevertheless, the snobbery is quite involuntary. Mrs. McKelvey and Babbitt are not talking up or down to their hosts, they are far too democratic for that. However, the outcome is worse than if they had made a few tactful concessions to class differences. This is, however, beyond George Babbitt's idea of himself and his city. Yet he is not an insensitive man. He protects his artist-manqué friend, who, miserable in Zenith, is not a good mixer and is therefore regarded as a snob and eccentric. What makes Zenith so interesting is that even Lewis, who wanted to show a city in the grip of a coercive conformity, revealed considerable social variety. These given differences in wealth, experience, and style mean involuntary snobbery. Who has not, in fact, ever committed such an act? I remember telling a woman whom I had just met that our new house was a "big barn." No sooner had I said it than I realized that she would have loved to be able to live on that street and in that house and that my manners, though only too natural, must have seemed to her mocking and mean. I felt like two cents, or less, but it was too late. We learn ways of talking at home and in our immediate circle, and they are not always suitable or unsnobbish.

Zenith also has an intellectual lawyer, who is the very model of a Progressive—a local reform politician called Seneca Doane. When Babbitt, a staunch Republican, sits down next to him, he discovers that Doane is no monster and he is mightily impressed by all the titled reformers and professors whom Doane knows in Europe. Doane is, in fact, a name-dropper of considerable energy and by no means untouched by "primary" snobbery, although he professes to prefer Zenith to class-ridden Britain and does run for mayor in his home town. Although Babbitt is briefly drawn to the liberal ideas of this man, he is pressured to give them up. But then, Lewis took no pains to make the polished Doane particularly likeable. He also is ambiguously a snob.

The only perfectly "genuine" heroes in Lewis's novels are German Jewish scientists, especially Max Gottlieb in *Ar-*

rowsmith. Such a figure makes a brief appearance in *Babbitt* under the name of Kurt Yavitch. These characters became a fixture in American fiction, but Lewis wrote about them a dozen years before Hitler and the arrival of numerous German Jews in the United States. What Lewis needed and found was the utter, absolute, and complete outsider. Max Gottlieb is an alien socially because he is a foreigner, culturally because he has had a deeply humane education, and spiritually because his devotion to pure science is incorruptibly perfect. Nothing in the United States could command Lewis's full respect in the 1920s, and so he resorted to this idealized figure above all the levels of local society. In due course, the Gottliebs became a part of American university life and even contributed to some of its snobberies, but in Lewis's America they are quite beyond caste and class; for they are not part of society. They belong to a transcendent order of pure science. There was nowhere else for Lewis to turn; for although Zenith has its villains, Babbitt is not really one of them. His snobberies, like those of the rich, the loners, and the reformers, are all wholly inadvertent and unavoidable, the result of diversities and inequalities even in this most "standardized" of cities. "Secondary" snobbery, the result of differences that exclude and "put down" the disadvantaged outsider, is endemic and by no means only at the uppermost levels of society, but everywhere except at the very bottom. That is unfair, which is why Andrew Undershaft, the orphaned, classless millionaire and supercapitalist hero of Shaw's *Major Barbara*, arranges opportunities for snobbery for everyone in his model village. He hates condescension, but he knows that no self-respecting worker wants to associate with someone who makes a few shillings less. Only Undershaft, at the very top of his pyramid, can afford to dispense with snobbery entirely, and he grew up without a family, a foundling. To be like him, our manners would have to be very undemocratic, attuned to every nuance of social standing. We would have to consider the social place and sensibilities of everyone we met, rather than assuming that they were all just our fellow citizens. Daily democracy would be dead.

The snobbery of actual and far-from-perfect democracy is effortless and disorderly, unlike Undershaft's company town. In keeping with its nonstructure and confusion of social standards, there are any number of unequal and dissimilar groups and snobberies. Neither their intentional nor their unavoidable exclusions would, however, have any great force without the indestructible remnants of "primary" snobbery. A plurality of cliques does indeed inspire all sorts of anxieties about one's social standing, but these worries owe most of their intensity to the experience of being snubbed by someone who is placed above one on some recognizable social ladder. There are, after all, many hierarchical organizations which, even when they absorb much individual diversity, remain endemically snobbish. One need only think of universities. It may seem odd that institutions of higher learning should be such a splendid stage for snobbery; but compared to the displays of Veblen's old upper-upper middle class, they have far greater subtleties and nuances. The leisured classes are not as idle as they were in Veblen's day, and they have adopted far more austere forms of distinction, but their games of exclusion and inclusion remain basically unaltered. In conspicuously consuming "society," there appears to be an anxious quest to be in the "right" place and to do the "in" things in matters of dress, housing, food, cars, vacations, schools, and even culture. These are not quite the real snobberies of Veblen's day. At present, this is often the hard work necessary to attract the attention of the media in order to advertise and sell the goods that these people produce or distribute. Publicity for its own sake may be sought as a form of fame, but mostly it sells newspapers, and in turn other commodities. Celebrities must be seen constantly to promote films, clothing, and other luxury goods for profit. This certainly does exploit the snobbish proclivities of consumers, but it is not itself snobbery. It is, in fact, very functional in the marketplace. The wine snob, the clotheshorse, and the gourmet-food junkie are often happy show-offs untainted by malice, and very necessary to the economy. They perform exactly the same wholesome services as the culture snobs, without whom the arts would starve in the United States. Innocently they can be the subjects of many jokes and uncharitable humor. If they seem snobbish it is because we tend to regard any distinction other than that of income as illegitimate and undemocratic. And of course there *is* something silly about these pretensions, especially in their imitations. Nevertheless, these snobberies pay their way in the expenditures and fun they provide.

Academic Snobs

These luxury market transactions are simple compared to academic snobbery. That is so not because university professors are rich, or because their work is inherently snobbish. Science and scholarship—what Veblen called "the higher learning"—are, as he knew, the result of "idle curiosity" which has no place in the world of production or of commerce.[25] If they are to flourish, as even he came to wish, they must be insulated from and protected against these overwhelmingly important concerns of society. Theirs is a nonutilitarian scarcity value; and, like all solitaries, scholars appear snobbish in a joiners' world. At most, they form little societies that do not mitigate their reputation for a false aloofness. Yet no one respects education more than Babbitt, especially when he sends his children to college. He admires degrees, but, more genuinely, he knows that knowledge beats ignorance. Babbitt is divided; he likes learning but distrusts its consequences, and so, at his worst, he sounds like Spiro Agnew. But these ill-humors have always been a by-product of the very existence of higher learning. Babbitt lives outside its borders; he is not taken into account. The opinion of one's fellow scientists and scholars always counts far more professionally than any other judgment. That is, however, not primarily snobbish, though it is exclusive. To care only for the opinion of one's academic peers is not snobbery because, in principle, the values at stake are not social but scientific and scholarly. Expertise and great learning are always very scarce, and though they feel like snobbery to the layman, they are not meant to be so. Arrogance on the part of a great scientist would be as unfortunate as on the part of anyone else. But the fact remains that some people know far more than most of us, whether they be modest or boastful. Babbitt need not suffer in silence, but he is not really facing snobbery. To be sure, any specialization is a system of inclusions and exclusions that can induce fawning and snubbing, especially when social prestige is attached to our various occupations. But in spite of appearances, snobbery is not built into academic work, and certainly not into learning. It just attaches itself to them.

The *real* university snob cares more about his society than about his knowledge. Thackeray already knew him well. This snob thinks his university is the center of the world. He does not cringe to the great; often he patronizes them and reminds them that *he* began as a scholarship student, just to show how clever he is. This is the true snobbery of those who are really convinced that their university is the only institution that matters. What is good for that university is good for the nation and mankind. Harvard is the whole world for some of its members, and everything is measured by its closeness to or distance from it. This amounts to imposing a single ladder of worth. At the top is not learning itself—just Harvard. In a country with no educational system, but only a jumble of dissimilar institutions and objectives, such an effort to single out one center of merit amounts to ignorance induced by vanity. It is a snobbery that does not follow from the recognized fact that Harvard is indeed a very great university, perhaps the greatest, but from the fancy that it is the only one that matters.

If a too rigid view of academic worth may induce habits of snobbery, these can flourish just as well when there are no clearly defined standards at all. Scientists have relatively certain, or at least shared, criteria of judging each other. Priority of discovery, the number and importance of published papers, the initiation of new projects—all these add up to a "good" scientist. Among the humanists, nothing nearly as reliable exists; opinions diverge more and standards are wholly incompatible. Above a certain accepted level of competence, there often is no obvious way of distinguishing the very good scholars from the merely good, and then unscholarly, personal preferences come into play. And these are often social and political or snobbish, either upwardly or invertedly. This temptation is rendered all the more powerful by the subjects of scholarship in the humanities. They are traditional, and those who teach them are the heirs of medieval institutions. Europhilia is likely to be strong among them, as well as nostalgia for the aristocratic past. That is why Jacksonian critics of university culture thought that snobbery was inherent in the very task of transmitting the literary culture of the feudal ages. But it is not likely that the literary imagination all by itself could have so profound an effect on social conduct. In fact, there is more than just nostalgia at work here. More fatally, there are at a university like Harvard, for example, many undergraduates who are the children of rich and famous parents. To teach these and to be associated with them stirs the snobbery already latent in the humanist. Scientists are, as a rule, far less likely to see many of the children of these classes, so even if they are inclined to social snobbery, the occasion does not arise so frequently. The humanist is disposed to respond to social distinctions, and they are thrown in his way. The looks, the family, the style of education, and much else will determine his judgment of a younger fellow-scholar, and lacking a firm set of scholarly standards, he will choose snobbishly. The rule of "publish or perish," harsh as it seems, is a rough and ready way to avoid this, which is why those who champion "other qualities" dislike it.

Just as uncertainties of social status tend on occasion to encourage a nervous snobbery, so also do ill-defined intellectual standards. However, a too rigid and exclusive scale of values and sense of worth may have the same effect. Both extremes encourage snobbery. In both cases there is much to tempt Thackeray's other college snob, the intelligent middle-class boy who takes to toadying to the "great" people in his class and gets into debt and trouble. This affectation is still usual among students, especially in colleges where exclusive fraternities and clubs play a great part in students' social life. It is also not unknown among scholars, which is unfortunate, because they do by word and deed direct the young. The consoling thought that a professorial snob is in many ways completely ridiculous usually comes far too late, if ever, to his pupils, who are either hurt or misled by him. What the young see is a confusing adult, half of whom lives in the past, in an imaginary aristocratic Britain, while the other half sits among the more elegant American students. To teach the daughters and sons of a president or a multimillionaire has its attractions for scholars, who almost always come from relatively modest homes. If they come to an eastern, Ivy League college from the Midwest, they may also suffer from debilitating culture shocks. That combination is enough to awaken both self-contempt and snobbery. Among Jewish scholars this used to be extremely common, to the point of reducing them to a painful conformity of manners and even a repression of their ideas, lest their novelty offend. A fair number of acerbic and highly original minds were reduced to bland triviality by this costly desire to please their putative superiors.

These most deplorable manifestations of snobbery are passed on from one generation of scholars to the next by the severities of departmental socialization. Young scholars are quite spontaneously molded into the shapes of elders whom they admire, and self-interest and the hope of promotion more than suffice to induce conformity. Often, however, older scholars humiliate the young as part of a system of snobbery, which is not only intellectually crushing but also self-perpetuating, as the victims internalize the habits of their tormentors. Each generation becomes only too eager to pass the humiliations of their own youth on to the next generation. It is as if the old had the right to humiliate the young as a sort of earned compensation for their own former degradation. There is also much self-hatred in this. Many older scholars do not wish to be reminded of their own younger selves, especially if they long to be part of that opulent and socially remote world of their undergraduate pupils and their families. Young men who remind them of their own modest youth, of their families, and indeed of their actual position do not warm their hearts. And scholars who hate themselves are likely to spread their misery. When this temper was common, as it was in the 1950s, it often created an atmosphere of exceptional vulgarity. Scholars deprived of self-respect are likely to pretend that they are not intellectuals at all. Sports, front-page politics, and uncivilized gossip were the only permitted topics of conversation. Studious and intellectually gifted undergraduates were snubbed, graduate students intimidated, and a woman could expect only rudeness. Here was snobbery gone wild, because self-hatred created manners that were not only gross, but wholly remote from the sporting, rich, upper-class world of which these clever and learned slobs dreamed so pathetically. It never occurred to them that the mental world and habits of a business elite could not be recreated in a university and that their aspirations were grotesque rather than aristocratic.

The effort to seem worldly and rough-hewn was usually accompanied by conservative politics. A Boston Brahmin, whether genuine or bogus, is expected, not always correctly, to have "sound views." Radical snobbery is, however, not unknown among American academics. Here again, Europhilia has played its baleful part. Today, Seneca Doane would be more likely to be at a university than in Zenith. Many an ardent young American who has studied at Oxbridge has been overwhelmed by the possibilities that were revealed there. More than one has longed to imitate the careers of socialist dons who could expect to join the Labour Party and rise in it even to the Cabinet. They might even have been the sons of aristocratic families, and educated at famous public schools. Above all, they seemed to evoke an unforced deference from almost all other Englishmen. To be both radical and successful to such a degree is, of course, a dazzling prospect. It is not at all surprising that it should go to the head of a bright young reform-minded American. It does, however, create political expectations and daily manners that are useless and indeed self-defeating in America. The most recent public display of these illusory hopes was by the servile and fantasy-ridden court that gathered around President Kennedy. At worst, such displays mean frustrated ambition and again an introduction of social snobberies into the university. This is, nevertheless, politically legitimate conduct in a free and democratic society, and does not deserve the fear and loathing it invites from Babbitt in a choleric mood of university bashing.

As a response to the periodic assaults that are mounted against America's intellectual communities, snobbery, whether radical or conservative, is self-defeating. An occasionally endangered minority needs fortitude and self-respect, not the demoralization and self-hatred of snobbery. Scholars might indeed require a high level of self-esteem that goes beyond a justified pride in achievement. Knowledge is, after all, rare; acquiring it is very hard work; few people are willing to undertake it; and even when it is useless, it is far superior to ignorance—a point no one denies. Scholars need protective pride because from time to time Babbitt threatens them by going on an anti-intellectual rampage. This is a recurrent peril; for there are political advantages in attacking universities. Scholars do not directly serve the intangible or material interests of most citizens, but they offend the sensibilities and aspirations of many. The fears and angers that can be deployed against intellectual societies are formidable, and there are always reasons for universities to worry about them. The causes of their endemic unpopularity are, moreover, so numerous and varied that no single policy can be expected to protect scholars permanently. It may be that many people have unpleasant memories of their own schooldays; and who loves the teacher? There have always been religious reasons for looking askance at secular learning, and, as one senator once put it, "admission to the Kingdom of Heaven does not depend upon the results of a competitive examination."[26] The will to believe and the will to question confront each other here. The academic intellectual as a remote agent of cultural change is not a wholly imaginary figure. As such, he manages to offend both the egalitarian and conservative inclinations of democratic citizens. Distrust may be the price he has to pay for his independence. It may also be a cost incurred by any very good university. The more academically distinguished a university is, the more demanding and exclusive it must be. Even if none of its members are practicing snobs, it will still acquire a reputation for snobbery among all those who resent its aloofness and the restless and disquieting activity of its scholars. This is not altered by the endless economic and technological services that universities render to any modern society. Nothing is, moreover, to be gained by making scholars pretend that they are "regular fellows." These efforts, very common since Veblen's day, have made timid academics ridiculous, especially those who champion college athletics. This is an internal threat to the primacy of learning in the academy that is far greater even than the snobbery of the humanists, for many rich alumni encourage and support it, not least in order to display their hearty and muscular contempt for those who remain in the library and laboratory. But these displays of what Veblen called "exploit" have not really done much to satisfy those who distrust academic institutions. It is not likely that any society of scholars could placate them. Academics must always become an excluding group, and even if they should never stoop to personal snobbery, they would still appear snobbish to suspicious outsiders. An actively self-humiliating stance of anti-elitism would hardly serve; it can only disrupt the inner life of learning without really altering the actual situation of the university, which is always visibly apart.

The effort to be hearty and jovially conservative was common already among Veblen's contemporaries, and it had no other consequence than to sacrifice science and scholarship. Veblen regarded these efforts as the snobbery of administrators who thought of themselves as "captains of learning." There have since then been other outbursts of anti-elitism, often radically defiant rather than timidly conservative and conforming; but in their way, these seemingly egalitarian efforts have been self-defeating. To understand why this should have been so, one must again look at the Europhilia of some American rebels. Even Bismarck's Germany was capable of radicalizing young Americans who went there to study.[27] The prestige, naively mistaken for political power, of French intellectuals, has naturally been an even greater stimulant. In both cases, misplaced envy proved a strong motive. Among American radicals, there is thus always a lament that in the absence of a feudal past there has never been real revolutionary radicalism in the United States. To these frustrated class-warriors, "the great Mr. Locke" is no hero, but a lingering disease. The lack of a vanguard party and of a proletarian revolutionary culture makes all American reform and rebellion seem insipid and worthless to them. It is never the real thing. As it happens, there is no Marxian proletariat anywhere, since the original model bore no resemblance to any actual group of industrial workers. Marx simply wished upon them the characteristics of the old aristocracy—specifically, an intense class consciousness, military courage, and a willingness to lead and exercise uninhibited political power. Not surprisingly, this aristocratized working class did not materialize. The actual conduct of Europe's and America's working populations was so disappointing that many radicals lost hope in them and saw them not as a class at all, but as just a "mass" of homogeneous and reactive automata, alternately febrile and passive. For more resolute Marxists, the prolonged absence of the revolutionary proletariat did not enfeeble the myth of its eventual advent. Its glamour is an offshoot of "primary snobbery," that hostile encounter between the poor aristocrat and the rich bourgeois. The would-be gentleman of the past may now choose to be a would-be revolutionary proletarian. This was very usual among the student radicals of the 1960s and 1970s, who professed to be extremely "anti-elitist" but in fact managed to practice new forms of snobbery.

The fate of Students for a Democratic Society (SDS) is a chapter in the political history of both snobbery and the effort to eradicate it.[28] It failed on both counts. It began with the Port Huron Statement, which was a call for participatory democracy, for people to control their own lives, and for a rejection of every trace of elitism. In pursuit of the last goal,

SDS began with self-reform. There were to be no leaders, no procedural forms, no top-down rules, and no elected officials, in an atmosphere of perfectly spontaneous equality. This was to be especially so during the summer months, when SDS members would go into the slums to organize the local community. Their experience was politically painful. They were despised and rejected. They failed to notice that whatever their manners, they came from the top of society to its bottom, and that this could scarcely escape "the people"—especially in the fall, when SDS members went back to college. The influence of mass-society ideology had done its work among SDS as well. The members assumed that only the ghetto, the rural South, and the universities had escaped the blight of becoming middle class and protofascist. There was, they reasoned, a natural affinity between the top and the bottom of American society. If they proved their democratic manners and their anti-elitist convictions, the distance between the extremes would simply go away. Never has antisnobbery shown more clearly not merely its futility, but also its tendency to enhance the evil it wants to extirpate. Back on campus SDS members tended to form minuscule committees, to avoid any emerging elite of outstanding individuals in their participatory midst. To organize the rest of the student body, of course, required other skills, and in fact SDS was exceptionally manipulative in its tactics. Anti-elitism turned out to be self-purifying, but in political practice not very different from any other sort of ideologically intense politics. Eventually the remnants of SDS became a violent vanguard movement acting on behalf of the silent masses in a new form of *noblesse oblige.* SDS's elitism had always been real, even though its anti-elitism was also perfectly sincere. *Noblesse oblige* simply has no place in a democracy, and SDS's end was written into its beginnings. In the longer run, the upheavals of the sixties and seventies, of which SDS was but a small part, did create a less snobbish climate in the universities, which may or may not be lasting. Their predecessors, the Jacksonian democrats, did, after all, leave indelible marks on American politics.

Should Americans, then, worry about snobbery? Can we ignore it? What can be said, first of all, on behalf of "primary" snobbery, the remnant of aristocratic disdain and bourgeois toadying? Surely nothing. Its worst outcomes are humiliation and self-hatred, and even if its class and psychological sources are ineradicable, this is a kind of snobbery we can lessen, in ourselves and around us. At the very least, we need not stimulate it. Humor and a certain easy tolerance can do much to lighten this blight, but the intentional snub that hurts and enrages, and is then internalized to be turned against oneself, is not a joke. It is often very cruel morally. The difficulty is that systematic efforts not to be snobbish at all may turn back upon us in a mortifying way. If we disregard differences, we will be tactless; and if we are too class-conscious, we will not be democratic. Moreover, as long as snobbery does exist, we may have to protect ourselves against its barbs. Here the example of Cléonte may serve us well. Pride and more pride is the best defense. Whoever feels that he belongs to a group that would arouse the snobbish ire of some potential father-in-law, or his equivalent, ought to muster all the personal honor of which he is capable. Neither his rights nor his "true merits," whatever these may be, will serve him well. What one needs is the courage to be loyal to one's own, which is a way to live, not a way to alter the conduct of other people. In a world of multiple moral hierarchies, this is not only feasible but an act of fidelity to the democratic polity as well as to oneself. Humility is not a democratic virtue.[29]

"Secondary" snobbery, the mark of a society of many cliques, is not edifying, and it does not do much for anyone's character; but it does have very real indirect worth—quite unlike "primary" snobbery, which is an assault on any democratic order and its citizens. Our most genuine experiences of equality, of intimacy, and of fraternity occur only within a "clique"—that is, in an excluding group of like-minded people, modeled on that most irreducible and necessary of all societies, the family. Many groups do not have exclusion as their main object, and some are hardly aware of it; but whatever their real ends may be, they exclude by including selectively. Snobbery is the by-product of this multiplicity, and it is a personal price that must occasionally be paid for the sake of freedom. Not all doors are or can be open. Certainly, gentlemanly manners are no answer to inequality and diversity in a democratic society. The traditional gentleman is aware of the feelings of his inferiors and takes pains not to hurt them. Such fine distinctions are wholly out of keeping with the democracy of everyday life, which depends on treating everyone identically and with easy spontaneity. That does result in inadvertent snobbery and roughness, but these are nevertheless the best manners in America, because they are the only ones in keeping with the customs and the spirit of the people. There is no place in the United States for either condescension or deference, and to show them is ill-bred because it is incongruous and jarring. The gentleman is simply irrelevant to the world of "secondary" snobbery. That is why Cooper's politically candid democratic gentleman does so little in public life. Candor is not a political virtue in a democracy; successful persuasion is. Jefferson had a far better grasp of its manners than Cooper, when he urged his young grandson to imitate "Dr. Franklin, the most amiable of men in society," because Franklin never contradicted anybody. Do not argue, but listen to other people, Jefferson advised the boy, and "do your best to make them pleased with us as well as themselves."[30] And as we know, Franklin was no Monsieur Jourdain, but a self-confident self-made man, sure of his achievements and ready to do his best to make self-reliance the democratic virtue and part of "good behavior."

It may well be that even in the most democratic societies, there must be a counterpoint between equality and hierarchy, and that some elements of the latter are required both in private and public. If that should be the case, then a Madisonian solution to the exclusiveness of groups and their unavoidable and unintended snobberies presents itself. They must be multiplied so that all can have some occasion for inclusion and exclusion, which should make it far easier for everyone to bear. The desire to get on in society and pride in achievement lead to public inequality, while the wish to be with one's like and the pleasures of intimacy bring us a private equality which simply excludes the outsider. Each line of conduct is too gratifying to be given up. The demands of efficiency and functional coherence, the psychological needs of families, and the universal desire to separate friends from strangers make us close ranks as a matter of recognized social rights and necessities. Snobbery can and may have to accompany them, even if only inadvertently. That Americans entangle themselves in the oldest snobberies by trying to destroy the newer ones is less obvious, but it is a real lesson to be learned from the experience of daily life no less than from history. It cannot be helped, and Americans often make matters worse by ineptly fighting snobbery. It might be better to disregard it and just concentrate on that "simplicity" of manners that has justly been celebrated as the great achievement of democracy, especially when compared to the elaborate distinctions of aristocratic conduct. For as Thackeray already knew, it is impossible "not to be sometimes a snob," however much people may try to avoid it. Nevertheless, because it is a form of betrayal, both in private and in public, snobbery is hard to bear. It is at its worst a rejection of friends who are no longer sufficiently affluent, and in America it is a repudiation of every democratic value. As with hypocrisy, it may be difficult to fully grasp the intensity of human reactions to such an expression of falseness unless it is thought of as a form of treachery. And betrayal is not only one of Montaigne's and our commonplace vices, but one that many people have always "put first," because it causes so much psychic pain.

The ambiguities of betrayal

Good neighbors I have had,
and I have met with bad:
and in trust I have found treason.

—Queen Elizabeth I, Speech to
Parliament, 1586

4

WHO HAS NOT BEEN betrayed or betrayed someone? Betrayal is so common that its scope can scarcely be imagined. It is the main theme of our literature and history. Perfidy stalks through our greatest poetry and prose. If we were to think only of infidelities in marriage and politics, we would be overwhelmed by their number and variety, and yet they are only a part of the full range of possible treacheries. There are too many of even these betrayals to put them in any coherent order. Indeed, if we merely think of the motives and opportunities for marital and political betrayal, their ordinariness and frequency, we may simply lose interest in the matter, dulled by the volume of incidence. Examples and recitals are tiresome when they seem endless. And yet the immediate response to the direct experience of betrayal, personal or public, is sharp and intense: we all hate being betrayed. The public reaction is as acute as the private. "No crime can more excite and agitate the passions of men than treason," wrote Justice John Marshall.[1]

When we think of treachery, we stand, as it were, between intellectual incoherence and passionate feeling. The difficulty is not lessened when we recall that just governments and reflective people generally know that betrayal cannot be judged on mere impulse. For acts of treachery are often very ambiguous and difficult either simply to condemn or condone. In law, as in the most personal of relations, perfidy becomes fascinating, not because we are so used to it but because it is often enormously puzzling. It has its place in our experience both as a simple and as an infinitely complex vice.

What exactly is treachery? The dictionary is expansive; its entry is long: "deceit, cheating, perfidy, violation of faith, betrayal of trust." Betrayal, we learn, is to place another person "in the power of an enemy, by treachery or disloyalty," and also "to prove false to, to disappoint the hopes or expectations of." This, I think, should include breaking an appointment that means much to the other person, neglecting those who depend on our care, and talking maliciously about our friends. We may otherwise forget how utterly commonplace the vice is, and how much pain it inflicts every day. The dictionary continues with "to mislead, seduce, deceive" and "to disclose or reveal with breach of faith." This is by no means all that the *Oxford English Dictionary* has to say, but it is enough. What the dictionary cannot tell us is why we react so intensely to betrayal. Why is "traitor" such a word of contempt? There is, as the dictionary does show us, an irreducible experience in betrayal: desertion. That brings into play the greatest of childhood anxieties, the fear of abandonment. In quitting a bonded group, an equally primeval fear is stirred: of the failure to distinguish kin and stranger, the latter almost always called "enemy" as well.[2] To reject a blood relationship for a new and alien association, or for none at all, is to deny the most elementary of social ties. Finally, there may be the fear of the gods, when oaths and divinely sanctioned bonds are broken.

Feeling Betrayed and Acts of Betrayal

The fairy tale of Hansel and Gretel derives a great part of its enduring hold on the imagination because it is the epitome of what children fear most: that they will be abandoned by their parents. Contemporary psychology has shown us over and over again how deep and enduring and significant for our whole life this earliest of terrors is.[3] Whenever our friends desert us that unquenchable uneasiness wells up in us, and we, however momentarily, are infants again. What abandonment is to each former child, the bonds of kinship are to societies. From Roman ancestor worship to the nation-states, "this is my own, my native land" (or tribe) is still, however metaphorically, a union of common descent. And its betrayal must be blotted out in some way. Treason is the only crime mentioned in the United States Constitution. The standard text on the law of public order in Great Britain is clear: "Treason is the most serious crime offensive against the state and as such it carries the mandatory sentence of the death penalty."[4] In both countries, levying war against the state and adhering to its enemies and giving them aid and comfort are, as they have always been, at the center of public treachery. Subversion of the constitutional form of government, especially if it be with foreign aid, is no less feared and abominated. There is, finally, an element of impiety that has traditionally made betrayal particularly odious. There is often an oath, an engagement to obey God, involved in marriages and public offices. God is therefore betrayed as well, when a desertion of friends and countrymen takes place. At the very least, it is felt that a divine principle of harmony is offended when trust is violated. Oaths are merely a sign of recognition, however casual, of this link between us and the whole order of things. That is why they can bind even agnostics. To betray God directly is, of course, the most intolerable offense for a believer. The heretic who abandons a creed is therefore disdained and punished, while the pagan is merely an object of solicitude. Judas Iscariot was throughout the Middle Ages the lowest of the low, and treason was the worst of sins, the pit of the *Inferno*, because of him.

It is easy to see why we hate treachery; but that does not, in itself, tell us much about the kinds of encounters or exchanges between people that make one or the other party feel betrayed. The one irreducible experience surely is having an expectation disappointed. For a simple act of betrayal, one person should have both intentionally convinced another person of his future loyalty and then deliberately rejected him. The latter then, not surprisingly, feels betrayed. There is nothing ambiguous about this, the hard core of treachery. And indeed its ambiguities do not arise from the simple act itself. Betrayals become ambiguous as a part of complicating psychological or social situations. One thinks at once of genuine conflicts of loyalty, which force us to betray someone or something. My friend or my lover, my convictions or my people, are the most obvious choices of that kind. One may also be torn by conflicting ethical demands. In some societies vengeance and loyalty are equally obligatory, and one may have to betray one's friends to avenge one's kin or one's own honor. Then, too, external circumstances may justify or stimulate betrayals. One ought to betray oppressors, personal or public. Less obviously, there are societies so sleazy that everyone habitually betrays everyone else. It becomes hard to pick out an individual traitor there. Less drastically, social mobility, which is prized, also tempts people to desert their less successful families and friends. This is the world of Balzac's Paris and Dreiser's America, and also the world of snobbery. To some, betrayal seems less culpable if it is done to achieve a "high" rather than a "low" object. Sex and money do not, as a rule, justify betrayal; but selfless political or other beliefs often do, which may well be a completely irrational judgment, if one considers consequences at all. It is difficult to see why fanaticism is excusable, but personal ambition is not. In any case, motives and purposes count for much.

When we turn to the victims of treachery, all kinds of difficulty appear as well. There is a dissonance between feeling betrayed and actually being betrayed. We can feel betrayed without any identifiable traitor. People and societies change. One can suddenly discover that the man or woman at the breakfast table is not the same person one married twenty years ago. More difficult to grasp is the likelihood that the rules one was brought up to obey will quite unexpectedly become ridiculous and objects of derision. One feels betrayed; but who is to blame? Nor are those who feel betrayed always simply victims. People may also invite betrayals or force them on others. If one idolizes or imposes excessive moral demands on one's friends, one may well be betrayed unintentionally by the overburdened person. It is one of the many painful experiences of our adolescence to discover that the adults whom we admire most are far inferior to our expectations. They may well be unreliable, but they may also have been quite unaware of our worship. It is not the idol's fault that he has feet of clay. There are, in short, asymmetries between our expectations and our normal world which make us feel betrayed. Nor is that all. Some people are so passive and so unaware of the character and activities of their friends that they virtually collaborate in their own betrayals. The complaisant husband used to be such a figure; but a careless, class-bound intelligence service, such as the British, is no different.

Deceit certainly does make betrayal worse, but it is not always clear that its absence improves matters. The two are often confused. Deception accompanies betrayal in order to conceal it. Unfaithful spouses do not want a fuss. Spies lose their usefulness and their lives when they are discovered. Nevertheless, there are two quite distinct actions involved: a violation of trust and protective secrecy. If a relationship depends on honesty and others rely on it, then lying can be an act of betrayal. Scientists who falsify their results betray their fellow researchers and their vocation. The deception in such a case is the betrayal. There are, however, betrayers who do not choose to conceal their behavior at all, either because they are brave or utterly contemptuous of their victims. Spouses often simply desert their families. Nevertheless, the presence or absence of deception does make a difference, because it tells us much about the whole character of the betrayer, and this may well affect the meaning one attributes to his acts.

The character of traitors is so significant because although all of us occasionally violate trust, we are not all of us treacherous characters. Of these there are many. Some people are just unreliable—philanderers of some sort or other. Much as they love you on Monday, by Wednesday there is someone else. They move from job to job, from one political party to another, and they adore fashion. At most, they tend to exasperate. There is, however, a far more sinister character, who is a pure traitor. This is someone who betrays in order to exercise power over those whom he can hurt by violating their trust. The despotic parent who promises a child a gift or an outing, only to withdraw it at the last moment; the experienced seducer who enchants teenagers mainly in order to leave them quickly; the confidence man who preys on elderly women, for fun as much as for gain— all these and their like are really treacherous characters. They and those whom we call "dishonorable" because they have no inhibitions about pursuing their ends are relatively uncomplicated betrayers. And indeed, often irresponsible people come close to that as well. Our difficulties may begin with them. It is, after all, not easy to decide what one is to make of Mozart's Don Giovanni. Is he just a rover who gives the women as good a time, even if only briefly, as they give him? Or is he out to demonstrate his sexual powers by betraying them? He is hard to decipher, but the difficulty he presents is small compared to the ambiguity of steady characters who commit betrayals out of cowardice or some other weakness, and who hate themselves for it. One thinks of Conrad's Lord Jim. There are also characters who would have to betray themselves if they did not betray others, like the hero of Conrad's story *The Secret Sharer*. Shakespeare's Coriolanus, who deserts his people, the Romans, because they demand a democratic demeanor from him, claims that he had to be untrue either to his own character or to them. These men each betrayed a public trust, but they were not perfidious characters at all, which is what makes them ambiguous, though their acts are really quite simple betrayals.

In *Lord Jim*, Conrad makes us care far more about his hero's possible regeneration than about his treachery. And he does this to his readers over and over again. Jim is a coward. He deserts the passengers of a sinking ship to run away with his fellow officers, possibly killing a man to get away in time. He has betrayed his charges, betrayed his obligation as a white man among the natives of the Empire, and above all betrayed his own ideal self. He is no cynic, and he does not equivocate; but he might still be contemptible until the end, when he dies courageously and with demonstrative honor. At no point, however, do we fail to identify with this weak and often fatuous boy, or think seriously of the plight of the passengers whom he deserted. We would probably care even less about them if Jim were torn by a genuine conflict of loyalties, not just by simple cowardice. For in *The Secret Sharer* the young captain of a ship shelters a murderer who, he recognizes, might easily have been himself. To let that man escape safely and, more significantly, to prove his own courage, fidelity, and self-reliance, he endangers the ship and its crew. He is lucky and everyone emerges safely from the ordeal. What if everyone had drowned? He had betrayed the men in his own care in order to be true to himself, and Conrad has us cheer him on. Can we really all shake off our responsibilities in order to "find ourselves"? Is it really, in principle, more important that a man be true to himself than to his fellows? That is what Coriolanus said when he scorned the Roman voters, and that is what every ideological traitor claims, quite genuinely.

Shakespeare's Coriolanus is an open and frank traitor, and so we do not hate him. Yet on second thought he allows us to see just why traitors who go over to the enemy in war are so hated. He abandons his people by imagining that he can wish his instincts away, "As if a man were author of himself / And knew no other kin" (V, 3). And if it is not enough to deny one's father, he also dreams that "There is a world elsewhere" beyond his city—indeed, beyond the world of ordinary men and their undistinguished lives. There is no "world elsewhere" for any of us, but Coriolanus suggests that every traitor is a self-deceiving, self-made alien. It appears, in fact, that convicted traitors never think of themselves as such, but as residents of "a world elsewhere." Their kinsmen do not, however, go away, and *they* know that bonds which cannot be severed have been overtly disdained. Everyone has parents and other relatives, to be betrayed or not; we cannot replace them with other "authors." The public traitor is therefore a threat to the very existence of his society, and is so both because he leaves it to join its enemies, and because he denies its reality, its very definition as his place of origin. Whatever his personal character, in his public presence Coriolanus is a terrifying monster of dissociation. Nevertheless, he imposes mixed responses upon us, because he is far from being base, dishonest, or craven. He is not a treacherous man.

Coriolanus is also subversive, because he scorns elections. And subversion is much feared in republics. Partly it is only another rejection of his "own," the forms of government peculiar to free citizens. Republics, and liberal democracies especially, rely on mutual trust between governments and citizens to an unusual degree. Threats to the established constitution, even when no foreign state is involved in the enterprise, are therefore perceived as attacks on every established political relationship and every social agreement. Unlike Shakespeare's tormented hero, Plutarch's Coriolanus emerges as a far simpler traitor, condemned by his political incompetence and folly far more than by his military treason. Here there is no real ambiguity at all: Plutarch's Coriolanus is just a bad citizen and an undisciplined commander who threatens the public peace of Rome.

When we are uncertain not only of the character but also of the intentions of a betrayer, his act may have no clear meanings, though we may well detest him and his ways. Even when one observes despotic and cruel parents, it is not always clear that they are simply betraying their children's trust. Ambiguity may haunt the suffering of the weak sometimes. Consider Dr. Sloper in Henry James's *Washington Square*. He does not love his daughter and he destroys her happiness when he tells her fortune-hunting suitor that he will disinherit Catherine if they marry. The man deserts Catherine and she is doubly betrayed because she loved both men. Dr. Sloper does not, however, think of himself as a traitor, though he has clearly revealed his disdain for his child and is far from honest. But it is not clear that Catherine would not have suffered more betrayals than these had she married her untrustworthy suitor. Dr. Sloper could have said that perfidy used against perfidy is quite justifiable. Even patriarchal tyranny in its most typical betrayal of expected affection cannot be judged apart from its circumstances, so that we detest the traitor but not his deed. Betrayal owes much of its coloration to its specific social environment, not only to the character of the actors.

In a tricky and unstable world, fidelity may be in such short supply that betrayals become the norm. That does not excuse them, perhaps, but if disloyalty is expected, betrayal must lose its primitive horror. It cannot mean much to the participants who are used to it. The Slopers do not, in fact, live in so unreliable an environment, but Balzac claimed that parts of Parisian society were like that. Here it is not the personality of the betrayers that makes betrayals ambiguous, but the relationships between people who have no real sense of mutual obligation. Ambition, snobbery, and social mobility have eroded the bonds of family loyalty, so children readily betray parents. The parents are not naive. Balzac's Old Goriot has made his money deviously in this new and speculative economic world until he has become very rich. He then spends it all on his worthless daughters, society matrons who will have nothing to do with their lower-class father. He, however, not only continues to dote on them, but pays their enormous debts. He obviously rejoices in their social rise, in their upward social mobility; but its cost to him, as we see it, is awful. Is there betrayal here when one of his daughters will not even allow his name to be mentioned in her mansion? Balzac wants us to believe that as far as this society goes, all expectations are being met. The last pages of remorse carry no conviction. No lover is faithful to his mistress here; young men squander their mothers' money under false pretenses and disreputable bankers ruin everyone. What precisely is betrayal in this corrupted Paris, if Balzac's picture is right? The poor country relatives, the simple-minded faithful and trusting mother in the provinces—these, to be sure, are betrayed; but her son lives in a city where he cannot get ahead honestly, since he went there to climb up its social ladder as best he could. His immediate society must now share the blame. It does not absolve him, even though it is made up of psychological and moral confederates in betrayal, and judgment does shift from him to his society.

Individual betrayers who go beyond the normal levels of unreliability in competitive worlds may well plead that they are not wholly responsible. This will rarely be granted by a self-protecting society, even if it be as crooked as the pre-1929 New York Stock Exchange. Nevertheless, betrayal is ambiguous in a society that rewards the very characteristics that make people treacherous. The prevailing sense of honor is too conditional for simple condemnations. It is as if each individual were just one strand in a web of betrayals. The honor codes of college do not apply to the Stock Exchange, an upright banker tells a New Deal reformer in Louis Auchincloss's novel *The Embezzler*. The actual felon explains that he cannot see why one should play the Roman patriot, and thinks his friends should pay his debts even though these were incurred when he sold securities that had been put in his safekeeping by his club and his relatives. His friends are upset mainly because he has brought down a Jewish New Deal investigator upon them. In a similar tale, Frank Norris's *The Pit*, the organizer of a clique that wants to prevent the hero from cornering the wheat market sells out without telling his fellow speculators, as soon as he sees that they cannot succeed. The rest are ruined, but he is undisturbed, because he figures that this is how one must behave in the each-man-for-himself world of the Chicago Wheat Exchange. In both cases we feel that the reluctance of the betrayers to feel the slightest guilt is not wholly self-deceiving. They do live in that kind of world. The embezzler may be unrealistic about the obligations of his fellow brokers to help him out, but they are not much better than he, when they run into competitors whom they fear and dislike, or the government's agents. In both these cases betrayal involves deception; but do we really care about lack of honor among the semi-honest? The reigning habits and impinging conditions are such as to rub off on each one, and betrayal is muted by the sordidness all around it.

That sort of society need not be as public as the business world. Families and friends, too, can create their little world of mutual unreliability. In his wicked comedy of manners, *Betrayal*, Harold Pinter treats us to just such a circle of well-bred betrayers. A married man betrays his best friend by having a secret affair with the latter's wife. The wife betrays her lover by telling the husband all about it. The husband betrays the wife with a string of affairs about which he tells her only when he wants a divorce, which is amicably arranged. Nevertheless, the lover feels betrayed because his secret was let out, and the wife because her husband was not as candid as she herself was and expected him to be. Betrayals multiply in this little world; and although its members may feel betrayed, we really cannot tell why they should, and who, if anyone, is to be blamed. These three people have created a little society built on betrayal. Each act has multiple meanings, even if each one is a betrayal.

The Social World of Treachery

Although every society, large or minuscule, can change the meaning of betrayal, it is political circumstances that bear down most heavily upon our reliability. Of all extenuating circumstances, the pressure of military force is the most irresistible. Fear of persecution makes all of us potentially treacherous. Who is to condemn the Soviet citizen who shuts his door and heart to a dissident who once was his friend? It is the self-righteous, far more than the craven, who are unjust. Public fear, even more than personal circumstances, makes us treacherous; and it also excuses us, because danger summons us to look out for ourselves and our families. Heroism is very rare, and no one is obliged to rise to such heights. When someone does, he is praised precisely for being more than merely good. Because some were indeed exceptionally brave during the Nazi occupation, the question of how much courage and fidelity one ought to expect of ordinary civilians became a matter of practical importance after the Second World War. Most of the casual

nondemonstrative passive collaborators were only interested in surviving, unlike some of their more principled and
daring fellow citizens. Dr. Joost Merloo, a Dutch psychia-
trist who interviewed and knew many such people, reported
that most of them felt that they had done nothing wrong.
They did not come to see themselves as their angry accusers
did, and in fact it is not clear that they were given to more
than normal cowardice. With the end of the passions of the
war and of the need for a symbolic purification and renewal,
most collaborators were quietly pardoned, and it was
accepted that resistance to terror is not a duty and that
fear under protracted threats must inevitably wear down
all but the heroic few.[5] Betrayal became a habit, a way of
life in Nazi Europe, as it is today in Soviet Russia and its
empire.

There are, moreover, less political and far more tem-
porary situations that make us scurry to save our own: in
natural disasters such as floods and fires, most obviously, in
which cooperative behavior begins only after everyone has
looked after himself and his family. Even those who have
special public duties, such as policemen and firemen, will
eventually leave their tasks to look after their families.
Here, one would think, is betrayal pure and simple—worse
than military desertion, since the soldier may be an involuntary conscript but, in fact, family feeling is always given
its due.[6]

Danger and habit: both create environments in which the
climate of betrayal is so pervasive that individual acts of betrayal, however simple and pure, acquire an uncertain
meaning and make judgment doubtful. What of divided
loyalties, the staple of every melodrama? Who has not seen
Ingrid Bergman betraying Humphrey Bogart in *Casablanca* as
she returns to her husband, who is on the run from the
Nazis. What if she had decided to remain with her lover instead? The husband could still have escaped. In either case
someone would have to be betrayed and in either case one
weeps for the losers. Traditionally, when women were
thought of as objects to be "stolen" rather than as people
with their own choices to be made and unmade, the great

149

conflict was between friendship and love. And friendship, always between males, was meant to triumph, in a victory of the higher over the lower self. It was a favorite theme of Elizabethan and Jacobean drama. The man who has fallen in love with his friend's mistress must give her up, or receive her from the friend in a show of generosity. The true friend was not supposed to give in to passionate love. He must leave the woman to the friend: "I were not worthy to be call'd his friend / Whom I preferred not to a mistress."[7] Yet if he really loves the woman, turning away from her might at the very least be an act of self-betrayal. The unfaithful friend in Shakespeare's *Two Gentlemen of Verona* makes just that argument. He therefore asks, "In love, who respects friend?" and decides to pursue the girl. Everyone else takes his treachery ill, and so he eventually retreats. Friendship triumphs, as it is supposed to. The real claim here is that friendship is a supreme bond and that whatever interferes with it must be abjured, especially love. The conflict for the individual is between his better self and his lesser self, and he is expected to see it as a question of will, not of divided loyalties. What, however, if the woman has a genuine choice and prefers the second lover? What, indeed, if we do not accept male friendship as superior to love between the sexes? Then there is a serious conflict of loyalties and someone must suffer betrayal.

When religion and race compete with sexual loyalty, the conflict becomes utterly hopeless. Although one or the other side in such cases feels the deepest rage and hurt in being rejected, the onlooker may not be able to take sides at all. Until recently it was thought to be a betrayal of faith for Jews to marry gentiles. If one thinks that marriage is a matter of personal choice, then the claims of love and compatibility are just as compelling as those of religion and tradition. Someone will be betrayed and will react with justifiable fury; but can it be helped? Perhaps the most dramatic of these ambiguities arises from the racial obsession of the South. One of the most enduring themes of Southern fiction, from Kate Chopin to William Faulkner, is racial betrayal. In Chopin's *Désirée's Baby* a white father discovers that his newborn child has negroid features. He assumes that his wife must have a black ancestor and deserts her at once. She kills herself and the baby. He then finds an old letter which discloses that he, in fact, has "black blood," but he simply burns the letter. Far more compelling is Faulkner's telling of this basic myth in *Absalom, Absalom!* Henry Sutpen comes to love his half-brother Charles Bon with a complete and passionate devotion. He is quite ready to overlook incest and legal bigamy to let Charles Bon marry his sister, Judith Sutpen. But when their father tells him that Charles is partly black, Henry shoots his brother dead, to prevent the marriage and to end his own intense loyalty to an impure idol. If we do not share their racial terrors, we think that Désirée's husband and Henry Sutpen betrayed a wife and brother respectively. However, they were sure that they had been betrayed by the "impure." To discover blackness in a white wife or brother is for them a disruption of the most sacred, elementary expectation. The fact of or feeling of betrayal is there, but one might well reject its validity if one is not a racist. If one is, one may still think loyalty to wife and friend supremely important, though it may be shaken by racial fears.

Not all conflicts of loyalty in the family are so harrowing as those of a Southern family at its most gothic, but they can occur in any marriage. They are not, however, the only occasions for ambiguous domestic betrayal. In many cases, people feel betrayed even though no betrayal has occurred at all. Comedy knows no more common plot than the one about an elderly husband who has married a meek and mild young woman, only to discover that she is a spendthrift shrew. More commonly, people just change and become unglued. That cannot be foreseen, and we have to *trust* each other precisely because we cannot *know* all the changes that will affect us in the future. Trust is the response to the limits of foresight. Nevertheless, characters do alter and marriages fall apart. Both people may feel betrayed, and it is usually painful, but hardly culpable. If the couple has no religious objections, no-fault divorce is just the answer to a marriage of minds that are no longer at one. Disappointment is not the equivalent of betrayal, and some divorces really are as simple as those in John Updike's stories in *The New Yorker*. Some, however, are more difficult, do involve betrayal, and may be exceptionally ambiguous. Anyone who regards adultery as a sin will look upon divorce not merely as a wrong, but as part of the act of betrayal, and so it is. So also, however, is a marriage that is a perpetual domestic war, that betrays day after day the purposes of family life. To this state of affairs, there is, of course, no answer. It yields a rich store of ambiguities, as does the early history of divorce.

When divorce first intruded upon the tradition of monogamous marriage, it was seen less as a solution to miserable marriages than as a threat and as an opportunity for betrayal. William Dean Howells's *A Modern Instance* is a perfect mirror of such views in turn-of-the-century America. The villain is a plagiarist, unreliable in money matters, and a bad husband. He deserts a wife who absolutely adores him, and in due course he tries to divorce her, pretending that she has deserted him. This at last awakens the all-too-trusting woman, and after much melodrama she divorces him. More subtly, however, Howells suggests that she is not entirely blameless, though the husband is the betrayer; she has excused all his shoddy deeds and so has become his accomplice, in effect. The divorce is their joint contribution to a marriage based on self-deception and betrayal from the very first day. Is marital betrayal, on this evidence, a specific act, or a web of incremental dodges? It is not that each act is defensible, but that it is not isolated, and that it does not, therefore, stand out quite as starkly as those who "feel betrayed" think. Most divorces are little wars between two people who have been mutually betraying each other and themselves in many ways for some time. And even the most harrowing desertions are not always inflicted upon innocents.

In Howells's novel we begin to catch a hint of collaborative betrayal. The long-suffering wife encourages her feckless mate. And, indeed, psychological collaboration is a subtle alteration of simple betrayal that is far from rare. We can drive people to betray us—and even invite it—by passivity, indifference, blindness, and self-hatred. Moreover, untrustworthy people encourage each other. All of this occurs in one way or another in *Madame Bovary*. Charles Bovary is not an innocent; he is simply so passive and deliberately blind that he will not see that his wife has lovers. He is no stranger to deceit, however, for when he was a student he spent his parents' money on pleasures, while he made them believe that he was studying medicine. Eventually he settles down, but he betrays his patients, and he is not so obtuse that he could not easily have understood what was happening to his wife or what she was up to. He is too self-centered to recognize her or her growing troubles. Her infidelity to him is in any case a minor betrayal compared to the refusal of her two lovers to help her pay her debts. Within their world, however, they behave just as one might have expected. They are no more than conventional, and it is she who alone has misperceived the entire reality. What could be hoped for there? She has spent not just more money, but far more trust than she could afford, given this economy. It is as if betrayal were a way of life rather than an assault upon a victim; that is why self-destruction is Madame Bovary's only possible exit. Betrayal is built into any relationship where trust is placed in an imagined person, not an actual one. But who would not try to fantasize her way out of a situation as mean and dull as Emma Bovary's?

Madame Bovary was certainly neither the first nor the last woman fatally to misplace her trust. She thought far too well of her lovers; but she did not idolize them, as young people sometimes worship their elders or as some women adore one man. There is perhaps no tragedy of betrayal that can rival that of Euripides' Medea in making us recognize the devastation of love accepted and then scorned. It is not a simple story, partly because Jason and Medea are already implicated in so many betrayals that it seems raging folly for her not only to trust him, but to make him her whole world. Jason is not a man capable of responding to such overwhelming adoration; but is anyone? No woman ever felt more betrayed than Medea, and Jason is indeed an unprincipled adventurer. Medea does not, however, suffer as she does because she is a savage creature unprepared for Greek suavity. Jason is her whole life because she has no other, and that is so because she has for his sake betrayed a father, a brother, and a host. She also knows the meaning of trust quite well, for she reminds an Athenian friend of his obligations to her. When Medea's nurse, however, tells her that nothing is more usual than unfaithful husbands, she cannot listen, because Jason is not just a husband but her whole universe. Since he has now deprived her of it, she kills everything in sight, including their two children. In this she is only completing her career of treachery, to which her passion for Jason has led her. He has been her "world elsewhere," and when he pushes her out there is nothing left. Jason does not ask to be idolized (which does not absolve him from his greasy, self-serving, and self-satisfied desertion of his wife in favor of a Greek princess), but he does somehow make his perfidy look less glaring. Treachery among various kinds of traitors is not the same as among simple victims and betrayers. It has, as it were, "a place" in the moral world of that particular marriage. If Medea is self-betrayed and betraying, so is Jason. He has convinced himself that he loves his children and that he is marrying the princess only to improve their social standing and future. But the horror of the story is not to be found in his character, simple traitor though he be, but in Medea's unlimited, passionate devotion to him. To give up oneself so totally would burden a better man than slippery Jason.

If Medea's is a tragic betrayal by and of an idol, Evelyn Waugh presents us with a wry one. He, too, shows with particular subtlety that one may inflict a feeling of betrayal on oneself. In *Officers and Gentlemen* the hero, Guy, is too passive and too decent to manage his world. Often he is betrayed, but not always. Among his fellow officers he worships an obvious cad, whom he regards as the perfect English gentleman. This paragon deserts his men in battle, disobeying orders, and then lets a society woman cover up for him. England is less betrayed than our hero, who does not even choose to pursue the traitor, because his faith has been so shattered. He has had, however, no reason to admire this decadent representative of a frivolous culture, which Waugh does not spare. Indeed, even without the novel's explicitly religious tenor, we would know that only a saint like the hero's father would come through this morass without being tarnished or ridiculous. Guy could certainly have seen through his idol right away. There was only his need to believe in a world long melted away that allowed him to feel betrayed when he met a traitor among members of his own social circle.

Waugh's hero is particularly upset by the people who cannot be bothered to do anything about the villain. The traitor's friends even protect him against any possible punishment. If they were thoughtful people, which they are not, they might claim that personal relations matter more than any duty to one's country, even in war. They might point with horror at communists and Nazis who turned their friends over to the police, at fanatics who betrayed their benefactors and families for the sake of some ideology. They might recall the nationalist frenzy of the First World War which made common sense a public enemy, even in Great Britain. All this would be perfectly true. It has also to be kept in mind when one reads E. M. Forster's celebrated statement about the rival claims of friendship and the state; for otherwise it loses all its force, which was considerable in the age of the two world wars.

My Country or My Friends: Choosing Betrayal

"I hate the idea of causes," Forster wrote, "and if I had to choose between betraying my country and betraying my friend, I hope I should have the guts to betray my country . . . Still, there lies at the back of every creed something terrible and hard for which the worshipper may one day be required to suffer, and there is even a terror and a hardness in this creed of personal relationships, urbane and mild though it sounds. Love and loyalty can run to the claims of the state. When they do—down with the State, say I, which means that the State would down me."[8]

Even without its heroics, this is not an intelligent statement. It trivializes the bitterest of conflicts because it says
nothing about the kind of "state" involved or how one's
friends might betray it. It does not even seem to recognize
the difference between governments that try to avoid these
intolerable choices and those that force them upon people.
Under a decent legal system, like that of the United States
or Britain, spouses do not have to testify against each other
in criminal cases. In Soviet Russia and Nazi Germany they
and their children were encouraged to inform on each other.
For quite apart from how one chooses, the most important
political and personal aim must always be to live under laws
that do not force us to make intolerable choices. Parents and
children should simply not be put into such situations. So
first of all, Forster might have asked himself just what sort
of "state" he was saying "down" to. If he had begun with
that, he might not have had such an easy or self-enhancing
answer. Moreover, what was the friend's act? Was he sup-
porting Nazi Germany or Soviet Russia, or was his betrayal
of another sort? Was he making an anarchist gesture by
failing in his duty as a public health or safety officer? Was
he neglecting some official service and thus seriously en-
dangering many innocent citizens? Was he accepting money
from a foreign entrepreneur to spy on some state-owned industry? Was he a terrorist, "levying war"? Was he organiz-
ing a big race, or an anti-Semitic riot? If Forster meant what
he said, and if he really loved this personal friend, who
might be charming, well read, and good-looking, he would
fly to his defense and help him escape from the rigors of the
law in all these cases. He would assume that the well-being
of those whom he did not know directly, his anonymous
fellow citizens, counted for nothing compared to the safety
of a familiar, personally known friend. As a response to
those vast impersonal causes that scorned private devotion
of every kind, one can see Forster's outburst as a self-de-
fensive, perhaps even necessary antidote. But Forster did
not leave it at that; he spoke of a hard "creed" calling for
"guts." There is a very real difference between this and the
importance that a pluralistic society must always attach to

the sanctity of primary social bonds. Even judges often go far to meet that end. When the U.S. Supreme Court upheld Haupt's conviction for treason because he had overtly helped his saboteur son during the Second World War, Justice Murphy dissented. In a crime in which intention counts decisively, he argued, Haupt had acted as a loving father, not as a traitor to his country.[9] Justice Murphy was not, however, proposing any creed of personal relationships. He merely thought that psychologically Haupt was so overwhelmed by parenthood that he had not been able to recognize his public act as treason and so had not intended it. If Justice Murphy had thought Haupt capable of a considered choice, as the majority of the Supreme Court did, he would have had to join their opinion. It is the hard dogmatic self-righteousness of Forster's creed that makes it so mindless. In a sense, Forster was saying that if a friend is "mine," I need not give him up simply because "they" (society) punish him for a crime. It says something also about the class and cultural boundaries of his immediate circle, with its passion for exclusion, that he should have felt so remote from "the state"—which was, after all, the democratic government of Great Britain.

The most spectacular conflicts of loyalty, the greatest ambiguities of betrayal, are political. Forster's bravado is so hollow because he does not trouble himself with these difficulties. He is merely the obverse of the superpatriot and the ideological fanatic, who are impervious to any claims except those of their own creed. It is as if politics in general did not matter. To think of loyalty and treachery seriously, however, inevitably demands that one think about politics. The first great discussion of the tension between public and private obligations, Plato's *Crito*, makes that clear. One might well argue, in fact, that Socrates betrays his old friend by refusing to escape from an unjust death sentence. Poor Crito does not only raise the claims of a deep affection, but also of his personal honor, which would be tarnished if he failed to aid a friend; but he is never allowed to make a principled primacy-of-friendship argument. He is simply silenced with complex accounts of Socrates' familial and contractual obligations to Athens and to the ideal of a heroic philosopher, indifferent to death. But we do hear the question, omitted by Forster and by any "creed": "What sort of person am I, in making this choice?" Can one ever say in advance or categorically that one's character or life would be morally better if one always stuck to "the creed of personal relations" against the state, as Forster did? Will one be tarnished if one does not? Is there an answer? Surely one should ask.

Montesquieu was perhaps both peculiarly poignant and self-divided; hence he was instructive on this very point. He thought, as did many other Enlightenment thinkers, that only the claims of humanity as a whole should count, because the greater social unit must always have the prior claim on us. My family before myself, my country before my family, and mankind before my country. No wise man should have friends, he went on to say only too consistently, since it would deflect him from that impersonal moral rigor required by our duties as members of the human race. Unfortunately, he also noted that everything is "vulgar" and beastly without friendship and that his rigid ethical stance was a psychological disaster. Stoicism should not even be tried. Honor, the finest dispositions, and everything that is best in us as individuals would have to go, if we did the right thing.[10] Nevertheless, to betray society at large without concern would also be psychologically and politically too costly. Is it possible to be only for oneself and one's own? What would one be? Would one even be a good friend? This may well be the inevitable endpoint of asking such questions about friendship and politics. Montaigne's look at friendship reveals even deeper doubts, too deep to be a mere choice. If my friend is really another self, then anything he might do would be done by myself. If he had reasons for betrayal, then so would I. We would indeed be friends to one another before we were enemies or friends of our country, of ambition, of sedition, or of anything else.[11] That is simply an account of friendship, and sometimes of marriage. It is not an alternative obligation; one does not act *for* a friend, but for and as oneself. It is not a creed at all, and does not evoke the self-admiring "guts" of the creed of "personal relationships." What my friend does is done by myself, not by another, because perfect friendship is a form of self-love, not unlike that of a mother for her children, according to Aristotle.[12] To stand with them neither is a sign of "guts" nor does it lower politics on the ethical scale. The character necessary for friendship at all would be such that one would act with self-confidence in an impossible situation, in which one must move without any certainties or guidelines and in which even the idea of choice seems inapplicable. It is not a question of conflict of loyalties at all, but of being an actor in a complete and real tragedy. It is no longer betrayal that appears ambiguous then, but the whole structure of human relations, which forces one to suffer with others as if they were ourselves—more so, occasionally. But a person incapable of friendship would be not only miserable but incomplete. That is why friendship is both wholly self-oriented and entirely other-regarding, as Aristotle's account of friendship demonstrates. To engage in friendship is not therefore to adopt a creed but to have a specific character, one open to others without loss of self.

To look at conflicts of loyalties that must inevitably involve at least one betrayal, one ought not to look mainly at personal friendship, but at the conflicts we face as members of more than two hostile groups. We have seen, in the case of racial hatred, what sort of betrayals can occur when kinship groups are at war. In a less tragic vein, one need only think of the "ins" and "outs" of any group. I am unsparing in criticizing my university department to its other members, but let even a close friend from the outside sneer at its performance and I fly unthinkingly and dishonestly to its defense. To do less would be to betray "my own" to outsiders, presumed to be hostile. Everyone has these experiences. In John Galsworthy's play Loyalties, a Jewish visitor to a country house is robbed by another guest. All of the people there make it clear that they are not anti-Semites, but they rally around the thief, because they cannot believe that "one of us" would do such a thing. When it becomes obvious that he is guilty, he has to shoot himself precisely because he cannot face "his own" after he deceived them, though he thinks nothing of robbing an outsider.

Social comedy is not the only occasion for choices between such loyalties. The most famous betrayal in U.S. history was surely Robert E. Lee's decision to remain loyal to the South. The Confederacy as a whole may have been driven by economic and political self-interest, but not Lee. He was the most distinguished officer in the U.S. Army when the war broke out. He had been superintendent of West Point; he was on terms of friendship with most of the Northern generals and had even been offered the command of the Union forces by his old commander, Winfield Scott. Lee thought slavery wrong and the Union indissoluble, and he hated to see all of George Washington's "noble deeds" undone. Nevertheless, he wrote, "I have not been able to make up my mind to raise my hand against my relations, my children, my home," and so he decided to fight for Virginia.[13] To those who think we learn loyalty to our country locally, in Burke's "little platoons," Lee should come as a sobering thought. He also raises another ambiguity. If one thinks that he fought not only for his home but also for a thoroughly bad cause in which he did not even believe, and if one considers that his betrayal must have cost many lives as the war went on and on, one should despise Lee. He is nevertheless one of America's few classical heroes, universally admired, not because we have been duped by Southern historians but because we cannot help recognizing the human tragedy of such a man, with his knowledge of the consequences of his acts. Here again it is not creed but character that raises treachery out of its usual depth.

In the absence of personal nobility, even wise political betrayals are often judged very harshly. Richelieu, who betrayed his Church by siding with the Protestants in the Thirty Years War, and Bernadotte, who deserted Napoleon to save his Swedish throne, are not much admired. "Reason of state" does not somehow inspire approving responses, yet it has its merits. At its simplest, it is the doctrine that rulers must follow not their inclinations or personal loyalties, but only the coldly calculated interests of those whom they rule. This is the proclaimed ethos especially of absolute monarchs in the process of becoming legal sovereigns—that is, impersonal agents of their subjects, rather than dynastic self-aggrandizers. They are now "servants" of the state, even if they *are* the state. This self-serving doctrine requires that everything be subordinated to cold public calculation and that rulers must acquire the character required for such conduct. Pure reason of state can exist only when an individual political actor has a choice between personal and public betrayal, not just whenever any possible moral principle is at stake in the relations between states. The conflict has to be between two kinds of reasoning within one mind. It is not a choice of policies, but of personal or impersonal loyalties, one of which must be betrayed. The former is regarded as less rational because it is individual and falls outside the rules of state interest within a state system. Although this view is part of an overconfident rationalism, it is far from absurd, given its original context. Why then have historians responded less sympathetically to Richelieu and Bernadotte than to Lee? The two former did less damage and they did the best possible thing for their countries in betraying their faith and benefactor, respectively. They were, to be sure, not losers, but that would only, on their own terms, have made them contemptible. The difference is between characters. Historians do not look just at individual acts of treachery in isolation, but at the whole character of the traitor, as well as the quite specific circumstances under which he came to act as he did. Lee is thus perceived as an honorable hero, right out of neoclassical drama, and Richelieu and Bernadotte as a pair of excellent statesmen and awful men, which is an ambiguous judgment, but one that gives politics its due.

Conflicts of Loyalty: Honor and Obligation

One reason why any discussion of infidelity turns so quickly to politics is that of all the groups that may have claims upon us, it is the state that has usually demanded our primary loyalty and that has, correspondingly, been most readily betrayed. Treachery, of course, exists wherever and whenever trust is given or expected, but governments are the most conspicuous focus of both. Public treason is a significant, dramatic event that touches the imagination. It may, in fact, affect the lives of many people. Treason is, however, no less ambiguous than are personal betrayals, especially when it is a betrayal of an impersonal entity such as a bureaucratic state, or a constitution, as it now often is. It was not always so. In the feudal monarchies of Europe, treason was a personal affront inflicted upon one's liege lord, and the horror that the crime still arouses may owe something yet to that memory. Indeed, to understand current thinking about both treason and subversion, it helps to remember other mentalities. The bond between a king and his baron was, in theory, one of personal loyalty, and it was supposed to be unbreakable and unchallengeable. There was certainly much familiarity between rulers and barons during their youth, in battle, and at court. The upper layers of the hierarchy knew each other directly. They also hated each other frequently. And disloyalty, baronial in-fighting, and rebellion were far more common than civil upheavals in modern states. It was, of course, much easier. One ought not to indulge in wholly illusory sentimentalities about the sacredness or durability of bonds in face-to-face societies like the medieval monarchies. Here betrayal was both personal and endemic. The actions regarded as treasonable and the severity of the law make that abundantly clear. An ideology of personal fealty, in fact, is a response to the actuality of constant betrayals. In civil wars, as in despotic regimes, betrayal is so common that a yearning for trust arises from the very depth of hypocrisy and perfidy.

The ultimate basis of the English law of treason and the remote ancestor of its U.S. counterpart is the Treason Act of 1351, enacted in the reign of Edward III to stabilize prosecutions. Although it combines Roman elements of obedience to authority with Germanic notions of mutual fidelity, the overwhelming impression is one of personal duty to an individual king. Treason is a breach of feudal duty—part of an ethos structured by belief in the purity of blood descent, hierarchical fealty, and military values. Behind it stands the feudal web of personal pledges, of vassalage, of allegiance between lords and their men. Among the early Germans, to break one's troth was to outlaw oneself—indeed, to reduce oneself to a wolf. To this were eventually added Roman notions of respect due to authority, and then the Christians' oath to God, administered by a cleric. "Petty treason" reflected the whole hierarchy of duties of which this body politic was meant to be composed. It covered betrayals of masters by their servants, husbands by their wives, and bishops by lesser clerics. These were punished more severely than ordinary murderers. It is, however, high treason that is most revealing. It includes "compassing and imagining" the death of the king, of his queen, or of his heir. Violations of the women of the king's immediate family were treason. Punishment included not only beheading but also "the corruption" of the blood of the traitor.[14] This means that his noble blood was now held to have been soiled by his deed, and in practice that all his property reverted to the Crown, thus disinheriting his children. There was no benefit of clergy for men who had so gravely violated their oath. Judas Iscariot loomed in people's minds when they talked about treason. Treason to a king was a sacrilege, and doubly so, for the sacred oath was meant to ensure one's fidelity to the Lord's anointed, to a semi-sacred personage at the very least, even a vicar of Christ. In *Richard II*, Shakespeare recreates for us that mental world, which prevailed long before he wrote of it.[15]

As soon as we meet Richard II we are informed that he is not a competent ruler and that he has treacherously connived at the murder of his uncle. Trust is the last thing that he inspires. Yet we also recognize why he and his loyal followers think that he cannot be deposed and killed. He is not an ordinary man. He wears the majestic crown; all of his realm is on his head, and he is a vicar of the Lord. His greatest burden, however, is that he is also a man who needs friends and who feels every pain. When Bolingbroke rises

163

up against him, he has a just cause: Richard has taken his
inheritance away from him in a high-handed and malicious
manner. But even John of Salisbury, who considered tyran-
nicide justified under extreme circumstances, would not
have called Richard a tyrant. And even he thought *lèse ma-
jesté* the very worst crime.[16] Pious Richard is not a tyrant fit
for discarding. So when Richard laments, "I live with bread,
like you; feel want, / Taste grief, need friends" (III, 2) we
pity him; but he and we also know that he is more, and that
"The breath of worldly men cannot depose / The deputy
elected by the Lord" (III, 2), and that the rebels "break their
faith to God as well as us." One is soon drawn to him and to
his defenders. What is so revealing for us is how much the
familial haunts the person of the king. He wrongs and is
deposed by a cousin; another cousin stands by him valiantly; his uncles exhort him constantly; his wife and his immediate friends must fall with him. Yet this is not really a
man. He is a divine object and the ultimate military and
legal authority at the pinnacle of a hierarchy—and of a
country of which his uncle, John of Gaunt, speaks so mov-
ingly. These circumstances suffice to make treason ambiguous even when it is so loathed and dreaded. For Bolingbroke
is not a traitor, pure and simple. He is not an aristocratic
Iago in disguise. He is a resolute man who is likely to rule
more competently than Richard. We also know that his
claim to rule is not as good as Richard's, that he has no business killing him, and that even in his most generous moment, when he pardons his cousin who conspired on
Richard's behalf, he is just a "new prince," and acting like
one. We also know, retrospectively, that his treason was not
a good or solid basis for the Crown and that England was to
suffer for it long and horribly. *Richard II* is not about any
one political idea; but among its many themes, none stands
out more firmly than the difficulty of treason committed
against a weak man who is accepted as more than a man,
who is reduced and then displaced and killed by an able
and unjustly provoked kinsman. The victor must then rule
without the benefit of genuine reverence, personal or sacred. Bolingbroke is not merely a Machiavellian prince as a

man, but he puts himself into the position of such a ruler by an act of betrayal, whch we begin by applauding and end by doubting. Shakespeare's characters feel intensely about treason. Historically, there was never a time when treason meant more perhaps, and yet it was very uncertain in its actuality for those who had to deal with it. It was not clear-cut at all, only more personal, more agonizing. It was a public conflict that had all the marks of a family fight, and all its bitterness as well. In this it was unlike later, more impersonal ideological betrayals.

The uncertainties of early Tudor kingship seemed to call for public extirpation of treason. Treason as such was more reviled than at any other time, but unhappily there were also real conflicts among intensely loyal religious and political foes. The horror of treason was certainly enhanced by the savagery with which the Tudors sought out and punished traitors.[17] The reasons for their policy, fear of a return to civil war, uncertainties about the succession, and religious conflict, were such as to make most of their subjects apparently as afraid of treason as they were. The many condemned were guilty under the terms of the then existing law, but the law and its execution were horrifying in their scope and brutality. To predict the king's death was treason. Ben Jonson was not thinking just of Tiberius' Rome when he has a senator say in *Sejanus,* "We shall not shortly dare to tell our dreams, / Or think, but 't will be treason" (I, 1). Here speech with no act in sight was enough to convict. Even failure to denounce conspiracies was treason. Anything that could be "construed" as "compassing" the king's death was so "construed," and judges tended to bully juries if they seemed recalcitrant. It was decidedly a harsher law than that of the late Middle Ages, and it enhanced the sense of ubiquitous treachery. Treason was about, and the endless trials advertised it, so that from above and below, and at court especially, betrayal seemed to be everywhere. Yet the obligations of fidelity had not melted away; it was still "corruption of blood" to be a convicted traitor. The aristocratic idea of personal fidelity, of keeping oaths, of friendship and gratitude, especially to those above one, survived, as did faith in a just and clement rule. It was into this world of an already bruised aristocratic self-image that Machiavelli burst as a herald of bad social news. For he was shocking not just as an unchristian devil, but as a mocker of the very heart of the aristocratic ethos. He was the master of treachery. In a society in which oaths had proliferated in the desperate hope that they might rivet society, he laughed at them as just one more instrument of policy. It was this that Montaigne could not tolerate in him. Machiavelli was right as the world goes; treachery did indeed have its place in the world, and "perfidy to punish and betray perfidy" was justified there, Montaigne wrote. But even in the midst of a civil war, he preferred to be trusting rather than suspicious, and open in his dealings with princes, rather than tricky. It did not always work well, but he did morally disarm a man who had meant to abuse his hospitality and to murder him treacherously. Montaigne's open manner seemed to shame the villain into decency. Most of all, however, Montaigne did not choose to live in fear or to practice betrayal, because such a life just did not seem worth living at all. Personal honor was clearly the mainspring of Montaigne's fortitude.[18] So Locke was to say of keeping oaths that some did it out of fear of God or Leviathan, but that pagan philosophers thought that to break one's promises was "below the dignity of a man."[19] That had been Montaigne's choice. The answer to perfidy and its ambiguities may be a willingness to take risks.

Men already badly shaken by Tudor political actualities found it difficult to cope with Machiavelli. His enormous impact cannot be fully appreciated unless one recognizes the wounds he inflicted upon aristocratic sensibilities. The prince as a lion was not outrageous, but the prince as a fox was repulsive. No chapter of the *Discourses* seemed more troubling than the one that gave practical advice to conspirators.[20] Aristocratic readers might well retch when they were told that cruelty was futile without treachery, that princes should blame and get rid of their faithful servants whenever it seemed convenient, that they should break their oath whenever it seemed profitable, and generally ma-

nipulate everyone near them. They might share Machiavelli's view of Fortune as part of a different and difficult
stoic ethos, but they also knew, to their disgust, that she
was often invoked as a license for complete personal irresponsibility. That also was one of the uses of the doctrine of
political "necessity." The Elizabethan stage put all this before its audiences in the most lurid light.

What if one accepted Machiavelli's picture of the political
world as a wholly treacherous place? What if it were nothing
but a dense web of betrayals? What if courts were vipers'
nests and Machiavelli was just an honest, unhypocritical re-
porter? So Lord Bacon and Marlowe thought him to be. The
writer who observed such a scene and put it on the stage for
the public might be revolted by these realities; he might
protest; but he could not deny their truth. That is how Machiavelli came to cast so long a shadow on the Elizabethan
and Jacobean theater, and made everyone aware of the character of the new moral world. The poet Fulke Greville was
not speaking only for himself when he said that he wrote
not like the ancients, to illustrate the miseries of human life,
nor as the moderns did, to point out God's revenge on our
sins, but "to trace out the high ways of ambitious Governors, and to show in the practice the more audacity, advantage and good success such Sovereignties have, the more
they hasten their own desolation and ruin."[21] In most tragedies of the time, they also destroy everyone and everything
around them.

Marlowe's *Jew of Malta* could be a chapter out of Machiavelli. The ruler simply confiscates the property of the Jew
Barabas to pay an overdue tribute to the Turks. Barabas is
not wrong when he says of the governor and his men that

> I can see nothing in their faith
> But malice, falsehood and excessive pride,
> Which methinks fits not their profession.
>
> (I, 1)

But they are also right when they scorn his greed and perfidy, especially when he tricks two young men into a fatal
duel. He betrays the governor to the Turk, then the Turk to

the governor. The Christian governor deceives both Barabas and the Turk. Everyone has some excuse for treachery, chiefly the universal reign of dishonesty. "Oh happy they that never saw the court," says one of Webster's characters. For all courts seem to be like Malta, perhaps worse. There is nothing like the doctrine of reason of state yet—just a mass of personal passions. And the princes are almost invariably the chief perpetrators of treachery. They may be Italians but they are rulers in these plays, and they stand at the pinnacle of a hierarchy from which they make treachery a norm throughout court society. Is there an acceptable escape? Or just resignation? Or should one not join in the general treachery simply to survive?

What happens to men of honor in a detestable Machiavellian world? Ben Jonson seemed to suggest that they could only grumble and acquiesce in the treachery of their rulers, because there was no alternative. In *Sejanus*, Tiberius is easily persuaded to dispose of his inconvenient relations by trickery, but then, following Machiavelli's advice, he destroys Sejanus, his now far too powerful courtier and henchman. The fallen favorite is brutally killed by all his erstwhile hangers-on. A successor is already in place, and while the courtiers bemoan the good old days, they also have no choice but to go along with Tiberius, vile though his personal life may be. He is, at least, a shrewd prince. What else is there? Join in. That is the measure of Jonson's disgust. The great resort of personal friendship "chaste and masculine," as his fellow dramatist Chapman put it, remains the only haven. When Claremont, the hero of Chapman's *Revenge of Bussy D'Amboise*, discovers that his friend Guise has been ambushed and killed, he commits suicide. He has no place in the world of conniving courtiers who tell the king of France that

> Treachery for kings is truest loyalty;
> Nor is it to bear the name of treachery,
> But grave, deep policy. All acts that seem
> Ill in particular respects are good
> As they respect your universal rule.

THE AMBIGUITIES OF BETRAYAL

I will be honest and betray for you
Brother and father.   (III, 1)

These men are the winners; their treacheries are necessary but also intolerable. Tudor aristocratic political tragedies are about the victory of perfidy, about a society in which there are rarely more than one or two loyal people who can suffer in, comment on, and expose the character of this all-enveloping climate of mutual betrayal. It is not that the treachery in action is ambiguous here, but that at court there is no escape from it. One must simply resign oneself or flee, as best one can, from a political world that cannot, by definition, command the loyalty or honor of aristocrats, but for which there is no alternative. There are, therefore, usually only one or two genuine paragons in each play, for everyone knows that most noblemen are not, in fact, honorable. They are courtiers for sale to the highest bidder.

The courtiers who serve princes free from all normal restraints do not yet talk the real language of reason of state. They are the agents of an individual who may be new or born to the throne. In either case, he must be a self-made ruler, because his position is never secure and he maintains it as best he can. Only a post–civil war "absolute" monarch could pose, on and off the stage, as the personification of public values, as the "servant" of his state. In this service, aristocrats could honorably join. Reason of state was an ideology that made political "necessity," even betrayal, respectable. It resolved the awful war between honor and treason in such a way as to allow aristocrats to recover their morale at court. If the ruler is not an evil character, but the agent of order for his people, then one can serve him faithfully and honorably, even though he may be a calculating fox. Both he and the aristocracy now face the same moral tension between private and public duty. Treachery survives as a base personal weakness, unworthy of a member of a ruling class, but it also becomes a public obligation in the interest of public peace, grandeur, and order. For a century the aristocracy could enjoy plays that dealt beautifully with what they believed were their moral struggles. From Corneille's *Cid* to Mozart's *Clemency of Titus,* we see the way in which treacherous personal impulses must be overcome with great pain by a hero, who may fail or succeed, but who acts in a non-Machiavellian setting and who is not without support at court. Generally, he is torn between private inclination and public duty, which may be either to his sovereign or to his family or to both. No ruler may permit any personal ambitions or love to interfere with his political obligations. On the stage, service to the state is sanctified because it depersonalizes even a Roman emperor, though he has reached the throne by means of various crimes. Once he is in charge, a ruler must think rationally, objectively, and disinterestedly of the public good, which has but two aims: stability at home, victory abroad. For reason of state is not divorced from the fear of civil war. The rationality of state service is the successor of and cure for this, the worst of all wars. The need to end the Fronde and similar last-ditch aristocratic upheavals is its ultimate justification. Rulers are by no means always idealized in this classical drama, but what we see is a unified political ideal in which king and nobility are proud to share, precisely because it is so difficult and because so many have failed. Louis XIV can, in short, be admired for not being another Nero.

In Racine's *Britannicus* a still-wavering young Nero asks his old adviser, Burrhus, about the public: "Am I then emperor just to humour them?" The good man replies: "And is it not enough, my lord, for you / That public happiness on you depends?" An evil courtier, however, eggs Nero on: "Are you unmindful of your own desires, / Are you the only one you dare not trust?"[22] Nero, as we know, careens down the hill of corruption, killing and betraying everyone for his personal gratification. Yet noble Burrhus himself advises him to keep his mother at bay, since only "policy" must concern him. Unegotistical, institutionalized treachery has lost its Machiavellian sting. Its horror, especially when it is committed by rulers and conspiring noblemen for purely *personal* reasons, is enormous; but as a necessity of the *public* happiness, it becomes a lofty duty to abjure one's loyalties to one's family and old companions. Treachery as a public policy, dispassionate and even disinterested, has been civilized and rendered honorable. Royal and aristocratic audiences were relieved to watch dramas of personal moral conflict, believing that these were also their own. These plays reinforced the ethos of aristocratic honor in the service to a king who is a fox only to his and the state's enemies. In Corneille's *Cinna*, the young hero is torn between a promise to his bride to avenge her father by killing Augustus, and his duty to a gracious emperor. Augustus wants to resign his throne because he is weary of ruling. When he discovers Cinna's plot, he decides to forgive him and also to remain emperor. He thus demonstrates his aloofness both from personal vengeance and from such weaknesses as natural exhaustion. He now becomes a model emperor, which he has not been before, not least because his authority over his aristocratic subjects was not yet fully established. Cinna is duly grateful and so are the spectators, even though two questionable betrayals are required to bring about this happy end. Cinna does not avenge the death of his bride's father, and his plan is betrayed to the emperor by a fellow conspirator and friend. These personal treacheries are required for public honor and wisdom, and are now morally edifying. It is the final domestication of Machiavelli. In his earlier retelling of Cinna's story, Montaigne had come to a far more skeptical conclusion. Augustus was just lucky. Fortune had favored him. Other princes had been killed by those whom they had pardoned. Not reason of state, but chance ruled politics. There were, therefore, no rational political betrayals or pardons.[23]

If Machiavelli inspired nightmares of ubiquitous treason, making it baffling because it was so universal, reason of state reduced it to a respectable ambiguity again. In Tudor drama, treachery was committed by, for, and against recognizable personal rulers, often Italian, and was politically dreadful because it was still so individual, so familial. When treachery is depersonalized as selfless and passionless reason of state, it is no longer a tragic necessity, but a demand that aristocratic and royal honor can accept as a self-imposed burden. The conflict between treachery and honor is transformed into a struggle between basely personal passion and lofty public duty—a struggle that all noble men and women must to some degree experience. It is the victory of aristocratic honor within the individual that liberates him morally to do whatever the public happiness may demand in the way of political knavery. In fact, however, the difference between faith and betrayal did not go away; it was only insulated.

What honor itself meant for an aristocrat of the *Ancien Régime* can be readily discovered in Madame de Lafayette's famous novel *The Princess of Cleves*. The heroine would not feel worthy of herself or of her dead husband if she were to marry a man whom she loves and who has long loved her. Her husband has died of grief after discovering that his perfectly faithful wife does not love him. To her it seems that this is the equivalent of his having died in a duel. Austere though it be, she follows the path of duty to a convent. Anything else would make her unhappy and would be a dishonor to her husband's and her own name. This paragon is much loved at court, and plays her part in maintaining the monarchical order, as does her husband. Both behave as their rank and their own sense of it require. But nothing outside that circle can touch them—they have no obligations beyond its confines. That they are eventually wholly unable to compromise with or to understand the necessity of constitutional reform is predictable. And as always, of course, the reality is not what the ideal has suggested. In those days kings betrayed not only for their people, but for their own sake as well. Ministers came and went, and when Charles I abandoned Stratford he was doing nothing very uncommon. What was gone was the desolation created by the Machiavellian scramble, which had swallowed every aristocratic impulse to honor. With personal loyalties and betrayals now tamed, a depersonalized treachery abroad and at home could be underwritten by personal honor, fidelity, and devotion to public duty. Without a king, moreover, to act for and on behalf of the public and as a personalized state, this whole complex mixture of honor and state reason would collapse.

Betrayal in Republics Ancient and Modern

Impersonality is not the only way of coping with political betrayal. What happens in a republic, whether ancient or modern, when there is no personal focus of loyalty, and when both trust and treason are directed at the city and at one's fellow citizens? An ancient republic such as Athens or Rome certainly offered its free males many opportunities for democratic participation in politics, but leadership was very generally exercised by members of noble families. The many could frequently insult the few, and the proud could readily injure the many by acts of betrayal. The Athenian and Roman republican laws of treason were severe, and we have no reason at all to doubt that the crime was deeply resented by the people and ferociously punished. The ancient historians do not, however, always reflect this patriotic temper. Thucydides tells of three traitors: Pausanias, who betrayed Sparta, and Themistocles and Alcibiades, who were traitors to Athens. All three went over to the enemies of their respective cities, but Thucydides does not seem particularly shocked by their conduct, certainly not in the way that he was by the dissolution of all civilized restraints in the course of a civil war. Treason emerges as a decidedly aristocratic crime, not only because, then as now, important and powerful people have more opportunities for treason, but because they stand apart from the city as a whole. The politics of conflict between the rich and the poor in Athens provides the setting; for aristocrats frequently felt debased, and when they did they quit the city in disgust. Arrogance was in all cases the effective motive, according to Thucydides, but it had different implications in each case. He clearly did not think well of the Spartan Pausanias, who was certainly a great general but excessively proud and ambitious, and who was probably rightly suspected by the Spartans of wanting to be a tyrant. Pausanias sold his services to Xerxes, the king of Persia, and took to living in the Persian manner. Just as he thought Pausanias' character lamentable, quite apart from his treachery, so Thucydides admired Themistocles, because of his extraordinary intelligence. Themistocles had been exiled from Athens, but continued to have many friends in the city who remained devoted to him. Though he, too, went over to the Persians and became an important personage among them, Thucydides praised him with unusual ardor. More surprisingly, loyal and democratic Aristides, who under the same circumstances remained faithful to ungrateful Athens, is not even mentioned. Silence tells us nothing, except that an unaristocratic leader might be less given to betrayal of his people, and that this in itself made him uninteresting. And, indeed, good faith is not intellectually or emotionally very stirring. Themistocles was, at any rate, a great and fascinating man in Thucydides' view, and the ordinary standards did not apply to him. What of Alcibiades, the golden boy of Athens? Thucydides thought him an able man, but not in Themistocles' class, and also unbalanced, too ostentatious and lawless. He may have been treated unfairly by his enemies, but the extravagances of his personal life were bound to lead him into trouble, as did his recklessness as a military commander and as a diplomatic agent. The Spartans trusted him no more than did the Athenians or the Phoenicians. Therefore, when Alcibiades says in his own defense that the Athens he left was not the old Athens he had loved, and that a true patriot opposes his city when it is wrong, he fails to convince.[24] Since the only change and "fault" in Athens was its decision to condemn him, we can see that his argument is self-serving. In any case, his sense of his own and his family's social importance was such that he simply invited his own downfall. As we read Thucydides' accounts of these three towering traitors, it appears that he, at least, is more interested in their entire character, especially their whole political career, and not treason as an isolated act. Pausanias' venality, Themistocles' adaptability and judgment, and Alcibiades' self-infatuation color the course of

their treasonable activity. Plutarch saw the matter no dif-
ferently when he compared the lives of Alcibiades and
Coriolanus. The latter deserted Rome when its citizens refused to elect him to office. Alcibiades was indeed "ruined
by his own glory" and was very dissolute, but Plutarch felt
sorry for him and thought him superior to Coriolanus, who
had in his pride brought Rome to the brink of civil war.
Sallust had been no less cool about the corrupt Catiline,
whose subversive conspiracy was only the last of a long series of vicious acts. For none of these ancient historians was
treason the profound psychological or moral problem that it
was for Shakespeare in his plays, notably in *Richard II* and
Coriolanus. The latter especially differs from Plutarch's portrait. What they really dreaded was civil war. Thucydides
thought it the worst of all political disasters, as did Aristotle
after him; for he also discussed treason, if it can be called
that at all, only in the context of attacks on tyranny. It is
civil conflict—the dissolution of trust among citizens, subversion above all—that is the greatest of political threats.
That is what made Plutarch condemn Coriolanus so severely; he had out of pride almost ruined Rome, not by his
act of treason but by giving foolish and unacceptable offense to the people, thus opening the door to civil strife.

When religion is a real tie, however, the quality of treason seems to alter. Josephus was a military commander
who, like Alcibiades, went over to the enemy. He had never
approved of the Jewish war against Rome, but he had taken
command of one of the armies. Moreover, he could not
claim that he had been rejected, as Alcibiades had been.
Nevertheless, like the latter, he was deeply at odds with the
most anti-Roman factions in Jerusalem. When Josephus refused to commit suicide, as did all his defeated comrades,
and when he urged his people to give up their fight, and
then finally joined Vespasian, the future emperor, he was
reviled as a traitor, and he understood that he was one. His
excuse is not that of Alcibiades, even though he thought
himself just as superior to most men as did the Athenian
general. First of all, he argued that God must have given him
his ability to foretell the future for some purpose. He used it

175

to predict that Vespasian would become emperor, and on the strength of that was favored by the Roman commander, who invited him to betray the Jews. When he did so, Josephus still said, "I am not denying my birth or forgetting my heritage."[25] Indeed, the Jews should never have fought at all; for as God took them out of Egypt, he would now protect them, if only they did not take their fate, unfaithfully, into their own hands. As for collective suicide, however brave, it was an act contrary to nature and to God. Latterday apologists for Josephus have argued accordingly that survival then as now was more important than self-rule, especially since the many Jews who lived in the diaspora were also endangered by the uprising in and around Jerusalem. Even more remarkable is the suggestion that Josephus, though certainly a traitor by the standards of his time, redeemed himself by writing a history of the Jews that was ultimately of greater value to them as a people than his suicide, however noble, could possibly have been.[26] The difficulty is that Josephus could not have foreseen all that, great as his prophetic gifts were. Was it just moral luck in its consequences? Did he really try to save himself for posterity? He never said so, but that may not be significant. If he acted as he did in order to serve the collective memory, it is a matter of no small importance for the Jews, and it becomes as difficult to judge his treason as any that was ever committed. Should the people of Jerusalem, however, have forgiven him? Could they?

Josephus tells us, as Thucydides does not, just how profoundly treason was hated by a betrayed people. The Jews were not engaged in an ordinary war, to be sure, but rebelling against a conqueror who they thought threatened their faith no less than their independence. They were, moreover, not a political people. Their factions and quarrels always had a religious as well as a social character. Heresy, not merely treason, agitates such a people. When we return to the more purely political cities, we see that its historians and political scientists thought treason less significant than sedition, and the prevention of civil war more important than any incidence of treason. Even Cato thought so, according to Sallust.[27] That may well have been part of a common aristocratic outlook. In all these cases, whether it was Alcibiades, Coriolanus, or Josephus, the people were betrayed by one of its chosen aristocratic commanders. To the patriotic citizen their act was simple, arrogant treachery, but we cannot fail to recognize the ambiguities especially of Themistocles' and Josephus' betrayals. Both were acknowledged leaders—wiser, more far-seeing, and, to be sure, prouder than their less capable fellow citizens. Each understood the realities of the situation more clearly, and each was spurned by a people more patriotic but far less intelligent than he was. The ties of mutual trust, never very strong for exceptional people, were severed, and the traitor chose to act in accordance with his quite justified sense of his own capabilities, which had both raised and isolated him all along. Nevertheless, it is in republics—in which all are, in principle, fellow citizens—that treason and subversion are most thoroughly despised.

In classical republics, the ambiguity of treason is due to the unstable relation between the ordinary citizens and their aristocratic leaders, especially in times of war and danger. In a representative democracy, such as the United States, the difficulty is quite different, however. Freedom creates a whole new range of complexities. Subversion—and other threats to the constitutional order—have inherited all the odium that treason had aroused in the more personal republics of antiquity. Not the least important reason for this is that a Lockean political society depends on trust more than does any other, yet it may well lack the means to enforce it, if it is to remain free—that is, politically trustworthy. A free society is not at liberty to suppress disloyalty, because it will cease to be free if it does not restrain itself. Yet it depends on trust, and so suspicion is always rife. For where is treason if not in trust?

When America declared its independence it said goodbye in principle to the English Treason Statute of 1351, though some phrases from that old law survived. Nevertheless, some laws of treason were required at once, if only to prevent desertions from Washington's army. The American law of treason was, from the first, a creature of war. It was also the outcome of memories of loosely interpreted, "constructive" treason, of Tudor savagery, and of some severe sentences in the eighteenth century. The law was certainly far less harsh in eighteenth-century England than it had been previously, but Americans were determined that charges of treason must not become part of partisan political conflicts. Factions were not to wreak their "malignity on each other" by using "new-fangled" treasons, as Madison said in the Forty-third *Federalist*. George Washington's question "Can we subsist—did any state ever subsist without exterminating traitors?" was answered eventually, but it was not to be a very important part of American history. It is indeed remarkable that the federal government survived its early years without an army, significant patronage, or well-organized parties.[28] There were a few riots—the Whiskey Rebellion, most notably; some of its leaders were charged with treason, but it was a rare and isolated instance. What is really significant about the treason clause of the U.S. Constitution is that it contemplates only acts of violent rebellion and going over to an enemy in war. Article III, section 3 of the Constitution is quite clear about that: "Treason against the United States shall consist only in levying war against them, or in adhering to their enemies, giving them Aid and Comfort. No person shall be convicted of Treason unless on the testimony of two Witnesses to the same Overt Act, or on Confession in open court." The clause is, in fact, taken from a part of the existing English law, but divorced from the monarchical past. There are also less serious crimes of political betrayal than treason, especially espionage and subversion—the latter meaning, in the words of the Smith Act of 1940, "conspiring to teach, advocate or encourage the overthrow or destruction" of the government "by force or violence."[29]

The oft-expressed hopes of Ben Franklin, Madison, James Wilson, and John Marshall that the law of treason would not be used in partisan political quarrels, that it would be applied only rarely and with every safeguard to individual rights, were in fact fulfilled, though charges less severe than treason have done their mischief from time to time. Wilson was particularly influenced by Montesquieu's views on the matter. If the crime of treason "be indeterminate," we read in *The Spirit of the Laws*, "this is alone sufficient to make the government degenerate into arbitrary power." Moreover, only tyrants punish thoughts, rather than "overt acts"—and speech, in Montesquieu's view, was not such an act. A republic will destroy itself if it gives power to anyone to punish those who wish to subvert it. Bills of attainder are an outrage. In any event, not the rebel but rebellion should be attacked—or, one suspects, prevented, which was what Cato had already thought. It is evident that Montesquieu would have preferred to do away with the laws of treason, subversion, and espionage altogether. Nothing reveals his fear of governments more fully. His voice was surely heard in America, but his advice was only partially followed, though Justice Jackson was not in error when in the famous *Cramer* case of 1944 he noted that the United States had managed to survive very well with only the rarest resorts to the law of treason.[30] What has always aroused the public and the government of the United States, often to the point of frenzy, is not treason to an enemy in wartime, but subversion—surreptitious designs to destroy the people's trust in and allegiance to the constitutional system. Subversion is perceived as betrayal of constitutional government, of the people, and of the system of trust itself. That it is often thought to be part of a foreign-made plot only renders the basic threat more hateful. Treason has, in comparison, been a secondary offense. It is internal treachery, and threats to establish institutions that are really dreaded.

At the outset, there was some doubt whether treason could be committed against the United States, or only against the several states. That was finally settled once and for all by the force of arms. In spite of some efforts to do so, however, no Confederate leaders were tried for treason after the Civil War, though Jefferson Davis was under arrest for a time. In the end, the reintegration of the South into the

Union was recognized as more important than punishing a defeated army. Under the Fourteenth Amendment, those who had held federal office under oath to uphold the Constitution were debarred from holding such office in the future.[31] This itself is a significant comment on the importance of trust (which oaths signal) in this constitutional system. Later convictions for treason were all for aiding the enemy during the Second World War. And it is conceivably still possible to prosecute a U.S. citizen successfully for treason, if intent could be established beyond a doubt and if all the other constitutional conditions could be met in the most exact way. It would not be easy. Speaking for the Supreme Court in the *Cramer* case, Justice Jackson eloquently recalled Montesquieu, Jefferson, the generous treatment accorded to the Confederate leaders, and America's ability to prosper without the use of prosecutions for treason. Lesser laws would suffice, even in time of war. Presumably he had the espionage acts in mind, though it is not clear why he thought that these, with their far less stringent procedural requirements, posed no threat to individual liberty. In any case, it is not only treason but all degrees of betrayal and dissent that create problems for modern states, especially in times of war, which is when they typically occur. For war does not always unite a people. It can also exacerbate all of the deepest divisions within a country and inflame the most severe conflicts of loyalty. The Revolutionary War, the War of 1812, and the Civil War were partly or entirely internal wars. Not everyone was persuaded of the rightness of the First World War, not to mention the Vietnam War. Since the First World War, moreover, in every European country the nation as the focus of loyalty, and so of betrayal, has been challenged by other ideologies. American Nazis who supported Hitler during World War II thought of themselves not as traitors, but as patriots saving their country from Roosevelt and the Jewish menace. The communists who served the Soviet Union thought they were doing their best for the American proletariat no less than for every other. Subjective treason and legal treason do not coincide in cases of ideological betrayals of the nation-state. There is not even a conflict of loyalties in these cases; on the contrary, the agent may be deeply loyal to his cause.

Espionage for pay is not without its ambiguities now, either. The abstractness of betraying a bureaucratic organization creates its own puzzles. The psychological difference between selling industrial secrets relevant to defense and the practices of ordinary domestic business espionage is marginal. Employees regularly sell trade secrets and confidential information to the competitors of their firms, though this is a felony. There is, however, very little to be done about it, especially since executives and technicians are free to move from one company to another. Signed promises to maintain rules of confidentiality only lower morale. The government is now itself a large-scale employer—that is, just another boss. And the intent of the employee is not political when he sells a secret. Most Americans are not exactly inclined to think of the boss who pays for their work as a liege lord. Why should they? The relation is one of services rendered for pay, not one of loyalty at all. The attitude to the state-as-employer or contractor for production cannot therefore be one of deep allegiance. Even though most people know that it is a serious crime to sell secret industrial information to a Soviet or Japanese agent, the individual act itself is not all that remote from selling trade secrets to a rival U.S. company that may want to enter that line of production. Only the legal consequences differ. Needless to add, computers have made all this even more impersonal. When one, in short, betrays the U.S. government for cash, it is not a unique crime; the motive may be casual and mercenary, and will seem remote from Judas Iscariot's betrayal, or Brutus' stabbing of Caesar. To punish such spies severely in times of peace may have a deterrent effect, but the community will not be deeply concerned by such incidents, as Christopher Boyce's easy escape from prison already suggests.[32] Loyalty to a big business, which is what the government is, need not and cannot be demanded in a free and mobile society, though the law may try. To be sure, the very character of betrayal and so of loyalty is shaken, or at least clouded.

Government as an employer, little different from a private enterprise, is only the last step in the diffusion of political loyalty and betrayal. It is not altogether a new state of affairs. Immigration has for a long time now defined one's country as essentially an area of more or less abundant employment opportunities. Rebecca West reported that at the trial of William Joyce, who had daily broadcast Nazi propaganda to Britain and had tried to subvert prisoners of war in Nazi Germany, some spectators excused him because they thought that he had gone to Germany simply to get a better job.[33] The fact that he had worked for the national enemy did not seem to disturb them all that much, apparently. How much less offensive must it seem to add to one's income by selling a few classified trade secrets to a foreign agent, and not always one from a hostile country. The act is less ambiguous than insignificant.

Political Trust and the Fear of Subversion

It is not espionage or treason that really seems to upset the American public most. It is subversion, especially if it be alien and ideological, that causes outbursts of almost uncontrollable fear, when Americans go on what one might call a loyalty binge. What is dreaded is a conspiracy by domestic aliens, possibly with foreign aid, to overthrow the established constitutional order. And as in private experience, there is often a great gap between feeling betrayed and actual acts of treachery. There are perfectly good reasons for that. Although patriotism runs high in the United States, America is an immigrant society and its nationalism is always compromised by people with divided or no loyalties. That is the condition of its freedom, but it also assures insecurity. In a society whose members are free to move up and down, in and out, and across the social and geographic terrain of North America, ties of loyalty are readily made

and unmade. That, in addition to its multiple ethnic and religious groups, the latter not all equally nationalist in orien-
tation, does not make America a unitary nation-state. Everyone is beset by strangers at his gate, and that inspires
mutual suspicion. At a more profound level, moreover, a
Lockean liberal society requires more trust from more people than any other. Consent and promises were the sole ties
of Locke's constitutional vision. And if Americans resort to
oaths constantly, in order to contain their dissociation, they
are again only following Locke and attempting to establish
those relations of trust which they require politically, even
as their culture tends to destroy and threaten them at every
turn.

Patriotic fury is not unimportant in stimulating outbursts
against real or suspected subversion; but it is not everything. The inevitably divided loyalties of a pluralistic society are bound to create much uneasiness, especially in
time of war or international tension. Nor is it always clear
who is betraying whom in periods of suspicion. The Japa-
nese-Americans interned during the Second World War
were betrayed by their fellow citizens and their government. That almost all remained loyal to the United States is
a tribute to their faith in its constitutional government and
not to the patriotic fervor of those years. Indeed, much of
what passes for superpatriotism at any time is simply racism, anti-Semitism, and the remnants of a general Anglo-
Saxonism, more rampant in the years before the First World
War than in the second half of the twentieth century. However, the deepest ideological source of the fear of subversion in the United States is not a primitive, persecutive
patriotism. It is to be found in the very structure of politics
in a representative democracy, which depends deeply on
trust. One might begin by simply counting how often and in
what different ways John Locke used the word "trust" in the
Second Treatise.[34] His whole view of constitutional government requires it at every juncture. The contract itself is
based on mutual promises; but even if we dismiss that as a
fiction, majority rule and the relationship of electors to representatives—and of both to the executive—would still be

based on trust. The use of oaths in the United States does not, in fact, bespeak any degree of religiosity; it signals the many moments when trust is given and accepted. Legal government, constitutional government, a government that meets expectations is one that does not betray those who trust it, Locke argued. So the whole citizenry must be able to trust a majority to act for it; the majority deposits its trust in its elected representatives. If the legislature, entrusted with the authority to make laws, betrays its charge, the trust it holds on behalf of and from the people will be withdrawn. The executive, in the conduct of foreign relations and in using its prerogative, must be trusted by the people, else it cannot act effectively. But if the executive betrays the people—say, by becoming Catholic or by submitting to a foreign power—then, Locke thought, it has broken its trust. Above all, citizens must trust one another to constitute parties, electoral constituencies, and majorities. Mutual trust must exist between those chosen to rule and the electorate. Finally, when those in office betray their trust, citizens must trust one another enough to organize resistance to unlawful rule. Where there is so much reliance on trust, there must also be frequent betrayals.

Fear of subversion is simply built into this system, and especially fear of disloyal government. There is more than one way, after all, by which a government can pursue a treacherous foreign policy. Indeed, Locke was overwhelmingly concerned with betrayals from above, and so are Americans. He thought that natural sociability and fear of social censure and ostracism made most people trustworthy in their daily dealings. Betrayal is most likely to come from governments, which are always disposed to prey upon the rights of the individual citizen. And he was not far wrong. Elected representatives habitually make promises they do not keep, and distrust is as justified and even as necessary in electoral politics as is trust in the constitutional system as a whole. One of the reasons why foreigners often fail to understand why Americans felt so betrayed by Richard Nixon is that they do not understand the importance of trust even in a political climate in which distrust is endemic. Where there is trust, there must also be distrust, because betrayal is always possible, and threatening. Hence the fear of subversives in positions of power in government, and the fear of agents who will plot to undermine the existing forms of government. In effect, representative government is a fine balance between trust and distrust. The trouble is that feeling betrayed in politics does not, any more than in personal life, correspond to acts of betrayal, much less prove the existence of conspiracies to betray. As change is itself quite sufficient to create the sensation of betrayal in marriage, so also in politics. Altered arrangements and distributions of power and prestige are perceived as betrayals by those whom they affect adversely. The consequences of perceiving betrayal, however, may be—especially after wars—disproportionate, disturbing, unjust to individuals, and dangerous to public liberties.

The fear of betrayal may, in fact, become subversive of constitutional forms, as Montesquieu saw. At the very least, it leads to the imposition of test oaths, which have restrained no real traitor or subversive since Benedict Arnold but which do humiliate and frighten public employees. They do not convince the anarchist of his obligations to obey the state, and they do not rekindle loyalties in those who prefer a cause other than an undifferentiated nationalism. The oath, even when not used as a means of entrapping the unreliable is, however, also a sign of agreement, of willingness to trust and be trusted, and it is as such that it is important to many Americans. Nevertheless, as the Supreme Court decided in the justly celebrated flag-salute case, even demonstrations of public allegiance must give way to the right to exercise one's religious scruples.[35] One may, of course, argue that oath-taking has been trivialized by over-use. Indeed, one may well argue that demands for loyalty do not halt betrayals at all—that they merely diminish liberty. If liberty defends itself against betrayal with a suicidal fervor, it becomes self-betraying. That emerges with particular nastiness when one is confronted with demands for positive loyalty or for demonstrative patriotism. This has often, both in theory and practice, come as a call

185

for solidarity. As such, it is less a response to betrayals than to a fear of the normal disarrays of political freedom, but the two are obviously related. The shock of adjusting to the new and diverse culture that developed in the early years of the twentieth century deeply upset many thoughtful Americans. Henry Adams was only the most famous among those who lamented the end of the older Anglo-American society. His distress could also be expressed in yearnings for a new, consolidated, and truly loyal society—one that would recreate the unity of the past, but on a higher plane. Josiah Royce's *The Philosophy of Loyalty* is not a reassuring book, with its call for "loyalty to loyalty."[36] Loyalty means choosing something "higher than one's private self." It sets selfless goals. The perfect example of such loyal selflessness is the Japanese samurai. Mutually destructive loyalties will disappear as mankind rises higher and higher above itself; for conflicts of allegiance are the supreme evil. Americans especially will learn to subordinate themselves to their groups without fighting each other, not only for the sake of peace, but for loyalty as such. Royce's model was obviously martial in its origins. "Foreign immigrants" would learn patriotism, unions would give up class interests for national ends, and personal leadership might inspire us all to look upward—and help us to a unified state. What Americans needed was "the will to believe in something eternal." This must have sounded a lot less awful in 1908 than it does seventy-five years later. The dream of loyalty as a martial virtue that is to replace conventional and trivial religiosity cannot, in fact, go away, even when its fascist overtones have become well known. For as long as treason in war remains the model of all political betrayal, military loyalty, by a simple act of free association, must also seem the most evident expression of patriotism. That is why not just betrayal but also loyalty must be ambiguous in a liberal polity.

In spite of Royce and his age's longing for a more uniformly Anglo-Saxon culture, divided loyalties and disparate subcultures continue to make loyalty and betrayal indefinite in the United States. Liberal uncertainties are not, however, the main source of the ambiguities of treason in the twentieth century. The most spectacular acts of betrayal have not taken place against liberal states, but against terroristic regimes in time of war, when principled men found that they had to commit acts of treason that they dreaded and yet felt compelled to attempt for the sake of their country. The most famous instance of such treason is that of Count von Stauffenberg, who placed a bomb under Hitler's table on July 20, 1944.[37] He was a traditional officer, not originally averse to the Nazis on either political or religious grounds. Weimar did not claim his deep allegiance, and like almost all his fellow officers he readily took the oath of loyalty to Hitler personally. Indeed Hitler's repersonalization of loyalty obviously appealed to the considerable cultural remnants of the monarchical and feudal past. Stauffenberg was a practicing Roman Catholic, but he did not offer a religious justification for his act. He simply declared his conviction that he was committing high treason and that he expected to be reviled for it in the future, the victim of yet another "stab in the back" myth. He did not think that he was betraying his people, however, just the state and Hitler. Any oath meant much to men like him, and it took him some time to realize that God could not be invoked credibly by the Führer. Nevertheless, Stauffenberg acted not to halt the war, which was already completely lost, but to eliminate what he came to see as pure evil, and to make a start on some sort of moral and political recovery in Germany. Some military officers among the Allies apparently said that Stauffenberg, as an officer, was a traitor, however tyrannical Hitler might be. But on the whole, his memory has been honored and he emerged as a hero, especially after the brutal trial and execution of all the men of 20 July. He himself, however, would have retained his expressed doubts—and they were not insignificant. Stauffenberg had been a disciple of the poet Stefan George, and one may well suppose that honor meant much to him, more than just the class and military duty of the traditional aristocracy. He was pitched into a regime that knew nothing of that. To the extent that he saw himself implicated in an act of high treason, it was for him a crime, but it was also a duty to other, more honorable obligations. He was at least partially dishonored, but only in very few eyes. Few of the enemies and none of the adherents of Hitler's Third Reich could have had any notion of that old mentality. The total personal loyalty that Hitler demanded was simply the condition of his power, and that power was not circumscribed by honor or anything else that might interfere with his own and the racial domination at which he aimed. The sort of loyalties that made Stauffenberg a traitor and a hero were completely alien to the Nazi regime—and to most modern states. Indeed, the fact that he and his friends had to wait until 1944 to act does not speak well for their political awareness.

To most Germans it was clear in the last months of the war that Hitler had betrayed them, and that he was determined to destroy all of them, since they had failed to live up to his expectations. He said as much at the end, and it was clear that he had meant it all along. That is why, it is now said, the Germans were so easily disabused of Nazism after the war. Hitler's betrayal cured them. They had failed him and the mission he had proposed to them. But whoever betrayed whom, there was misplaced trust.[38] And in politics as in private life, that complicates betrayal; it is a collaboration, not one-sided. Only Count Stauffenberg can emerge as a hero, at the last moment, and that because he belonged to an ethical world other than that of his actual century. He was an actor in his world, not the contemporary one. This may be treason at its most ambiguous, but it occurs at such an extreme situation that it is unique, or at best not reproducible in any significant way.

Some of those who joined in the resistance against Hitler in Germany and in occupied Europe did not suffer any of Stauffenberg's conflicts. They fought for an ideology, which is far more usual in the twentieth century, when the nation is only one among several objects of loyalty and betrayal. If conflicts of political loyalty among citizens, and even within the mind of the individual, have become the rule, then betrayal may cease to be a public offense. One cannot betray an ideology or a party to which one has never belonged, and existing regimes are often no more than that for many of their citizens. In a pluralistic society like the United States, the constitutional order certainly does possess the allegiance of most of the citizens, but not exclusively so. Many live with divided loyalties and try as best they can to avoid betraying one or the other. Not all changes of political loyalty are betrayals, in any case. To change parties or convictions or even to emigrate may merely involve changes of mind. Just as marriages come apart as people alter gradually, so do political groups and parties. People change and they keep moving, as they should in a free and mobile society. That in itself should remind us that the inestimable contribution of pluralism to politics is that it sustains freedom, and not, as many writers have suggested, that it is a nursery of loyalty. Those "little platoons" may make loyal characters, and trustworthy family and club members, but that loyalty may not overflow into allegiances to such impersonal associations as government or the nation. Even class has not proven, in spite of all the ink spilled on its behalf, a particularly durable or even noticeable object of loyalty. Almost everyone is a class traitor in the eyes of some observers. Be that as it may, the loyalties that members of families, ethnic groups, and religious sects bring to their roots and faiths are direct and personal— and not transferable. What they do generate is divided loyalties and fractured betrayals, not a Burkean deferential order.

There will always be sturdy moralists who prefer to think of betrayal as simple wickedness. It is comforting to argue, as Rebecca West did, that the Nazis and communists who betrayed Britain and the United States were somehow more twisted psychologically and intellectually than more loyal people in their reference groups. One does not know. However, even if it were true, what set them apart was conviction, ideology, and political passion, not a special mindset that one can label "loser-traitor." If we accept that these people were only too loyal to their awful causes, we must agree with Raymond Aron that not only malice and spite, but faith also played its part here, and that these men, who did have many resentments, were nevertheless not traitors to their *own* causes. When there is no consensus about the legitimate regime, treason is psychologically diffused. Subjectively, these men were not at all disloyal, whatever the law said and did to them.[39] The conditions created by ideological war are, to be sure, extreme, but they do not render the character of betrayal more ambiguous than most of the situations discussed here. War only puts a spotlight on already existing mentalities. It is merely good fortune that allows those of us who live in a liberal society to avoid the most harrowing choices of loyalty and disloyalty.

Proud as Americans overwhelmingly are of the constitutional order, they must, thanks to its principles, accept an enormous diversity of beliefs and loyalties. From the first, the right to freedom of religion encompassed that. Nothing can, therefore, define loyalty or betrayal uniformly for every U.S. citizen. Americans live in a shaded area—neither treacherous nor entirely loyal. And it is therefore difficult either to punish or not to punish ideological or any sort of political betrayal. That is not an easy condition, especially in times of war. At all times, however, representative democracy depends on a fine balance between trust and distrust, with the fear of betrayal lurking in just those places where trust is most hoped for. That is what makes for ambiguity and doubt. The dissonance and distance between the intensity of Americans' resentment when we feel betrayed and the variety of acts and circumstances that can inspire our rage is insuperable. It haunts both our personal life and our public conduct. There is no reason why anyone should like being betrayed, but that does not in any way diminish these difficulties; on the contrary, it is their origin. For nothing can lessen the pain and anger of feeling betrayed by friends, fellow citizens, partners, and allies. That is as true of private as of public experiences of betrayal. The two are not different; both are equally complex. And the treacherous character is as destructive to his family as he is to his party and society generally. A personal career can be pursued as treacherously as a public policy, and we respond to them very similarly. At all times and in all places, moreover, the skeptical intelligence must intervene, to restrain despair, to prevent general misanthropy, and above all to stop the destruction of a liberal order that is too determined to avenge itself upon its betrayers.

M*isanthropy*

Is there no feeling, then, that I can
  trust,
In spite of what we have discussed?
                            Disgust.

—Thom Gunn, *Misanthropos*

5

"HE WHO HATES VICE hates mankind," wrote Pliny the Younger.[1] Was he exaggerating? Surely one can abominate all the
vices and yet love one's friends and tolerate imperfect mankind. Even the deepest contempt for the world does not
allow a Christian to forget that he must love his neighbor, or
the skeptic that he must remain tolerant. One may, as one
reads the daily news, ask oneself, "How can I bear to be
human?"—but that does not imply a lasting and implacable
hatred. Enduring and consistent misanthropy is surely rare.
Nevertheless, Pliny's remark is remembered for excellent
reasons. It is a warning that cannot be ignored, because misanthropy can be very threatening. For misanthropy is not
only an observer's response to endless displays of human
cruelty, dishonesty, and treachery. It can also inspire and
justify active violence against a detestable and corrupt humanity. At the very least, misanthropy can make us miserable and friendless, reduce us to spiritual nausea, and
deprive us of all pleasures except invective. That is what
Montaigne feared so. Even the calmest souls may, like him,
dread an upsurge of misanthropy, and recognize the truth
of Pliny's ancient sentence. Nevertheless, there may be
types of misanthropy that are intellectually unavoidable
and politically valuable. Distrust has its place in the world.

Misanthropy: Calm and Violent

Pliny was a tolerant and civilized man, and his letters are a monument to common sense. That is why one cannot leave misanthropy entirely to him. He could see only its dangers; but although it is not a comfortable human trait, misanthropy is a fountain of intellectual creativity. Satire and philosophy are simply unthinkable without the inspiring force of contempt. We would be deprived of the most sublime moments of speculative thought if no one had ever measured in bitterness the huge distance between what we are and what we could conceivably be. The last plays of Shakespeare, satire from Juvenal to Swift, and some of the finest pages of romantic poetry owe everything to a distaste for men and especially for women. Most moral psychology of any worth is a scream of disgust, as is much of what philosophers since Plato have told us about ourselves. It is not enough to think only, as Pliny did, of the scolds and the nags. It is not even enough to be repelled by that passion for personal inner purity that restlessly pursues a perfect honesty about oneself and all other people. These are not agreeable characteristics, but they fade before the review of intellectual achievements inspired by the loathing for humanity. It may make us intolerant, cruel, and, at the very least, socially impossible. But it is the victory of honesty over hope. The unhappy struggle against illusion and self-deception has not only bred ill-temper; it has also extended the boundaries of our understanding. That is why misanthropy is politically a paradox. Disdain and fear could and did serve as the basis of political decency, legal restraint, and the effort to create limited government that would attenuate the effects of the cruelty of those who rule. Misanthropy can, however, also initiate slaughter. Pliny was as wise as good sense can be, but misanthropy is more significant than mere meanness of spirit.

The self-righteous misanthrope of Pliny's letter is perhaps the most common specimen of the species, but there is more than one kind of misanthrope. Much depends on the origins of his disgust. Treachery is most likely to arouse the most extreme misanthropy—hatred that envelops all mankind and even oneself. Hypocrisy has a scarcely less intense effect upon those who cannot endure a mask, though they generally exempt themselves from contempt, pleased by their own inflamed sincerity. If one puts cruelty first, however, one will control one's loathing or turn it to humane use. Montesquieu was able to provide an essentially misanthropic basis for a liberalism that was meant to reduce fear and to eliminate the grossest cruelties. The misanthrope who cannot endure our perpetual cruelty is then very remote from one who cannot bear vanity, cowardice, dishonesty, and treachery. There are indeed so many variations that it is impossible to imagine a complete catalogue of misanthropic characters. There are, however, at least three outstanding types.

The most dramatic misanthrope hates himself and all humanity and does so passionately with his whole being. Shakespeare's Timon of Athens is such a character. Far more prevalent is the satirical misanthrope, who likes himself and who appears to enjoy the spectacle of human imbecility and of every kind of evil. He may turn actively and politically against his intolerable neighbors, especially the hypocrites, but he does not have to do so. He may even try to limit the damage they must do. All great satirists are like that. Last, there is the misanthrope who may hate only his contemporaries and his own immediate world, because he has some inner vision of a transformed humanity. He may think of himself as one of these purer and better beings, actually or potentially at least, and he often imagines that either in the past or in the future a better version of mankind did or will exist. This misanthrope may choose to retreat from a revolting society, but he also may decide to make war upon a failed humanity. One need only recall Molière's Alceste and Nietzsche to recognize the type. There are other misanthropes, but for politics the self-hating, the satirical, and the self-righteous are the ones who matter most. They have contributed enormously to our social self-knowledge. To hate mankind often impels one to reveal much that would otherwise remain hidden. And

while the passionate and active misanthrope is indeed a political menace, the purely intellectual and distrustful misanthrope is as likely as not to force us to acknowledge what
we know about ourselves and each other.

Misanthropy was much discussed in the Renaissance, not
least because it had acquired both personal and political
implications. When politics are highly personal, the characters of rulers and their entourages are a matter of enormous
importance. A weak or tyrannical king surrounded by rapa-
cious courtiers cannot be easily ignored. Here, personal dispositions, vice and virtue, are at the very center of politics.
Treachery was only one, though the most intolerable, of
these. And those who observed the mighty few no doubt
pondered the consequences of a misanthropically tempered
ruler. They may also have fallen into a misanthropic mood
themselves, as they considered him, his entourage, and his
policies. It is hardly surprising that man-hating malcontents appear as both Machiavellian villains and as bitter
commentators in so many Tudor and Jacobean dramas. One
of the reasons why *The Prince* touched the readers of that age
so deeply was that Machiavelli confirmed all their deepest
fears and most disturbing perceptions. "Deepe, deepe ob-
serving, sound brain'd Machiavel" (as one playwright called
him) explained what they already knew about politics and
rulers.[2] But since he also seemed to encourage treachery and
terroristic policies with his misanthropic dismissal of the
traditional rules, he was doubly frightening. Even his satirical pages were too dark, especially for those who, like
Montaigne, were ready to accept a competent "politique"
prince who would stand above all sects in order to put an
end to religious war. Fear of civil war was, in fact, the greatest single support of monarchical power. What, however,
was to relieve effectively the anxieties that personal government and life at a court must always create? What was to restrain such a ruler, if he made Machiavelli his guide?
Aloofness from religion was widely thought to breed "Machiavellian" rulers, even if that adjective became increasingly remote from anything Machiavelli had actually
written. And, indeed, Machiavelli's advice to personal

rulers, even apart from religion, was too misanthropic to be of any comfort to their subjects. They had every reason to worry about him and his influence. The institutionalized monarchy with its palliative "reason of state" was still far away. So was any form of impersonal government. The royal peace-guarantor might turn out to be a Machiavellian prince and surrounded by Machiavellian conspirators. Personal government is unpredictable, and it makes the political future uncertain, especially for anyone near the court. The wheel of Fortune was therefore more than a trite image; it stood for constant and real worry—worry about the moods of the prince, worry about the fate of patrons, and worry about betrayals in every corner. The wheel of Fortune not only spelled insecurity; it also provided an excuse for every sort of moral irresponsibility. Personal government thus fed both misanthropy and the fear of falling victim to the designs of others. The theater provided the stage on which all this could be expressed.

The drama shows the personal devastations of misanthropy in a lurid light. But Robert Burton's *Anatomy of Melancholy*, which is calm and clinical, is also vivid in depicting the depression caused by fickle fortune. Explicitly following Montaigne, he preferred to be a laughing misanthrope, a new Democritus, rather than a weeping one, such as Heraclitus. Again, like Montaigne, he wanted to overcome the melancholy disgust that his observations aroused, not least because he knew what misanthropes are inclined to do to those whom they hate. The intellectual misanthrope was, in fact, a well-known type; but if he was at all self-reflective, he recognized, as Burton and Montaigne did, that misanthropy was a dangerous state of mind for himself and for others.

In spite of these reasonable fears, a calm misanthropy may, at times, be politically entirely benign. Indeed, it may be a vice we ought to cultivate under certain political circumstances. When in the eighteenth century the theory and practice of government became more impersonal, misanthropy, particularly as a private passion, ceased to be an obvious public concern. A diffuse distrust of humanity became the basis of constitutional government, especially in America. That was one of Montesquieu's many contributions to politics. In underwriting his preferred free constitution, Montesquieu's moral psychology was thoroughly misanthropic. A government was to be designed so as to avoid its own worst vices, cruelty and injustice; and it was set up by and for people who could do no better than to indulge in lesser vices in order to avoid worse ones. The whole point of limited and representative government was that it would not matter much who performed its offices. A small bureaucracy and the separation of powers would create a division of political labor so minute that no particular agent could be significant. No great talents were required. Procedure replaced personality. "Rotation" in office, not distinction, was to matter. Ideally, judges with no discretion were to apply rigid rules which would allow selfish individuals to pursue their ends without hurting one another excessively. In a predictable and secure environment, no one need suffer fear or alarm. This was misanthropy's finest hour. It was put to work on behalf of the most humane of political systems. In its way, it was the answer to Pliny's warning. The very idea of the modern legal state was meant to prove that misanthropy need not express itself in personal despair or political violence. It was to be a shield against aggression. This is the misanthropy that laughs and exerts itself to avoid tears, bitterness, and an anguish that may drive us to the politics of destruction.

Convincing as Montesquieu's liberalism was, especially to Americans, the limits of his doctrine and of political impersonality soon became plain. Romantics of every kind had no use for unpoetic and uninspired policies, and neither justice nor efficiency pleased them. In the nineteenth century, liberalism was far more threatened by nostalgic romantics than by egalitarian radicals. It was constantly accused of being hypocritical, leveling, vulgar, passive, and the mere servant of the "masses." The very word "masses" was and is an expression of a revived misanthropy. The aesthetic and refined sensibility applied it to all classes of the modern age, signifying an overwhelming general disgust.

All these long-standing discontents came together in Nietzsche's outbursts. Of all the voices to be raised against the psychological deprivations and falseness of the liberal state, none has proven more durable than his. His assault against its indiscriminate effect upon individuality was not just an effort to bring more "honesty" into moral and political discourse. He also added his own overwhelming misanthropy. And everything in the experience of the generations succeeding him seemed to strengthen the case against mankind. Politics have in any case become personal again, as the ubiquitous relationship between leaders and followers reveals plainly enough—not least in democratic political systems—and with it, a certain disgust overcomes the honest observer. The endless cruelties and treacheries of oppressive governments have a different effect, also personal. They have stirred a new will to hate, punish, and pity. That makes agents and victims discernible personalities. Less ominously, courts and courtiers are now again easily recognized, even in the most constitutional governments, not to mention in dictatorial regimes of every conceivable kind. We can hardly escape some faces. Misanthropy, along with all the vices to which it is related, has become interesting again. Nietzsche has rather unexpectedly turned out to be a prophet, and the herald of a whole literature of cultural disgust. This, however, has been relatively harmless, compared to the cult of ruthlessness which his misanthropy also called forth. Amid our butcheries, Montaigne's cruel hatred of cruelty again recommends itself. For us, also, the question of how to bear misanthropy has become vital. We have again become familiar with Montaigne's world and its typical characters—among them misanthropes, both the raging and the laughing kind.

The jeering cynic and the tragic solitary have been well known since classical antiquity. The latter had almost always been identified with the semimythical Timon of Athens, who reemerged in the Renaissance to become immortal as the hero of Shakespeare's play.[3] He is the total misanthrope, with both a public and personal face. Wherever we meet him, he is friendless and abusive. The absence

of friendship might well serve as a definition of misanthropy, and it is seen as an awful condition. Timon, the supreme misanthrope, loathed all men, and made no
exception of himself. He unconditionally detested all mankind. One can only shudder at the enormity of his hatred.
Suicide was logical for Timon, and an apocalypse was his
best hope. Such all-inclusive hatred is psychologically unusual. Cicero thought that some sort of fear was at the bottom of it, and both he and Pliny the Elder regarded
misanthropy as a psychic malady, along with other sorts of
self-isolation such as misogyny and inhospitality. Plutarch
presented Timon as homosexual and dissolute. Lucian, in a
satire, tells us that he squandered a fortune on worthless
people who then ran away when he was poor. His hatred of
mankind was only an expression of the shame and humiliation he felt in poverty. In the Renaissance, when Timon returned, Montaigne thought that such a hatred took
mankind too seriously, that Timon had felt it all too deeply
and ought not to be imitated. Timon, in short, cut a considerable literary figure even before Shakespeare gave him his
final form. His fame is, one suspects, due in part to the fear
he arouses. His must have been the kind of "sullen hatred
of the whole human race" that Tacitus ascribed to the
Christians of his day, presumably because they looked
forward to an end of the world.[4] And indeed there is something frightening in so unmitigated a will to destruction.

We do not really know how Shakespeare's Timon acquired his character. When the play opens, he is a rich and
honored Athenian who lavishly entertains his many friends
and showers all sorts of expensive gifts upon them. When
he has spent himself into debt he expects his friends to
come to his aid, and when they all rebuff him, he curses
them and turns his back upon Athens to eat roots, alone, in
a cave. Their betrayal does them no honor, but one does not
expect anyone to be loyal to Timon, either. In his cave
Timon discovers a pile of gold, useless and inedible, which
he hurls at the visitors who now flock to him. Among them
is Alcibiades, who has his own quarrel with Athens. Timon
gives him all the gold he will need to conquer and destroy

the city. With this hope and in bitter hatred of all mankind, he finally goes off to die. This, however, is merely an account of what happens to Timon. The tragedy is not in the events that stimulate his rage, but in himself. Timon is first and foremost a classical tyrant who hates himself because he cannot control his passion for debasing other people. His generosity is a cannibalistic gesture rather than a friendly exchange. It is the very denial of friendship. Nietzsche thought that this sort of greedy eating of men was bound to lead to misanthropy. In fact, it is already an expression of a misanthropic turn of mind. He was even closer to the mark when he observed that universal hospitality permits no single friendship at all.[5] Indeed, Timon does not even care for himself, as his refusal to pay the slightest attention to his own affairs reveals plainly enough. And he behaves as if he were determined to avoid every one of the possible forms of genuine friendship that Aristotle had described. His tyranny is at the root of this, and it is peculiar in only one respect: Timon does not use force to frighten other people; he employs money to dominate and corrupt them. Even in his anger he does not resort to arms, but pays Alcibiades to act for him. The effect of tyranny is, however, the same. He is all alone.

Timon's awful isolation is apparent even to himself as he sits among his guzzling guests. He wishes that he were less wealthy so that he might be closer to them and need their friendship. For he thinks that friendship is a matter of utility, unaware of how brittle such contractual friendships often are. But his relationship to his clients is even more tenuous because the benefits are wholly one-sided. Timon's guests serve no material or emotional purpose except to gratify his possessiveness. They are passive objects of his extravagance. Karl Marx was fond of quoting Timon's later diatribe against gold, because gold levels all differences and destroys all natural distinctions among men.[6] It is not the gold that is so destructive, though, but the way in which Timon from the first uses his wealth. All his guests are to be made identical at his table. He does not want to see them as individuals. Though he all but forces jewelry on them, he

barely acknowledges the gifts he receives from them and refuses to accept the money that one of his debtors tries to return to him. No wonder this man later refuses to help him!
When Timon has run out of gold and cries out "unwisely
but not ignobly have I given," he shows no self-under-
standing. He was, in his prosperity, neither unwise nor
noble, but cold and remote, an impression that is all the
more powerful since he is a misogynist and a homosexual
who trembles with sexual disgust. Grotesque dancing Ama-
zons entertain him, which is unpleasant enough, but even
more so is the gold with which he tries to bind men to him.
For as gold is infertile and unnatural, so are all of Timon's
approaches, and the perfidy of his guests is only to be expected. These men may have been the immediate sources of
his self-hatred, but he has really been a misanthrope all
along, friendless and tyrannical. In his prosperity, his imperial fantasy was that he could "deal kingdoms to my
friends / And ne'er be weary." In effect, he wanted to overwhelm them and to reduce them to an indistinguishable
crowd below him. His megalomania never abates, so that in
the end, when he is about to die, all alone, he cries out,
"sun, hide thy beams! Timon hath done his reign."

If Timon's character as a tyrant is consistent both in his
munificent and in his furious moods, there is, nevertheless,
a clear difference between the manipulative and the raging
man. Timon does change when the wheel of Fortune turns
against him. As soon as he loses all his wealth, he suddenly
comes alive. He changes from a passive misanthrope into an
active, cursing one. And unique among misanthropes, he
hates himself as loudly as the rest of mankind. "His sem-
blable, yea himself, Timon disdains." Alone in his cave, he
finds "the unkindest beast more kinder than mankind." Not
that he has a high opinion of the animal world. The animals
also prey one upon another. Indeed, the entire universe is
hateful and hating. Hatred is the very law of motion, the
source of life itself. Even the fecund earth is but "the common whore of mankind." All nature is a spectacle of preda-
tory activity, and Timon in his misanthropy is the perfect
voice of such a cosmos. Yet he never does anything violent.

At worst he throws stones and then gold at his false guests. Only when he urges Alcibiades to drown Athens in blood can we see how his misanthropy justifies cruelty. "Religious canon, civil law are cruel? Then what should war be?" He does not choose to be a warrior again; his hatred is too perfect for any action now. In his own view, his final curses are but an echo of the dissonance of the spheres. Even the exercise of power that gold makes so easy loses its allure for him. He neither has nor wants an audience to whom to display a misanthropy that he has turned against himself. Nevertheless, like any tyrant, he does want to be remembered after his death. He also seeks fame of a sort, and so he writes a message on his tombstone before he dies, to make sure that his hatred will not be forgotten. To the end he is a public figure, a political character.

There is a second misanthrope in Shakespeare's play—one who laughs and sneers, and so reveals, as Montaigne had already noted, the two possible ways of hating mankind. Apemàntus is a pure Diogenes figure. He is something of a public entertainer—an intellectual, in fact, who can easily afford to laugh and mock, since he likes himself well enough. Generally, he makes himself conspicuous at Timon's palace by his abuse of the assembled company and by his rude and crude behavior, often laced with very dirty jokes. Although far too vain and distrustful to have any friends, he neither feels nor arouses any great hostility. His hatred is, unlike Timon's, selective, concentrated on greed and flattery. And he simply thinks that everyone except himself is depraved and depraving. Apemantus is no courtier, and he does not exploit the rich Timon. Instead he gives him some friendly and very sensible, if cynical, advice. But when Timon becomes an angry misanthrope, Apemantus furiously turns upon him. For now he perceives a rival in Timon who is a far more resolute misanthrope than himself, and so a threat to his own pure, philosophic brand of misanthropy. "Thou dost affect my manners," he shouts at Timon, and warns him not to "assume my likeness." The new and more intense misanthrope puts Apemantus' own cynicism in doubt, and so he tries to see only a habitual extravagance in Timon. But in his angry encounter with Timon, Apemantus also reveals the extent of his own misanthropy. He may have begun by hating only the vices of grasping, treacherous leeches, but we now see that he hates everyone, including the now intellectually alert Timon, whom he upbraids for his lack of balance. "The middle of humanity thou never knowst." Apemantus, in turn, is a problem for Timon, because this intellectual is indifferent to offers of gold. A friendship between misanthropes is clearly impossible, since each is an obstacle to the other. Apemantus has merely inherited his misanthropy, according to Timon; he does not really feel hatred. And in a way, Timon is right. For although Apemantus would be very glad to let the beasts inherit the earth, he wants that to happen only after he is dead. His misanthropy is more cerebral and far less intense than Timon's. He is, moreover, so self-infatuated that he is easily dismissed by the public. That was, perhaps, Shakespeare's comment on philosophers as a class. And, indeed, Apemantus' misanthropy has one notable feature that distinguishes it from Timon's emotional hatred: it is an expression of a passionate honesty. Apemantus' obscenities are his way of being honest about what he sees. And it is not only disguised viciousness that sets Apemantus off; the open sight of cruelty and treachery also evokes his misanthropic need for candor. Its appeal to the intelligent and humane is obvious, but it has its dangers. It can easily become a source of moral cruelty, when, as in Apemantus, it finally is not aimed selectively at intolerably dishonest, mean, and cruel individuals, but at mankind generally. That is what Pliny, Montaigne, and Burton feared. The laughing misanthrope then becomes the friendless moral scourge who scolds and humiliates. He is the snob who scorns his inferiors and the traitor who enjoys the discomfiture of those whose expectations he has disappointed. He is every domestic tyrant, and even if he does not burst out into violence, he is nobody's friend.

Neither Timon nor Apemantus is remote from us. They are merely the finest examples of a long and lasting line of misanthropes in life and on the stage. That the Tudor drama should have had such a direct impact upon the bitterest writers of the interwar years is not at all surprising. Both Artaud and Brecht, whom the First World War made into desperate misanthropes, drew upon it, and it continues to be our stage. Shakespeare's Apemantus, especially, even more than Timon, was not to be the last of his kind. The Tudor and Jacobean drama is full of such men, and its enduring impact owes much to them, misanthropes all. Some of these are licensed court philosophers permitted to interrupt the monotony of courtly etiquette and dissembling. Some are simply angry because they are dissatisfied with their place in society. Others find the society in which they live unbearable. Because such malcontents can imagine a better order of human affairs, their misanthropy is not as pure or as comprehensive as Apemantus'; but many are politically more active—Machiavellians in their own right. Why, they ask, should they be decent when the world, especially the court, is so vile? These malcontents are presented as minor Machiavellians who use misanthropy as an excuse for their own schemes. They are not figures out of Machiavelli's great political writings, for they do not aspire to glory, or to the state of princes, but only to small social advantages. Machiavelli did know these types well enough, however. They people his satirical writings, especially his plays and those of his great pupil, Ben Jonson. In tragedies, however, these courtier misanthropes sometimes become enormous criminals, such as Webster's Bosola, who tortures and strangles the Duchess of Malfi and her children. The small-time political misanthrope is obviously a very dangerous man. Bosola is not just a hired killer; he takes part in a political as well as a personal struggle. His employers are certainly moved by private passions, but they are public men, a duke and a cardinal, who object to their sister's failure to maintain her status as a ruling duchess.

Machiavellian Misanthropy

This utterly horrible mixture of personal and public violence is perhaps too much to endure in a tragedy for anyone but a twentieth-century misanthrope. To relish misanthropy we turn to satire, which is preeminently the literature of honesty in disgust. Its political intent and impact have always been obvious and easier to bear. That is easily recognized in that acknowledged masterpiece of English misanthropic satirical drama, John Marston's *Malcontent*, written during the last years of Elizabeth I's reign. The misanthropic hero is one Altofront, who is a deposed duke, now in disguise and acting the part of Malevole at the court of his successor. He is allowed to rant as an accepted entertainer. There is, however, nothing assumed in Malevole's bile as he watches the usurper of his throne in turn being deposed by one of the original conspirators. In the end, Altofront-Malevole outwits them all and in an uncharacteristic gesture forgives them. We need not take the mawkish ending too seriously, for Altofront-Malevole has told us early on that he knows why he lost his throne originally. He "wanted those old instruments of State / Dissemblance and suspect." He also knows that "we are all philosophical monarchs or natural fools"—and "philosophical" means cynical here. In this, Altofront-Malevole does not differ at all from his adversary, the archvillain whom he eventually defeats. We also begin to recognize in him a genuine pupil of Machiavelli. He is always aware of the ups and downs of fortune: like buckets over a well, one goes down empty as another comes up full. Friendship is always false, and trust is misplaced except in "usurers and brokers, they deceive no man: men take them for bloodsuckers, and so they are." The average courtier's religion is whatever he expects the ruler's to be, while the people are base and unreliable in all respects. As one might expect, there is plenty of sexual revulsion. In sum, "World! . . . there is nothing perfect in it, but extreme, extreme calamity." Calamity, in this case, refers to the nature of people and not of events. Altofront-Malevole does not choose to triumph over "peasants' graves," because his misanthropy is too deep. Reflective disgust, not Timon's passion, is at work here; but in his litany of loathing, he makes what is undeniably one of the greatest speeches:

> This earth is the only grave and Golgotha
> wherein all things that live must rot . . .
> Man is the slime of this dung pit,
> and princes are the governors of these men.
>
> (IV, 5)

Clearly, this malcontent is too revolted to look forward with much zest to being a ruler. He is not, in fact, one of Machiavelli's princes, but only the latter's "philosophic" disciple. And in keeping with that stance, whatever Malevole chooses to be and do, he is always perfectly honest. That is why he is not just pretending to be a malcontent. That also is why he may fail again as a prince, even though he knows exactly what he ought to do with this "slime" which he will govern.

To be a successful Machiavellian prince, one would have to be a far hardier and less reflective misanthrope than this Malevole, who lacks the ferocity to put his political knowledge to work. He evidently does not possess the single-minded passion required of a new prince. Glory would have to be his sole aim, and Marston's hero has none of Machiavelli's energetic misanthropy. He is just a cerebral cynic. To fully appreciate political misanthropy, one must read Machiavelli himself. For Machiavelli, glory was not just a worthy ambition, but a metaphor for all the values of his self-made, demythologized, wholly human order. It was, moreover, an inherently misanthropic aspiration. To hate men was not difficult for Machiavelli, who had all the honesty of the satirist and the bitterness of the failed politician. He found it easy to ignore the victims of his prince's march to power. Most men will remain politically inert as long as their women and their property are not disturbed. Princes are distinguished from this human trash by their ambition to achieve something else—glory. To be famous even after one's death is the elevating passion of the few, their substitute for eternal bliss. All the rest of mankind serves as either an audience for, or as the victims of, this princely performance. Without them glory is, of course, impossible, but it cannot be achieved without that princely contempt which puts them into their assigned parts. Heroes are set apart from other people by being sent to school with centaurs, so that they may also become half-animals, and as such far apart from mere human beings. The prince must be two kinds of animal, a lion and a fox. Animal imagery is always at the very heart of our self-appraisal. Machiavelli's admiration for the qualities of beasts was, as it always is, a misanthropic thought. And to call a prince a noble animal is to distance him so far from his subjects and victims that he can simply treat them as Machiavelli thought he should, cruelly. As beast, he is their superior. It is the last word in contempt of men. It is a great mistake to read Machiavelli as another Hobbes—a bit wry, but wishing mankind well. The fact is that *The Prince* is a celebration of violence to achieve glory for one man—at the expense of all the rest. There is much of Timon in Machiavelli. His new prince is to destroy all those incompetent, contemptible princes who have had neither the will nor the wit to be the creators of their own realms and rules.

It was always natural to shudder at Machiavelli's prince when one thought of his treacheries, but it is just as easy to forget them and to find him fascinating. A "new" prince, then as now, is inherently exciting: men follow him out of greed, but also with passionate attachment. Cruelty can be glamourous. One need only consider Marlowe's Tamburlaine the Great to recognize the animal attraction that a Machiavellian prince can radiate on the stage, just as multitudes adore the murderous "leaders" of today. Tamburlaine is a mass murderer whom we do not hate. We wish him well, in fact. This hero begins as a Scythian shepherd and, with a mixture of guile, courage, and military genius, conquers Persia, Arabia, and Egypt. He has loyal followers, whom he generously rewards. He is even a successful lover. He marries his adored and adoring Zenocrate after overcoming her father on the field of battle. At no time can his lieutenants or his wife influence his conduct in the slightest. Unmoved by any feeling or personal inclination, he never wavers in his march to glory. He is Machiavellian "virtue" personified and he knows it: "For virtue is the fount whence honour springs / And they are worthy she investeth kings" (IV, 4). Birth has nothing to do with it. "Virtue solely is the sum of glory." And "virtue" is "the love of fame, of valor and of victory." He is not a "slaughtering terror" for its own sake, but a man with a megalomanic end in view; he will be his own god.

> A god is not so glorious as a king:
> I think the pleasure they enjoy in heaven,
> Cannot compare to kingly joys in earth;—
> To wear a crown enchas'd with pearl and gold,
> Whose virtues carry with it life and death;
> To ask and have, command and be obey'd.
>
> (II, 5)

When in the second part of his dramatic career Tamburlaine speaks of himself as "the scourge of God," destined to exterminate mankind, we have no reason to doubt that he is the only god there is. This "terror of the world" now only wants to display himself "in war, in blood, in death, in cruelty." Yet we continue to be drawn to him, for the Christians whom he overcomes are dishonest hypocrites who give his candor and courage a certain glamour. In the end he can be vanquished only by death, the one inescapable turn of fortune for all men. Before he has done, however, he has "waded up to the chin in blood," his throne "sprinkled with the brains of slaughter'd men." All of this is necessary to advance to a "royal chair of state." Until the end, he has been "his fortune's master and the King of men." He never regrets all this. After all, did not mighty Jove become god by mutilating and killing his father and all his rivals? Treachery, not fidelity, is in fact what prevails in the cosmic order as on the sublunar scene, and to be trusting or faithful is indeed to be a cosmic fool.

Tamburlaine is far more a "princely lion" than a fox. Marlowe did not care much for the scheming part of Ma-

chiavelli's prince, but he hated hypocrisy most of all. His leonine prince was to be the scourge of both hypocrites and
traitors. When he put Machiavelli on the stage, he had him
say that he knew of "no sin but ignorance" and made him
jeer at the hypocrisy of those who rejected his teachings
loudly while following them in practice. *The Jew of Malta*,
which Machiavelli introduces so bravely, is meant to enhance his reputation, because the play itself is about a tan-
gle of petty traitors, all of them perfectly unexceptional and
commonplace. Three religions are realistically represented.
It is all very far from Tamburlaine and glory of any kind.
Could Tamburlaine have escaped enfeebling private motives? By the end, even that is no longer clear. In Ben Jonson's skeptical rendering of that theme, the antihero,
Tiberius, is made to excuse himself with a claim that the
pursuit of immortal fame is what distinguishes princes from
all other men decisively:

> The rest of mortal men
> In all their drifts and counsels pursue profit
> Princes alone are of a different sort
> Directing all their main actions still to fame.
>
> > (*Sejanus*, II, 2)

From Tiberius, such sentiments can imply only the opposite—that personal passions exactly like those of the most
ordinary people moved princes as well. Only the consequences were more dreadful. As the infamous Bosola puts
it, "Some would think the souls of princes were brought
forth by some more weighty cause than those of meaner
persons: they are deceiv'd, there's the same hand to them;
the like passions sway them; the same reason that makes a
vicar go to law for a tithe-pig, and undo his neighbors,
makes them spoil a whole province, and batter down
goodly cities with the canon" (*The Duchess of Malfi*, II, 1).

The picture of the classical tyrant had always been based
on Bosola's entirely plausible assumptions, and there is no
reason to suppose that a Machiavellian prince would really
be a lion and a fox all the time and not become just another
unrestrained despot. Hating cowardice as much as Tambur-

laine does, any "new" prince must be utterly repelled by everyone except those few of his contemporaries who possess the "virtue" needed to pursue glory. He has no particular reason to be anything other than a butcher, even when he maintains his perfect self-discipline. If the possession of power must inevitably relax this self-control and calculation, then he would simply destroy everyone, possibly even himself. Ideology, as we know, does not supply any constraint. Most princes are not different from the disgusting humanity (Marston's "slime") that they dominate. What *The Prince* has always needed is a good dose of demythologizing.

There is, in fact, an enormous psychological optimism in the very idea of combining the lion and the fox into a single hero. These are not really compatible qualities. Bosola was more astute than Machiavelli. The great foxes are not new princes, as a rule, but established rulers, like Ben Jonson's Tiberius, whose schemes are accepted because they promise something resembling civil order. This is the germ of "reason of state." Even more improbable than a prince who is both daring and calculating is the notion of princely meta-honesty. For the genuine "new prince" was expected by his fantasy-ridden inventor to be free from self-deceptions. He lies and cheats honestly—that is, consciously, knowing exactly what he is doing. In this he is to emulate Machiavelli's own supposed candor in recognizing the necessities facing a new prince. Action, in fact, requires a measure of illusion, and Machiavelli's vision of the uniquely qualified prince is simply a response to his bitter sense of the inadequacy of all actual princes. That is also why Marlowe's Machiavelli, who scorns "ignorance," was a response to the dominion of hypocrisy. They are mirrors in reverse.

The Machiavellians who strut about the Tudor stage are misanthropic commentators on a world dominated by a variety of other misanthropes. They are hate-filled observers of the conduct of men and women who are also consumed by hatred. The plays in which they act out their violent projects were surely meant to shock, but not to demoralize the audiences for whom they were written. That is not a trivial matter, for it distinguishes them from the works of some of their most influential admirers today. It was by overlooking their intentions that Antonin Artaud found in them predecessors for his theater of cruelty. When he proclaimed that there could be no celebration without cruelty and no creation without violent destruction, he echoed Nietzsche, to be sure, but that was protective covering. What he really wanted to present was "a gigantic liquidation," like the plague that would tear off the masks and divulge "our world's lies, aimlessness, meanness and even two-facedness." We would then admit openly that we are fit only "for chaos, famine, bloodshed, war and epidemics." The violent action would act like lyricism to release a "bloodshed" of images. The carnage, finally, was to be only secondary, for real cruelty is in submission, in displays of enslavement that torture merely introduces.[7] Artaud has many admirers today, but his manifestos are a mirror of the First World War, and it was that war, the source of all our subsequent destruction and misery, that brought out a misanthropy not unlike that of the age of Machiavellian religious strife. It is convenient to quote Artaud because he wrote manifestos, making clear what is implicit in the novels of Céline and in the early plays of Brecht. The latter's *Threepenny Opera* remains one of the most popular entertainments, so one might as well recall its best chorus: "What keeps mankind alive? Mankind is kept alive by bestial acts." Brecht's post–World War II alterations of this play and his later works, embellished by communist platitudes, should remind us of how the age began. How could one be anything but some sort of misanthrope after that endless incompetent slaughter? Was not the Second World War merely the continuation of the First? Were not Hitler and Stalin, and their armies of perfectly sincere followers, but a part of a convulsion that they had not in any way begun? As for the dreams of the half-mad Artaud and Céline, and the early Brecht, they were certainly not aberrant. Both the "lyrical" misanthropy of the first and the "epic" of the second were to be acted out by those for whom the war had never ceased—indeed, had hardly begun. That at present there should be nostalgic admirers of these latter-day Timons, especially Céline, is to be expected. The urge to loathe and destroy that moves across every page of his novels is far from quelled among his ardent readers today. Nuclear arms have made the political expression of these feelings less plausible for us, but the temper is still alive and in flame. Except in science fiction, literary destruction is on a lesser scale; but as we still live among the most ravaging cruelties and multiple betrayals, we, too, have our misanthropic impulses to contend with. Machiavelli is our much-appreciated contemporary, not because he was right about the primacy of war in politics, but because he and his latest readers are quite alike. Both sport a stylish and ironic misanthropy and find a certain satisfaction in the unending spectacle of human depravity.

That Machiavelli should be so popular has at least one advantage: it has brought Montaigne's response back with it. Montaigne was as little shocked by Machiavelli's impiety as we are. He thought that religious zealots were to be the first beneficiaries of Machiavelli's doctrines. More significantly, he was just as determined to avoid intellectual illusion and hypocrisy as Machiavelli had been. He was just as superbly honest. Experience had, however, convinced him that rulers did not need Machiavelli's advice to encourage them in drowning their subjects in bloodbaths. Montaigne was not deaf to Machiavelli's subtleties, but, as we have seen, he did challenge them. Given Machiavelli's own misanthropy, why should one care for glory? It is just a matter of fortune. Does glory really look as marvelous as Machiavelli pretends? Those faults of character required to win it cannot be obliterated. They, too, get into the lasting record. Montaigne found it impossible to overlook the puerility and pettiness of the ever-competitive Alexander playing chess. And the endless deceit to which Machiavelli's new prince must resort in his pursuit of glory is not only "ugly"; it also dissolves all the ties of society. For what holds society together, Montaigne asked, if not the stable meaning of words and our trust in our common speech? It seemed to Montaigne that nothing could ever wipe away the disfigurement of a craven slyness and dishonesty. Nor can the bonds of society, broken by rulers who lie to everyone, be readily repaired. Montaigne was right. Machiavelli's disdain is, in the end, self-defeating. He could see no function for mankind at all except to make the occasional life of glory possible; but what is glory if not ruling over such men, "the slime"? The fate of Timon lurks behind the showy effort of *The Prince*. A tyrant would in the end be overwhelmed by his contempt for those whom he ruled—and also for himself.

The Machiavellian prince was, after all, not the first misanthropic ruler. The lives of his predecessors were not marked by inextinguishable political virtue. Montaigne thought that tyrants were driven from cruelty to cruelty as their fears of real and fancied enemies increased with each one of their crimes.[8] The very idea of an economically rational use of cruelty was and is a psychological fantasy and a part of the illusion of violent efficiency. Cruelty, fear, and revenge simply escalate. What else has the present century taught us, if not that "the economy of violence" is the ideological beginning of an interminable cycle of terror? Uzbek, the Persian tyrant in Montesquieu's novel *The Persian Letters*, is a perfect illustration of Montaigne's view. He begins as a misogynist, but becomes increasingly bored, indifferent to his friends, and obsessed by fears about the disorders in his seraglio-court. He finally says that "he can find his own personality" only when jealousy "arouses his fear, suspicion, hate, and regret."[9] His fury against his despised wives has created such a vacuum around him that he can think of nothing to do with himself except to shut himself up with them while he ill-treats them. He does not brutalize them himself, of course, but employs eunuchs to rule the women with physical and moral terror. Sadism has nothing to do with it. Uzbek's tyranny is all politics, not sex. And his mistreatment of his wives is merely an instance of misanthropic omnipotence as it flows out of royal courts. Because he is a ruler, Uzbek's solitude is in the end just like Timon's. He begins as an all-too-honest intellectual, a candid Apemantus, in search of personal purity and enlightenment; but given his power over the seraglio, he loses his enlightened intellectual and cynical sneer to the rage of primitive domination. He is not a military hero, as a truly Machiavellian prince must be, but he is what any prince will be as a political ruler over helpless subjects.

Liberal Misanthropy: Limiting Government

In spite of his enormous psychological understanding of the dynamics of misanthropy, Montesquieu did not look to personal cures for any political impact. Only public reform can have an effect. Montesquieu had a public alternative to Uzbek: legal government. Friendship has no public function. There are no personal checks on the reign of misanthropic rulers or on any other political terrorists. Only the abolition of seraglios and personal government as such would make it possible to devise laws to protect the potential victims against the inevitable aggressors. This is the liberalism of fear, and of law as the alternative to violence. Montaigne's arguments for derisive mockery may perhaps have suggested to Montesquieu that he ought to put his darkest thoughts into an entertaining satirical novel in which individual characters could have their full play. His historical works are quite different. They dispense with individuals and concentrate on groups and their reactions to their environment and to each other. Montesquieu's political science is a highly depersonalized account of social phenomena.

Both Montaigne and Machiavelli seem remote from Montesquieu because they still thought of politics in entirely personal terms. Theirs were still the politics of character, however different the qualities they admired. The distance between them and Montesquieu is historically so significant because misanthropy also changed its meaning and scope when it was transferred from the personal government of princes to the world of political systems. Friendship was for Montaigne, for example, the greatest palliative of both our private and public suffering and wrongs. It is our defense against misanthropy. Montesquieu, however, thought of it as a dangerous feeling for those who rule, since it might interfere with the primary obligations of justice. That is a profound departure from Montaigne. In Montesquieu's impersonal state, personal qualities no longer make a difference. Political men cannot afford them.

One cannot, in fact, imagine Montaigne's moral world in impersonal terms at all. He weighed only character. Thus, in spite of all his admiration for personal courage, he had a profound sense of the limits of valor and the danger of letting it reign as the supreme personal virtue, as it does in war. The comradeship that binds brave men in friendship saves the soldier from being a butcher. Friendship for his fellow soldiers makes the difference, though war remains a cruel business. Friendship also, such as Montaigne's for La Boétie, ultimately preserved him from a misanthropy as deep as Machiavelli's. When his disdain for his fellow men reached such a point that even writing his essays seemed futile, he would remember his friend and that would restore him. Personal friendship was, for him, the irreducible, inexplicable experience that put a halt to nauseating doubt and contempt. It demands that perfect openness which misanthropy closes off. Friendship resists that avalanche of disgust which can at any moment overwhelm anyone.[10] To be sure, friendship is not available to everyone, as Aristotle explained; it is a state of character, not an activity. Politically powerful people make use of or enjoy the presence of others, but they are not as a rule capable of friendship. Montaigne's adversary, Machiavelli's prince, of course knows nothing of the frankness of friends. He is utterly friendless and he does not expect friendship to flourish among the victims. Otherwise he could not hope to manipulate them so effectively. Machiavelli had no doubts on that score. Those who do not aspire to glory are no more likely to be friends than those who do. Most men can be expected to prefer their patrimony even to their own fathers, and friendship is clearly beyond them. The prince should act with that in mind, and so should every other sane person. Indeed, misanthropy even at its most liberal and peaceful is an obstacle to friendship. Kant's pages on the subject are simply impoverished, with their harping on the conflict between love and respect, and the rarity of unblemished confidence.[11]

However much they differed about friendship and enmity, Machiavelli and Montaigne still thought in equivalent terms, in contrast to Montesquieu and Kant. They both thought of political persons directly, while Montesquieu and Kant were not interested in the achievements or characters of individual rulers, but only in a public philosophy that looked to the general condition of ordinary individuals and to their release from fear, rather than to glorious or extravagant aspirations. In retrospect, one can see that putting cruelty first was the beginning of that theory of systematic politics which step by step eliminated personalities from public concerns. That is why the psychological reform of princes who were to acquire a second mentality, a depersonalized "reason of state," seemed fraudulent and implausible to Montesquieu. Uzbek is the perfect enlightened despot, a walking contradiction whose violence breaks out as soon as his omnipotence is challenged. Only a system of liberty in which power is dispersed among intermediary groups could support an impersonal legal system to protect each citizen by limiting the opportunities for violence. No great demands are made on anyone's virtue or intelligence. Instead of living with their fibers frozen with fear, men will engage in benign and inglorious commercial activities. That was, as Montesquieu saw it, the only alternative to despotism: the reign of fear and uninhibited cruelty. The most startling feature of this theory is, however, not its public expectations, but its enormous underlying misanthropy. It is, to be sure, a new misanthropy, as dispassionate as the system it was meant to support. Montesquieu did not speak with any deeply felt loathing. At most there are occasional sardonic passages. Among the other founders of liberalism, Kant perhaps spoke a little more bitterly, and Madison rather less so. In a fable and in a few general passages, Montesquieu made it very plain that mankind's moral powers are so inadequate that men are always in danger of mutual destruction. Inferior to the animals, which do not have our intelligence and fears, we are free to be engines of aggression. We would be well-advised to think of ourselves merely as sentient beings, for it might bring us to the peaceful level of animal life.

This diffuse contempt is entirely unlike Timon's passionate hatred. It is a political form of the Democritus-Apemantus brand of misanthropy, though less mordant. But it does begin, just as Pliny said, with a hatred of vice; to be exact, of one vice—cruelty—particularly public cruelty. Instead of being overwhelmed by the spectacle of human iniquity, however, it goes on to seek public cures for the most extreme excesses of depravity. It does so not out of a sudden afflatus of philanthropy, but because of a specific ranking of the vices in which cruelty is put first, with dishonesty and treachery trailing far behind. One must add a perhaps inexplicable belief that the earth and all its inhabitants ought to be preserved, possibly because God created them or just because one cannot bear to be another Timon, as Montaigne had suggested. If one does not wish to suffer as Timon did, one must at least take some small pleasure in the natural world. Montesquieu followed Montaigne in this as in much else. And it was only by ranking the vices in a descending order of awfulness that they could fully respond to the warning of Pliny's words. For unless one does grade the vices as they did and react to them accordingly in a measured manner, one must indeed end up with an unlimited hatred, with all its Timonic private melancholy and Machiavellian projects for public violence.

It is with these assumptions that Montesquieu could begin with a general contempt for mankind and go on to build a fortress against tyranny. For him, the questions of politics were simply no longer a matter of good and evil persons at all, but of weak and strong groups. He had no use for imaginary states of nature, such as Hobbes's, in which human equality is at the root of an incessant insecurity. He would clearly have appreciated the defense of wolves offered by one of Lord Shaftesbury's more misanthropic characters: "For to say in disparagement of man that he is to man a wolf appears somewhat absurd, when one considers that wolves are to wolves very kind and loving creatures." What one should say is that men behave to each other as wolves do to sheep, because some men are "innocent and mild" while others are not.[12] The political misanthrope assumes these inequalities to be normal and concentrates on creating institutions that protect the security of the "mild" citizens against the ever-predatory incursions of those who govern. We need guaranteed freedom because the "ebb and flow of domination and subjection" of which Montesquieu spoke, cannot be halted in any other way.[13] The choice is between Uzbek's rule and a division and diffusion of power that will permit the flow of political cruelty to be dammed up. There is no trust, no friendship, and no virtue required or expected. To assume misanthropically that abuses of power are inevitable unless carefully restrained is the whole basis of this kind of liberalism. It is the very perfection of a generalized misanthropy that makes no exceptions, is contemptuous of fame, and has no faith in military valor. It looks to a balancing of ambitions that will make physical cruelty difficult and persuade men to concentrate their energies on the less lethal pursuit of wealth and peace. Such ends are entirely within the limits of their diminutive moral powers. Montesquieu was, indeed, as d'Alembert was to say in his eulogy, "the legislator of the nations." He was, moreover, not alone in thinking so mordantly of mankind's moral talents. Kant agreed with him entirely. Men may be crooked sticks at best, but it is only a question of "the organization of the state (which does lie in man's power), whereby the powers of each selfish inclination are so arranged in opposition that one moderates or destroys the ruinous effect of the other . . . and man is forced to be a good citizen even if not a morally good person."[14]

Montesquieu went even beyond Kant in thinking that bad men, which is what the English generally were, might be able to build the best institutions and to be the most free and fair citizens. James Madison, in turn, could build his hope for a just republic on the wholesome effects of the factional interplay of greed and sectarianism. These unattractive traits are, however, no longer displayed at the courts of princes. They are common qualities evenly distributed among all members at all levels of a modern state, with no one in a position to give full expression to his baseness. Not only physical power but also moral passion is redistributed more equitably. The clergy may no longer claim a place in government, and those who possess any degree of political or military power may not impose intellectual or moral rules. Ideally, there were to be a few general laws, administered by a magistracy so impartial and so devoid of any discretion as to be reduced to a mechanical fairness. Procedures, not persons, reign here. No virtue matters except justice, and justice is above feeling. Indeed, most moral relationships, such as pity, and love of one's country, are purely private and may not affect the one supreme public virtue. Even moderation, which is a private virtue, had for Montesquieu a public meaning wholly unrelated to its personal definition. With regard to legislation, it is the ability to combine, balance, and temper various powers—in short, to create "un système."[15] The English are not moderate as people. They are a nation of ill-tempered egoists with a penchant for suicide; but they have, in the absence of any sort of moderate personality, created the only free and moderate political order. Even education has no public function here, even though all other regimes depend on the appropriate training of subjects. In free England, people need only insist on their rights and express their opinions freely, however irrational these might be. In monarchical regimes, in contrast, men must be brought up to defend their honor, a mentality Montesquieu deplored along with everything else that went on in royal courts. The courts of law over which legally single-minded judge-magistrates presided were to replace the courts of princes where personal passions and public policy were joined in a destructive pageant.

The impersonality of the legal state was long accepted as the proof of its rationality. It created an island of reason in the sea of human irrationality. That absolved the "système" from vice and virtue. Civilized political life, it was generally agreed, was possible only if the legal order was protected from the vagaries of personal preferences and attitudes. And that order was expected to encompass all public activity eventually. But, in fact, it was in the political system which accepted Montesquieu's ideas most readily, the United States, that its limits soon became evident. In spite of every impulse to turn political disputes into legal cases, to be impartially decided by judges, and in spite of an enduring dream of "a government of laws, not of man," representative government involves highly personalized politics. They are not those of the monarchical past, but trust and distrust, loyalty and betrayal, are very much a part of electoral politics. Every candidate presents his character to an electorate that must be persuaded not only by arguments, but even more by emotional preferences. In spite of the early engineers of equilibrated institutions and factions, the liberal order was not a self-regulating "système." Democratic politics are not impersonal. And although our first presidents were not flamboyant, Andrew Jackson put showy leadership on the political stage of America. He saw himself as having a deep bond with "the people" as a whole, whose trustee and protector he proclaimed himself to be. Leadership turned out to be not accidental, but inherent in all organizational activity. And rulers, presidents, and lesser elected leaders who cannot satisfy the affective demands of the electorate will not be sufficiently trusted to weather the strains imposed on a government by such disasters as war and economic depressions.[16] Neither in small groups nor in state governments can policies be framed or implemented without leadership. And that requires dependencies of a far from rational or legalistic sort. One need only recall what Roosevelt's "fireside chats" were able to achieve, and how personal the response to Kennedy's assassination was in the United States. Personal political authority is based on something close to love which is unstable and incalculable, and it has made the liberal state far less procedural and far less predictable than its first designers had hoped. Nevertheless, a balance of trust and distrust, of hope and fear, of benevolence and misanthropy has underwritten this disorderly political nonsystem, and its liberal outcome. It has even preserved a degree of judicial impartiality.

Electoral politics as an avenue to personal leadership do not always have a liberal outcome. In the immediately post-monarchical régimes of Europe, they proved disastrous. From the first, sociologists and psychologists—Weber and Freud, to name only the greatest—knew that personal leadership would not disappear, and that the years after the First World War would be marked by emotionally charged leader-and-follower politics and with them the destruction of the impersonal state, especially its judicial part. From the very first, Europeans doubted whether the liberal state could live up to its claims and whether it had not been a sham all along. Was the impersonal state not just a cover for either the exploited or exploiting interests? Was it not rotten with hypocrisy? Was it not just a machine that crushed individuality in the interests of commercial enterprise and entrepreneurial vulgarity? Had it not ground every tradition down and had it not enslaved rather than freed those who labored for their daily bread? Indeed, impersonal government was not nearly as faceless, as fair, or as free as its defenders had hoped. It was merely the least cruel and the least oppressive of known regimes. But even its best impulses could not survive the shocks of the First World War.

The Assault on Impersonal Government

These failures of impersonal government generally, and of liberalism particularly, opened the gates to all their intellectual enemies. With them came their misanthropy, rooted not in a loathing for physical cruelty, but in a loathing for the moral blight of hypocrisy, snobbery, and betrayal. Dishonesty and betrayal put first invite the misanthropy of Timon and Alceste. Molière's unhappy hero withdraws with

a dramatic gesture, but Timon can lead or pay for the politics of mass destruction. Like Alceste's friends, we may feel
sorry to hear him say:

> Come then: man's villainy is too much to bear,
> Let's leave this jungle and this jackal's lair.
> Yes! treacherous and savage race of men
> You shall not look upon my face again. (V, 1)

But we might well wonder what he would do if he came
back at the head of a platoon of like-minded people. We
need not wonder about Timon: we know. He pays Alcibiades to raze Athens, and he would enjoy doing it himself,
because he was betrayed by a hypocritical world, was
snubbed, rejected, and assaulted by his inferiors. And in
our own age, even before the First World War, which
created all their opportunities, Timon's heirs, the political
misanthropes, had a philosophy to support their rage. For
contemporary misanthropy, not surprisingly, Nietzsche remains the most significant and active presence. He was the
real thing, not merely a part-time "angry young man." One
finds in him not only the misogyny and sexual disgust, but
also that utter loathing for the hypocrisy of all the feeble
and mean masses of mankind. Zarathustra's contempt is
bardic, like that of an Old Testament prophet in reverse.
God and man are not just false; they are dangerous enemies
of health and creativity. Nietzsche knew very well what
these notions implied. As he noted, "The fool interrupts:
The writer of this book is no misanthrope; today one pays
too dearly for hatred of man. To hate Timonically, wholly
without exception, with full heart . . . one would have to renounce contempt."[17] The fool was no doubt the one in
Timon of Athens, a very intelligent fellow, particularly adept
at reading character. Nietzsche did not give up his contempt, but he was not always eager to be another Diogenes.
He thought the cynic's friendlessness too high a price to pay
for independence. Mostly, however, he was quite ready to
celebrate solitude, for the sight of man simply nauseated
him. The contempt hurt, and as he noted over and over,
perpetual nausea is extremely disagreeable. It also is a dis-

ease. Nietzsche knew himself to be every bit as sick as the culture at which he jeered. The only people whom he could conceivably love were imaginary heroes or men already on the way to their own destruction. The latter are to make way for the emergence of an "overman." Living men are at best a bridge between an animal past and a future, perfected race of wholly self-created and honest men. The hope for the "overman" is not a historic expectation; it is a contemptuous reflection on actual sick, faith-ridden, illusioned mankind and an immense longing for its extinction, an apocalyptic warning. Nietzsche was, in spite of his disclaimers, more like Timon in his suffering hatred than like the vain and self-satisfied Apemantus. When he scorned other bitter idealists, it was an act of self-rejection; for his own "overman" was also a figure of humanity perfected, even if without realization. The "overman" may suggest only a new object of worship. He is only the final recognition that there is nothing to revere except mankind's own finest creations; but at least he suggests glory, and with this vision there goes a bitter indictment and curse. And that is Zarathustra's real dream. Whatever stands in the way of the mere possibility of strong and healthy men is to be discarded. The feeble and unwholesome are already rolling downhill, so why not help them along with a kick? It is cruel to them, but not to the "overman" who must replace them. Why not kick mankind as it is now? What is it but "an ugly stone"?[18] All signs of violence and energy are to be welcomed if they serve to obliterate the memory of a dead god and of the enfeebling and mistaken ethos that dominates a degenerate culture. The "overman" may be only an intimation, but cruelty, honesty, and self-expression would be his marks, instead of self-torment, hypocrisy, and a repressed will to power. Cruelty there must be, because it is part of creativity.

This was not meant to stimulate a bloodbath. It was a call to honesty about Europe's decadence and about what human aspirations might be. It was also a public renunciation of all faith in "given" truth, and a turn to honesty and self-recognition, as acts of liberation and purification. To the extent that there was a political element in Nietzsche, it was pure Machiavelli. He preferred the genuine Machiavellian article. Better an honest Napoleon than a hypocritical "servant of the people," whether he be a king or an elected parliamentary representative.[19] For ruling, as Nietzsche thought of it, should be a personal and creative activity, not the impersonal and blandly leveling policy of the modern legal state. A new philosophy and a new ruler must impose standards and discipline on the multitude, as the pursuit of his own individual projects. Both the philosopher and the emperor are called to honesty, not only as part of their will to power, but also in order to take up a struggle to unmask and dominate, and so cure the world made sick by its hypocritical culture—a culture made by men who refused to recognize that they had made their own prison. This grandiose appeal is less political than a metaphor for misanthropy. Nietzsche was, unlike most of his readers, not particularly interested in military or civilian politics. His scope was far broader, embracing the entire cultural and even biological history of Europe's peoples. When he saw the past and present as a gigantic struggle between the noble and the base, he did not think of these antagonists in martial terms. His avenging and recreating "overman" is just a name for supramoral physical and psychic health, designed not for policy, but to express an outrage beyond words. Aggressive despair and its honesty are, however, also a part of the will to power, and that is how Nietzsche was posthumously able to play every discordant chord of Europe's mental keyboard: in the heroic and cruel phase of his misanthropy, he clearly speaks to every terroristic impulse. In a more passive mode, Nietzsche encourages waves of contempt and nausea in those who fear the very shadow of an illusion, lest it hide the actualities of a world too corrupt to bear, or reveal their own human weakness.

Does honesty compel us to hate mankind and be cruel? Or can we share Montaigne's cruel hatred of cruelty and so avoid misanthropy? Montaigne did not think of cruelty as only a public vice. Private life is no better than public in that respect.[20] That is why he refused to accept Machiavelli's suggestion that the tender-minded should retreat from the world of politics. There is no library so secure that one can escape from cruelty. A man of honor, such as Montaigne, could in any event not choose to abandon his friends and his prince. And the retreat from politics, even had it been possible in a civil war, would not have allowed him to forget the victims. Cruelty, lying, tyranny, and treason were all therefore inseparably public and personal, our ordinary vices. It is a view that still has much to recommend it. For it reminds one that it is not impersonal forces or institutions that commit atrocities: it is always a human being who is cruel and another who is a victim. That is why misanthropy did appeal to Montaigne, but also why he could valiantly ward it off by remembering personal friendship and the occasional hero of the moral life. Sustained by them, he was able to remain a self-reliant skeptic. Often touched by misanthropy, appalled by his fellow men, he maintained a moral balance. He would prove Pliny almost wrong. For it is not only the hatred of vice, but which vices are hated most and the form and intensity of such a hatred that decides the character of the misanthrope. We may not always have to shun distrust and contempt, as Pliny thought we should. But like Montaigne, we can avoid the inhumanity of those misanthropes who, like Timon and Nietzsche, put all their moral energy into hating betrayal and dishonesty. They indeed remind us not of the truth of Pliny's saying, but of its wisdom.

Bad characters for good liberals

It is the logic of our times
No subject for immortal verse—
That we who lived by honest dreams
Defend the bad against the worse.

—C. Day Lewis, *Where Are the War Poets?*

6

THIS HAS BEEN a tour of perplexities, not a guide for the perplexed. These chapters have been inquiries into difficulties, and they are not held together by a continuous argument moving on to a destined goal. I have contributed nothing to the homiletic literature, and I have not harangued "modern man." At most I have tried to do what I take to be the job of political theory: to make our conversations and convictions about our society more complete and coherent and to review critically the judgments we ordinarily make and the possibilities we usually see. To question our customs is not a substitute for action, and I have not chosen to join any branch of the counseling industry. Indeed, I cannot think why any readers of this book would ask for my advice on how to conduct themselves or about what policies they should choose. I have merely undertaken an exploration of some types of characters and manners that we often—ordinarily, in fact—condemn. I speak quite deliberately of "us," for I have not pretended that I was writing a letter from some distant ethical galaxy or addressing strangers. These are our ordinary vices and our commonplace thinking about them.

Who are the "we" of whom I seem to talk so confidently?

I have assumed that I live among people who are familiar with the political practices of the United States and who show their adherence to them by discussing them critically, indeed relentlessly. We have been educated as is now only possible in liberal democracies and we have a fund of historical and literary memories on which we can draw as we contemplate ruling and being ruled. The institutions of constitutional government and representative democracy are our political givens, but we can draw on a considerable range of other possibilities to sharpen our political imagination. As a result, we can talk to, as well as at, each other intelligibly. Whether we disagree or are at one, we can know quite well why it is so. There is nothing in the least unusual about such an enterprise. After all, Aristotle said "we," frequently. He was not addressing the Persians or future generations of barbarians, nor did he probably expect Diogenes and his kind to pay much attention to his lectures on ethics and politics. And he also did not seem to ask his audience of "we" to necessarily agree with him. They were, rather, to enter directly into the general spirit of his discourse. That is all that "we" means here. What distinguishes this book, however, is my consciousness of conflict among "us" as both ineluctable and tolerable, and entirely necessary for any degree of freedom. Indeed, I have tried to make "us" even more aware of our incompatibilities and their consequences.

To write for and about "us" does not limit one to an immediate time or circle of people. Quite on the contrary, political theory is at any moment aware that it is an integral part of a historical continuum—that one of its tasks is to join past to present thinking about governing and being governed. That does not necessarily mean that one must write history always, important though that often is. I have not traced the development of attitudes to vice through the ages, nor fixed the exact historical context of various doctrines. I have used "then" and "now" only for purposes of comparison and illumination. A historian would, of course, be far more concerned with why something was said at a given time and not earlier or later. To refer to the political past, because it appears to be both like and unlike the present in ways that make us see ourselves anew, is to use, not to write, history, though of course it does not have to do violence to accuracy.

If I have not written intellectual history, I have obviously also not engaged in that part of political theory that analyzes concepts and fits specific ideas or practices to an established grid or model. Again I have taken another road not in order to criticize or reject meta-ethics, but merely to seek a more concrete way of thinking about politics, one closer to men and events and to our historical preoccupations and institutions. To do this I have given up some rigor of exposition and precision of usage, but I do not think that this has made my narrative more obscure, even if I have spent relatively little time on distinctions and definitions. I am not at all sure that this is for the best; "only fools are cocksure," according to Montaigne. And since he has been so much the hero of these essays, I have followed him rather than the many historians and political thinkers whom I admire among my contemporaries. I, too, have told stories, as he did, in the hope that they could carry messages to the reader and then suggest some more.

Some of the stories I have told were taken from plays and novels, others from the works of philosophers. In the latter case also I did it, as Montaigne did, "to express my own ideas more clearly," not to cover myself "with another's armor." In putting Machiavelli or Montesquieu or Nietzsche before the reader, I was not hiding behind the backs of these venerable giants; neither was I using their authority to bolster my arguments and intimidate those who might not agree with me. I have only made the great men useful to me by talking about them. Interpretation is an act of representation, of bringing an absent speaker into a discussion which occurs too late for him to join, but to which he has implicitly much to contribute. There is, to be perfectly honest, a certain amount of patricidal rage in these interpretive resuscitations, especially when they claim to be perfect reproductions of the original, like police reports of his statements. The interpreter is perhaps least aggressive when he treats these writers as less authoritative figures who can help us think something through, as when I appealed to Montaigne to find out what putting cruelty first might mean. I hope I have treated him decently so that he remains recognizably himself, even though altered, in the tales I have told about and with him.

I have told and retold stories that are not interpretations of or about the philosophers, but incidents from novels and plays. Partly I have done so to illustrate some general moral or political propositions. All philosophers do that, too. Aristotle relied very heavily on Homer and Euripides. Kant made up his own anecdotes, not very successfully, especially when he told stories about the evils of lying. Hegel took whatever he could find in the treasure house of our literature, and in this respect, at least, he has served as my guide and teacher. I have, in short, allowed the greatest of the story tellers to do some of my work for me, as I borrowed their most telling characters and scenes as examples.

Among the stories, there are some that do not serve to illustrate anything. They are told in order to reveal something directly. These illuminations are not meant to prove anything or to make it easier to grasp some general idea. They are there for their own sake, for their ability to force us to acknowledge what we already know imperfectly. They make us recognize something as if it were obvious. A great story brings us to that point. I have not made Molière, Hawthorne, or Shakespeare help me to push an argument along or to make it less abstract. No such subordinations, no such humble functions are fit for them! They impose understandings upon us, sooner or later, by removing the covers we may have put on the mind's eye. What, after all, is *Anna Karenina* supposed to illustrate? Surely it makes more sense to say, "I am Isabel Archer," than to treat Henry James's *Portrait of a Lady* as a sample of American womanhood in Europe. What I have tried to do is not to put some characters on the stage here to incarnate misanthropy or betrayal. I have not asked Timon or Alceste to put flesh on some abstract bones. They do not, in fact, tell us how to think, but what to think about, and make us "see things as they are."

At the other end of the imaginative spectrum, there are also stories to be told. I have found many opinions and types in less exalted places. There is more than statistics in published survey research, and legal cases have long been an anecdotal gold mine. This is the very matter to which political theory must apply itself in any event, but especially if it wishes to be about something concrete. The great intellectual advantage of telling stories is that it does not rationalize the irrationality of actual experience and of history. Indecision, incoherence, and inconsistency are not ironed out or put between brackets. All our conflicts are preserved in all their inconclusiveness. They can be rendered intelligible by epitomizing them in a scene or a character. Stories expose rather than create order, and in so doing they can render explicit much that is inarticulate. There are many significant habits and attitudes that cannot be easily discerned because they are expressed only in conduct, ritual, and casual conversations. They have to be structured for us before we can speak about them as part of a theoretical discussion. Without the poets in prose and verse, we would not know how to approach these characteristic features of the less than fully speaking person or group. It is often said that literature is not life; but though that seems obvious, it does not really matter much. Historical narratives are not like personal experiences of men and events, either. And although the rules of evidence clearly mark a history off from a novel, the difference is one of degree, and its biographical elements are often psychologically less plausible than the work of a great novelist. In any case, a book about vices can use both kinds of story without the slightest loss of footing in human experience. Our history books, like our "life," are certainly full enough of cruelty, hypocrisy, and betrayal, but to find their essence in a moment or a character we must look to literature.

There are, of course, limits to what story telling can achieve. It is best at seeing politics as a scenario of subtle interactions, and it is therefore an addition, not a substitute, for more abstract modes of analysis. To establish general laws or models to explain and judge political conduct is particularly necessary for assessing the rational consistency and consequences of specific decisions or policy choices. There is, however, much ritual, display, social exchanging, and acting out in the public arena by officials and citizens, and here story telling may offer more appropriate theories. The drama is saturated with politics not only because the subject is inherently fascinating. The subject also lends itself to the stage because it is almost prepackaged for that purpose. Especially when politics and morals, the public and the personal, meet, as in the case of the vices I have discussed, we can do worse than find the right character to perform and endure all the implications of any net of ideas, as *Tamburlaine the Great* plays out Machiavelli's politics. Active embodiment can bring out all the improvisations, dodges, adaptations, twists, and turns of politics, and also, of course, its enormous violence.

This defense of story telling is really only a reminder of something political philosophers used to do quite normally. I mention Plato as a matter of pure reverence, but among more modern theorists, Montesquieu's *Spirit of the Laws* is one story after another, and its penetrating qualities owe much to the author's skill as a novelist. Other philosophers have preferred to copy the theologians more closely, and they have attended more to fixing exactly the grounds for praise and blame in politics. They have been less successful in dealing with change and character than with judgments, enactments, and strategies. There is, actually, no reason why one cannot do both sorts of theory. Story telling is adaptable; it is philosophically very fine. In writing about vices and bad characters, one does not have to choose irrevocably between utilitarianism and its many critics. Either side could do it, if it could take an interest in the structure of character and manners, as both Bentham and Kant did. And it is to the place of character, especially vicious character, in thinking about politics that most stories such as those of Montesquieu ultimately refer.

The word "character" tends to be identified instantly with Aristotle. There is, indeed, a long tradition of character studies that seek to identify the essence of various kinds of men, in imitation of Aristotle's accounts of individual audiences in the *Rhetoric*. When moral philosophers point to Aristotle, however, they mean more than that. His, it is said quite rightly, is an ethic of character building. And it is then inevitably, and on the whole superficially, opposed to Kant's ethics of duty. In fact, Kant has also supplied us with an ethic of character in *The Metaphysical Principles of Virtue.* For although he thought that modeling oneself on the image of a perfectly wise man was a second-best morality, inferior to doing one's duty for its own sake as an expression of reason in action, he thought also that we would never be sufficiently free from irrational inclinations to be able to act freely and choose duty. Instead we must strive to approximate the state of true dutifulness. And that means choosing the right dispositions, which is exactly how Aristotle defined virtue. The differences between their respective characters are enormous, but it is a matter of politics, not of method. It is also a contrast that is particularly significant for liberalism, for it reveals the degree to which it may encompass a theory of character.

Although Aristotle and Kant agreed about character building as self-creation by choosing good dispositions, they were wholly at odds about the specific traits to be selected, and the final ensemble. Aristotle's self-sufficiently happy man can reach his political or contemplative perfection only if he is rich, fortunate, honored, and supported by slaves who do all the work that is not compatible with the aristocratic ideal of leisure and purity. Even his social virtues require wealth, so that he can be liberal. And for his own sake, he must be both magnanimous and magnificent—all of which requires unusual social distinction. He is, moreover, wholly self-concentrated, for he acts in accordance with a self-imposed vision of perfection even in choosing his friends. If he were to find his fulfillment in political activity, that too would be only one more item in the structure of the happiness of autonomy, which choosing his own character brings him.[1] This aloofness is inherent in any aristocratic project of self-perfection. Even Montaigne, so much more generous in his sympathies than Aristotle, created such a character for himself. And if he took to his library, he was only realizing what Aristotle in the end concluded—that true self-sufficiency was not compatible with the society of other people. The slaves, it must be recalled, are, after all, not really people but only living instruments.

Kant's character must proceed according to a very different blueprint. At all times, he must respect humanity, the rational moral element in himself and in *all* other men. For his own sake, he must choose to avoid all self-destructive and gross behavior, and, above all else, he must not lie. He also owes it to himself to avoid acts of wanton cruelty to animals. All such actions are beneath the dignity of humanity. To other men he owes no liberality or pity or *noblesse oblige* of any kind, because this might humiliate the recipients. What he does have to show them is a respect for their rights, decent manners, and an avoidance of calumny, pride, and malice. These also humiliate people. We must make an effort to be benevolent, for misanthropy, though certainly hard to resist, is "odious." We may not, finally, mutilate or inflict torture upon one another under the guise of punishment. Aristotle, we recall, thought only that torture was useless in trying to get the truth out of witnesses. He did not think it was an ethical or political issue at all. The real difference between him and Kant is glaringly obvious. Anyone can in principle aspire to become a Kantian good character. It requires no special gifts of intelligence, beauty, wealth, or good luck. You do not have to be an aristocratic, superbly endowed Greek male to be a decent character. This is a thoroughly democratic liberal character, built to preserve his own self-respect and that of others, neither demanding nor enduring servility.

Kant did not, however, argue that this character would be necessary to sustain or establish a liberal republic. Constitutional government and representative democracy could be run by intelligent devils, by any self-interested population at all.[2] It was, moreover, not the business of such governments to interfere with people's choices of disposition. Since a good character depends on being self-made, the interference of coercive authorities is inherently self-defeating and destructive. Why crass self-interest should be enough for representative republican institutions is, however, not so obvious. Clearly Kant meant to circumvent Machiavelli's argument that because men are evil they should be ruled by princes of his special kind. Since Kant knew most men to be as Machiavelli pictured them, he had to evade his conclusions, if he was to justify free government. Men are always ready for free institutions if the latter do not depend on virtue, if they are fueled by selfish impulses properly balanced, just as Madison had explained. That does not mean that freedom is without importance for character building. For if anything is clear, it is that the only opportunity, the only hope we can possibly have for self-improvement, is under conditions of freedom and the strict enforcement of legal rules. In the end, the purpose of politics is to serve our capacity, minuscule though it be, for putting together a better set of dispositions than we have done so far. And our best choices add up to a stunningly egalitarian character who is devoted to self-sufficient freedom in a different manner than Aristotle's great man. For Kant's purpose was to get vice-ridden men out of their Machiavellian world.

The liberal tendencies of this character emerge in another aspect. Kant's character is profoundly negative. We need the most intense moral fortitude to combat our evil impulses, and all our virtues are, in fact, avoidances of vices. Aristotle certainly mentions these, but his road to perfections is not very difficult for the lucky few, compared to what Kant thought all of us were up against. Partly that was his tribute to the power of vice, which, as we have seen, demanded freedom to give us an only chance to overcome it. But there is also a counter-ideal here. Moral fortitude is a democratic and wholly peaceful sort of heroism, the answer to that military courage that is so vital to every aristocratic character. All of which constitutes a deeper connection between personal character and liberal government than one might guess. For the absolute prohibition against any efforts by government to impose disposition, not to mention motives of duty, upon citizens remains in full force. It is by keeping its hands off our characters that governments provide the setting and conditions in which we just might begin our poor but epic battle against vice. To create such a government, however, demands no particular virtues at all. It is a government for men as they are, not as they might be.

Conceivably, Kant's picture of the struggle against vice might be an inheritance from Christian moral theology. However, not only did Kant very explicitly emphasize the wholly profane character of his vices and virtues, but his misanthropy was not due to a sense of sin. He thought of vice like Montesquieu, his irreverent fellow liberal. In both cases, vices were made to underwrite the impartial state in a brilliant evasion of Machiavelli's denouement. To be sure, Montesquieu went well beyond Kant in arguing that a bad character such as that common among the English was a positive support to free government. The good citizen is not a good man, except perhaps in small aristocratic republics. In the real age of personal freedom, when the burden of perpetual fear could be lifted, the good citizen certainly lacks all the classical and Christian virtues. Moreover, since in Montesquieu's subtle analyses character and government constantly mold each other, it can be said that a free government makes its citizens worse. Certainly, commercial greed and civic irascibility and pride are encouraged to replace their military equivalents. There is nothing in the way of temperance and personal moderation here. Some of the seven deadly sins seem to flourish, but not those that kill and maim. Lust seems to be contained, commerce makes citizens more gentle, and, finally, there is less political ferocity and cruelty. The real point for Montesquieu, however, as for Kant, is not to paint the free citizen as a virtuous person, but to insist that without freedom everyone is intolerably paralyzed or demeaned. In Montesquieu's eyes, fear is so terrible, so physiologically and psychologically damaging, that it cannot be redeemed by consequences. That is why there cannot be a price set on liberty. In Kant's view, despotism reduced its subjects to perpetual infancy, and that meant that they could not choose their characters at all. They would remain obedient children—and thoroughly nasty ones at that. Liberal government for bad characters did not promise us that freedom would make us good; it merely argued that it would remove the most horrible obstacles to any ethical undertaking that we might conceivably try. To demand more would not reduce vice. It would only shackle us again, and revive those pious pretenses and pious cruelties which a religious establishment had perfected and which Kant, no less than Montesquieu, regarded as one of the principal sources of public oppression. And although now, as then, every authoritarian critic of liberalism has found it easy to show that the citizens of free states are indeed very corrupt and lack both the classical martial and the Christian virtues, it is utterly impossible to claim that the subjects of more repressive, not to say terroristic and authoritarian, regimes are not worse people and far worse off. For their every impulse is hemmed in by fear, cruelty, and a massive dishonesty, which they share and which also accounts for their deference and governability. The character structure of all those slaves and metics who existed solely in order to make Aristotle's great-souled character possible is also easily imagined, and would not conform to any model of virtue. One would hope that they would all be as sly and conniving as the slaves we meet in Roman comedy, but we can be sure that they were just dull and miserable, for we know a lot about slavery. The admirers of Aristotle who find his noble hero irresistible might well reflect upon the cost to the rest of mankind, not excluding themselves from among those who would have to pay for him. The advantages of Montesquieu's self-assertive vices might correspondingly recommend themselves.

Kant and Montesquieu were, of course, not the only early liberals to think seriously about character. Clearly, Locke was a greater psychologist than either one of them. And, indeed, he gave the matter much thought. His good character is meant to be a good citizen of a liberal society. He is brought up to be neither servile nor domineering, and he is

habitually independent, truthful, and polite. We may suppose that he will have the strength to avoid false associations of ideas and to cope with the uneasiness that besets all
of us all the time. Liberal government does not, however,
exist only for the sake of this paragon. It is there for everyone, because we all can summon up enough rationality to
grasp and to act for our rights to life, liberty, and property.
It would be a great mistake to think that the author of the
Essay Concerning Human Understanding underestimated the
vices, but it is also true that the liberalism of rights is different, though entirely compatible with one that puts cruelty
first. I shall call the latter the liberalism of fear. It contributed as much to American liberal democracy as did the
"great Mr. Locke," powerful as his influence was.

Indeed, whenever I talk about putting cruelty first, I am
confronted by a rhetorical question and answer: "Why?"
"Because we have rights." That is, unhappily, a gross over-
simplification, possible only, I suspect, among people who
have relatively little experience of protracted and uninter-
rupted fear. To put cruelty first is not the same thing as just
objecting to it intensely. When one puts it first one re-
sponds, as Montaigne did, to the acknowledgment that one
fears nothing more than fear. The fear of fear does not require any further justification, because it is irreducible. It
can be both the beginning and an end of political institutions such as rights. The first right is to be protected against
the fear of cruelty. People have rights as a shield against this
greatest of public vices. This is the evil, the threat to be
avoided at all costs. Justice itself is only a web of legal arrangements required to keep cruelty in check, especially by
those who have most of the instruments of intimidation
closest at hand. That is why the liberalism of fear concentrates so single-mindedly on limited and predictable
government. The prevention of physical excess and arbi-
trariness is to be achieved by a series of legal and institutional measures designed to supply the restraints that
neither reason nor tradition can be expected to provide.
Among these are effective rights. Enforceable rights are the
legal powers that individual citizens in a liberal society can

bring to bear individually and collectively in order to defend themselves against threats backed by force. This is not the liberalism of natural rights, but it underwrites rights as the politically indispensable dispersion of power, which alone can check the reign of fear and cruelty. Montesquieu thus does not begin with rights, natural or other. He is concerned with imposition of laws that have one primary object: to relieve each one of us of the burden of fear, so that we can feel free because the government does not, indeed cannot, terrorize us.

The liberalism of fear does not suffer from any of the notorious weaknesses of utilitarianism or hedonism. Kant worried quite reasonably that if one puts happiness first, one may well choose a benevolent despotism rather than freedom. Indeed, Montesquieu before him had already tried to show that benevolent despotism was a contradiction in terms. Nevertheless, one can imagine only too readily that people might look forward to a state of material comfort without political responsibilities or the conflicts imposed by freedom. They might be, or at least might expect to become, happy under such circumstances. The liberalism of fear can never indulge in such fantasies. It begins with the assumption that the power to govern is the power to inflict fear and cruelty and that no amount of benevolence can ever suffice to protect an unarmed population against them. It therefore institutionalizes suspicion—and only a distrustful population can be relied on to watch out for its rights, to ward off fear, and to be able to make their own projects, whether these be modest or great.

The unique position of cruelty was indeed fully recognized by Montesquieu's and Locke's most distinguished heirs. The Eighth Amendment to the United States Constitution prohibits, among other things, the infliction of "cruel and unusual punishment."[3] Since this amendment has after its long dormancy suddenly come alive, its origins may be of special relevance. It is not that American governments have become more brutal—far from it—but that the experiences of this century have made many of us more aware of the cruelties that governments generally are capable of. The amendment itself was lifted word for word from the English Bill of Rights of 1689, but it had altered its meaning over the years and as it crossed the ocean. Originally it had meant only that no unprecedented, unlegislated, or disproportionate penalties, especially fines, be imposed. It was perfectly compatible with drawing and quartering, disemboweling, branding, slitting noses, cutting off ears, and burning female felons. The last was not abolished until 1790, the others much later; but Blackstone admitted that "the humanity of the English nation" no longer authorized judgments that "savor of torture or cruelty." When Patrick Henry and his fellow Virginians demanded a "no torture" clause, they had not novel or excessive penalties, but brutality in mind. To be sure, the phrase was vague, and some gentlemen in the First Congress worried about too much clemency, arguing that cutting off the ears of offenders might still be necessary. However, especially in the debates in the States, Beccaria, Montesquieu's humane disciple, was often invoked by the side that feared cruelty. It was one of the many ways in which Montesquieu came to join Locke in shaping that generation of Americans. The liberalism of fear came to be integrated with the liberalism of rights. But the difference remains, and Montesquieu did not speak the language of rights.

The turn against official cruelty was due to a long but steady moral transformation. I began this book with "putting cruelty first" partly because it is such a significant source of liberalism—for many, the most important. But it also marks a great moral turning point. Its consequences are, moreover, enduring because it remains a fecund source of diversity. It is no less responsible than the Reformation and the ideologies of the past century for making "us" so diverse and so hugely disagreeing. The question "Why put cruelty first?" may gain more from a historical than from a legalistic answer. Why did Montaigne do it? It seems to me that the answer lies within the dynamics of Christianity. Nietzsche argued very persuasively that Christian morality had always been a threat to faith. The demand for truth gnawed away at revealed religion until it ceased to be credi-

ble.[4] That part of Christian morality that demands unconditional charity was bound sooner or later to do something
similar to faith, and above all to an institutionalized religion. For it was the latter that seemed to express itself in fanaticism, violence, and the most devastating cruelties. At
the very least, it was clear that Christianity had not made its
adherents more charitable than other men. Montaigne may
well have retained a provisional belief in God, but he stood
outside the traditions of Christian religiosity. That is why
he never resorted to the normal forms of Christian self-criti-
cism. He never invoked, in the time-honored manner, the
memory of the Apostles and the purity of early Christianity
to shame his degenerate age. To put cruelty first, moreover,
was to turn away from the very idea of sin and to replace it
entirely with wrongs done to living beings. This is the truth
of an ex-Christian mental universe.

To see how great a departure putting cruelty first was,
one need only glance briefly at moral theology, especially
the seven deadly sins. All sins are directly or indirectly offenses against God. Saint Augustine placed cupidity first,
but cruelty came a close second. Nero is thus reproved for
his luxuries first, then for his cruelties. A benevolent, me-
dicinal, kindly meant cruelty is, moreover, a Christian duty,
especially when used to return the wayward to the true
faith. Saint Gregory's seven deadly sins certainly in no way
mitigate "pious cruelty," as John of Salisbury approvingly
called it. They do systematize the sins in order of their gravity and the punishment they will merit in the afterlife. The
capital sins, those at the head, are unique in giving rise to a
flock of lesser vices. The first one must always be pride, *su-
perbia*, for it is the sum of all sinning, a deliberate turning
away from God. But as Saint Thomas explains in his classic
account, pride has a lesser face as well: it is vainglory, pride
displayed to other men specifically. This arrogance is the
first and most creative sin among those to which pride gives
rise. Anger is not unlike it, and cruelty is one of its offspring. Saint Thomas found it no easier to dwell on cruelty
than had his master Aristotle. After noting that the word
was derived from "crude," "raw" in contrast to the soft and

"cooked," he too drifted off into a discussion of bestiality and savagery. He was, however, constrained to discuss excessively cruel punishments and the virtue of clemency. Nevertheless, neither lying nor cruelty is a capital sin, although both are condemned.[5] There are many Christians today, Catholic and Protestant, who, though they believe in sin, do not subscribe to either Saint Augustine's or Saint Thomas's list. Many wish that the former had talked a bit less about sex and a lot more about hypocrisy, and others would much prefer to hear moral and physical cruelty berated rather than vainglory or gluttony, which are also deadly sins. There seems to be less disagreement about envy and avarice. Nevertheless, sin is sin. It is not primarily a character flaw, or a transgression against the dignity of mankind, or a violation of the rights of man. It is a rejection of God; and though all the vices are offenses against reason in a philosopher's view, they are all sins theologically, because they offend God, according to Saint Thomas. That does not, of course, mean that all sins must be punished by public authorities. Indeed Saint Thomas is firm on the matter; rulers must select only those sins that cause public damage for criminal punishment. That is why a Thomist liberalism was eventually quite feasible. Putting cruelty first is, however, an altogether different matter. It is a turning away from sin entirely, and from divine punishment as well. It knows only two figures and one place: victimizers and victims here and now.

Having said all that about Montaigne's and then Montesquieu's radicalism, I must now also point to their profound debt to moral theology as a structure of thought. Fear plays the same function in Montaigne's thinking as pride does in Saint Thomas's, for instance. It is an undifferentiated evil in which all lesser vices and faults have their origin. It expresses itself particularly in a specific vice, cowardice, as vainglory is the first visible act of pride. But fear is broader and more general than cowardice, which is a quite limited vice, only one among many, and perhaps not the worst of our ordinary ones. Cruelty comes first, then lying and treachery. All, every single one, are the children of fear.

Fear is not just a vice, or a deformity of our character. It is the underlying psychological and moral medium that makes vice all but unavoidable. It is far more than just being afraid. One can be afraid of fear, because fear is the ultimately evil moral condition. It is so for the individual and for society, and that is what Montesquieu meant by despotism, the principle of which is fear.

Fearing fear may well drive us into our libraries or other places of withdrawal. Montesquieu had to recommend the vices that tend to bring us into public life and make us into free citizens. What else was there to arm us against despotism? Of rulers, therefore, no more is demanded than justice—no other virtues at all. That does, however, mean that they are required to live up to a higher standard of probity than are private persons. We are, of course, encouraged to cultivate the intellectual and social virtues, but only our legal obligations can be enforced. That is, in fact, the outlook of most Americans. We impose far higher standards of honesty and discipline upon public servants than upon people engaged in business or employed in any way in the private sector. That is a total reversal of the beliefs of Machiavelli and his disciples, who have always agreed that goodness is a private luxury that rulers cannot afford. Like them, Max Weber in this century has argued that there are two ethics, one obedient to the Sermon on the Mount, intent upon a pure conscience, and the other concerned only with outcomes and in pursuit of some political "cause." This stark choice between a public and a private ethos may seem especially real when one thinks about war and peace and similar life and death or public safety issues. In fact, the division of public and private imperatives is not so clear. Most politics are not a question of stark choices at all; they involve bargains, incremental decisions, adaptations, rituals, display, argument, persuasion, and the like. Decisions are rarely made by isolated and heroic individuals sacrificing their conscience and their honor. The Machiavellian ethical pathos and drama of choice are hardly ever relevant. A liberal government is expected to be more just and honest than its average citizens, and its agents are not charged with tasks that require them to be more vicious than, or even particularly different from, private citizens.

It is not possible to think of vices as simply either private or public. There are vices that are purely private, or that for the sake of political freedom are fenced off from even the scrutiny of public agents. But there are others that are both private and public. There are some that we tolerate only in public officials as agents of coercion. That means that the simple choice that Weber inherited from Machiavelli between a mere two roles, immoral politics and moral privacy, does not make much sense in a liberal democratic state. It is a leftover from the highly personal state of the early modern period, in which Weber often still seemed to live. His typical statesman is a heroic figure who must make enormous moral sacrifices for the sake of his country or ideology. His ethical conflicts are those of the aristocratic neoclassical drama of Corneille more than those that confront politicians in contemporary representative democracies. His were the politics of the great gesture, and they still appeal to those engaged intellectuals who like to think of "dirty hands" as a peculiarly shaking, personal, and spectacular crisis. This is a fantasy quite appropriate to the imaginary world, in which these people see themselves in full technicolor. Stark choices and great decisions are actually very rare in politics. The sorts of choices that occur in public regularly are no different from those that have to be made by every single person who is responsible *for* other people and not just *to* them. No mother of a family can cultivate her conscience only; and if she does not calculate the consequences of her actions in a cool matter-of-fact way, her children will suffer the effects. What we look for both in public officials and in our friends is character. Not a set of discrete, heroic, ethically significant decisions, but the imperceptible choices of dispositions that are manifest in the course of a lifetime. And character is an indissoluble amalgam of motives and calculations. No one specializes in that. Betrayal, especially, is built into relations of trust at every level of society—at home, in the office, and at war. As social actors, we all have unclean hands some of the time. It is not a glamourous melodramatic issue for conspicuous agents only. In matters of probity, far from permitting officials a great moral latitude, we are very strict about keeping their private hand out of the public till. The whole force of Weber's heroic drama is drawn from the obvious fact that there are special tasks that only public agents perform. Throughout history, war and punishment have been the primary functions of government. No liberal ever forgets that governments are coercive. Certainly, neither Kant nor Montesquieu nor Locke ignored this most undeniable of all facts. Weber chose to put it in a nutshell by defining the state as the holder of a monopoly on the legitimate use of force. It is not an adequate definition, but it does encourage demands for limited government and for justice as the sole public virtue, and underlines the political significance of putting cruelty first. All this and more is obviously an effort to reduce the threats that governmental force poses to liberty.

It is a mark of the ethical radicalism of Montesquieu and *The Federalist* that neither worried in the least about the consciences of rulers. They assumed that this was a moral relic that would cease to mean anything once absolute rulers and their confessors were replaced by an institutional "system" that demanded only justice from public officials. That, in effect, was too limited a vision of leadership. Whether it be a psychological necessity or only the effect of electoral politics, personal leadership appears to be inescapable, and this is especially so in circumstances of danger, in what are perceived as "crises" in international relations, intense domestic conflicts, or extreme economic disorders. Liberal democracies therefore continue to face the old threats of personalized politics, and they cannot ignore the character of conspicuous public figures. There has, after all, been only one incomparable George Washington. Not all the vices of public agents are therefore equally irrelevant, and that is why Montaigne's profound meditations upon cruelty and misanthropy, and his unconditional rejection of Machiavelli, even at the cost of unresolvable doubt, uncertainty, and conflict, seemed to me to be so enduringly relevant to the actualities of public force and coercion. It is clear, in short, that private characters in public places do not, as Weber saw it, have to choose between Christ and Caesar. It matters only that they be placed in circumstances and be subject to a process of selection that will moderate the most unacceptable vices and the worst characters.

One should add to Montaigne's unheroic realism Locke's instructions to his young gentleman. The boy is taught to look upon the military heroes of the past as the "great butchers of mankind," and his history lessons are about the institutions and laws of his country. To forget the mundane, the quotidian, is to forget liberal politics, which are the practices of peace and compromise, not of war and revolution—all, to be sure, within the limits of the possible. Locke's young gentleman is being trained to go to parliament and to play his part in his county. Today that part of politics is indissolubly a part of what we call pluralism, or polyarchy—the politics of groups. And the implications of private and public values are quite different when we think of liberalism as freely competing groups, rather than of government and the uses of force. The general welfare always meant more than war and punishment of criminals. Even government is not just an agent of fear, that primary object of liberal suspicion. Nevertheless, it was fear that originally linked liberalism to pluralistic politics. However watchful the citizens and however finely equilibrated institutions of government might be, the "blessings of liberty" were not safe enough. Montesquieu relied on intermediary powers to stem the expansive tendencies of coercive force. Madison saw competing interest groups, of which incompatible sects were his chief model, as the best safeguard against government by unrestrained majorities. It was not until Tocqueville came to America that voluntary associations were seen in a more positive light, as contributing much to the development of individuals, of manners, and of citizenship, and to political and social culture generally. Here private individuals move in and out of public roles continually, as a matter of course. Integration, competition, promotion of interests, and much else is at stake that is both private and public. This is where character is developed. And this is also where professional politicians, "leaders," in due course emerge. It is here, I have argued, that we cannot simply brush aside the public life of personal vices—especially hypocrisy, snobbery, and treachery, which have many faces. It is not whether they are the same or different at home and abroad that matters most for liberal politics, however. The difference may be small, but if public force is used to correct them, liberty will be jeopardized.

In writing about these vices, I have certainly not been original. I have learned much from a very remarkable literature about vicious characters. Its recognized parent was Theophrastus, Aristotle's pupil and successor, who wrote a series of character sketches, each one representing a single vice, such as flattery, or boorishness, or cowardice. He would begin by defining the vice, and then show us a man who displays it in a series of encounters. In the Middle Ages, the sins were often personified on the stage and in homilies, and there was also an "estates" literature in which a member of each of the social orders would act out its typical vices or virtues. But it was only after Theophrastus was translated that his art again came into its own in England and France. Early in the seventeenth century, Bishop Hall wrote a full set of characters, mostly bad, and his book was an instant bestseller, and much translated and imitated. Most of his successors were also Anglicans and aristocratic in their outlook, and soon "characters" became part of the polemics of the age. However, the hypocrite, the courtier, the busybody were never forgotten.[6] Thackeray's *Book of Snobs* is one of the last and finest productions of this genre, and he was particularly successful in joining occupation, class, and typical vices into a single portrait. But the great masterpiece of character literature remains La Bruyère's *Les Caractères*, which is a panorama of all the flawed social types of the France of the *Ancien Régime*, its courtiers, its great nobles, its rules, its unbelievers, and its bourgeoisie. It is here, indeed, that we meet the ultimate Timon. He does not rave or rant; he is "ceremonious"—so cold and polite that no familiarity is thinkable. He also has his place in such a world. I have as best I could, in a very different society and without their moral self-assurance, taken my cue from these extraordinary writers.

There is, to be sure, a difference between personifying a vice—speaking of "the hypocrite" or "the miser" or "the flatterer" as if the man were his flaw and nothing else—and speaking of character as the structure of all the human dispositions. To make an individual represent a single vice is not psychologically convincing to us, accustomed as we are to the refinements of the novel especially. There is always more to a human being than just one vice, even if it dominates his conduct. But what I have learned from Theophrastus and his heirs is that one puts characteristics in familiar settings and tells a story about what happens to them in the diverse but common encounters that are likely to occur there. It is they no less than Montaigne who taught me to appreciate the "ordinary" in following the vices around their daily course.

The vividness of these old "characters," their immediate resonance, has its own interest. The political distance between us and La Bruyère is huge, but we generally respond to his characters just as he expected us to do. We recognize these wayward individuals as if we had recently met them, and their manners offend us no less than those of our snobbish and hypocritical and egoistic contemporaries. How close these awful people are, and yet how very remote! For the public meaning of their acts in a pluralistic democracy is wholly different from the implications of these vices in La Bruyère's *Ancien Régime*, with its hierarchy of orders and sins. Those vices did not just mar character; they were also ranked within a Christian order of sins, which gave them their gravity. We learn to understand ourselves both by the distance and the closeness of the past to ourselves. The old hypocrisy is not like the new. Franklin would not have understood any more than La Bruyère the intensity of the quest for perfect sincerity that is built into our world of incoherence and mutual moral incomprehension and hostility. I have argued that we ought to give up not only our obsession with openness, but indeed go beyond the traditional horror of the hypocrite. The spiritual inner man, his motives, and his deepest impulses are not only no business of public authorities; they ought not to concern his fellow citizens, especially his ideological opponents or even people who do not share his system of associations, background, and loyalties. Hypocrisy is one of the few vices that bolsters liberal democracy. Of snobbery, however, it is impossible to approve. Who does not hate the moral cruelty, the cowardice of the snob? La Bruyère's models of the snob are certainly alive. It is not because they lack a Christian or aristocratic character, however, that we now hate snobs. It has a great deal more to do with our public ethos, with the moral demands of democracy and representative government. Nevertheless, pluralism also requires that we endure snobbery as an inescapable by-product not just of inequalities of prestige, but of diversity itself. We all snub and are snubbed as part of the process of our multiplicity of roles and groups, and it is here that a most unchristian personal pride particularly recommends itself. Finally, betrayal in a multireligious and multiethnic society has its ambiguities; but then, it never was a simple vice. Montaigne had already locked friendship into a purely private room of his life, and so it remains, but not without consequences to our public expectations and responses. The conflicts of loyalty and struggles against misanthropy have put us all in Montaigne's shoes now. The plural moral world has imposed Montaigne's burdens on us. That and his cruel hatred of cruelty have made him the hero of every page of this book.

The vices of character create individuals from whom we may shrink for any number of quite different personal or shared reasons. When we think of these vices, however, we must do what the tradition of character writers did: relate the vice bearer to a whole social and religious scheme. Ours is a nonscheme, and that is how I have looked at character. Liberal democracy is more than a set of political procedures. It is a culture of subcultures, a tradition of traditions, and an ethos of determined multiplicity. It puts enormous burdens of choice upon all of us, and it ought to be seen as very demanding. But it has never been easy to choose the dispositions required for a good character. No one has ever promised us an effortless moral life. Finally, ours is not the world of early modern Europe, and neither its manners nor its politics are ours. Even though we still scorn hypocrisy, snobbery, and treachery, we do not do so for the same reasons or in the same way. Given that as liberals we have abandoned certainty and agreement as goals worthy of free people, we have no need for simple lists of vices and virtues. On the contrary, it seems to me that liberalism imposes extraordinary ethical difficulties on us: to live with contradictions, unresolvable conflicts, and a balancing between public and private imperatives which are neither opposed to nor at one with each other. The ordinary vices, at the very least, reveal what we have to contend with if we want to be fully aware of what we think we already know.

N*otes*

1. Putting Cruelty First

1. D. P. Walker, *The Decline of Hell* (Chicago: University of Chicago Press, 1964). Arthur Danto of Columbia University looked for references to cruelty before Montaigne wrote his *Essays* at about the same time I did and came to the same conclusions. I have relied on his account as much as my own research, and I would like to express my thanks to him here. Keith Thomas, *Man and the Natural World, 1500–1800* (London: Alan Lane, 1983), does show that humanitarianism may have been more widespread (at least in England) than had been believed.

2. Montaigne, "Of the Art of Conversing," in *The Essays of Montaigne*, trans. E. J. Trechman, vol. 2 (New York: Oxford University Press, n.d.), p. 383.

3. Idem, "Of Democritus and Heraclitus," ibid., vol. 1, p. 296.

4. Idem, "Apology for Raimond Sebond," ibid., vol. 1, p. 434.

5. Montesquieu, *De l'Esprit des lois,* in *Oeuvres Complètes de Montesquieu*, ed. André Masson, vol. 1 (Paris: Nagel, 1950), pp. 330–331. My translation.

6. Montaigne, "On Some Lines of Vergil," in *Essays*, vol. 2, p. 303.

7. Idem, "Of Democritus," ibid., vol. 1, p. 291.

8. Idem, "Apology," ibid., vol. 1, pp. 464, 468.

9. Montesquieu, *Esprit*, in *Oeuvres*, vol. 1, p. 4.

10. Montaigne, "Apology," in *Essays*, vol. 1, p. 441.

11. Idem, "Of Coaches," ibid., vol. 2, p. 372.

12. Idem, "Apology," ibid., vol. 1, p. 466.

13. Bruno Bettelheim, *Surviving* (New York: Vintage, 1980), pp. 84–104, 246–254, 258–273, 274–314.

14. Jean-Paul Sartre, *Anti-Semite and Jew*, trans. George J. Becker (New York: Schocken, 1965).

15. Donald M. Frame, *Montaigne: A Biography* (New York: Harcourt, Brace and World, 1965), pp. 217–218.

16. Jean-Paul Sartre, *Being and Nothingness*, trans. Hazel E.

Barnes (New York: Washington Square Press, 1966), pp. 273–285, 315–370, 480–504, 513–526, 624–650, 672–681. Idem, Preface to Frantz Fanon, *The Wretched of the Earth* (New York: Grove Press, 1963), pp. 7–26.

17. Montaigne, "Of Fear," in *Essays*, vol. 1, p. 71.

18. Thucydides, *The Peloponnesian War*, trans. R. Crawley (New York: Modern Library, 1934), bk. 7, sect. 29.

19. Montaigne, "Of Cannibals," in *Essays*, vol. 1, pp. 205–206.

20. Montesquieu, *Esprit*, vol. 1, pp. 329–330, 338.

21. Montaigne, "Of the Inequality That Is among Us," in *Essays*, vol. 1, p. 255.

22. Euripides, *Hecuba*, trans. William Arrowsmith, and *Trojan Women*, trans. Richmond Lattimore, in *The Complete Greek Tragedies*, ed. David Grene and Richmond Lattimore (Chicago: University of Chicago Press, 1958).

23. Montaigne, "Of Vanity," in *Essays*, vol. 2, p. 423.

24. Idem, "Of Presumption," ibid., vol. 2, p. 107.

25. Ralph Waldo Emerson, *Representative Men*, in *English Traits and Other Essays* (London: J. M. Dent, 1908), pp. 237, 242.

26. Montesquieu, *Esprit*, vol. 2, p. 170.

27. Montaigne, "Of Husbanding One's Will," in *Essays*, vol. 2, p. 482.

28. A. V. Dicey, *Lectures on the Relations between Law and Public Opinion in England* (London: Macmillan, 1952), pp. 188–190, 309.

29. Jeremy Bentham, *Pauper Management Improved*, in *Works*, ed. John Bowering, vol. 8 (New York: Russell and Russell, 1962), pp. 369–439.

30. Norman S. Fiering, "Irresistible Compassion in the Eighteenth Century," *Journal of the History of Ideas* 37 (1976): 195–218.

31. Friedrich Nietzsche, *The Gay Science*, trans. Walter Kaufmann (New York: Vintage, 1974), sect. 352 and passim. Idem, *Beyond Good and Evil*, trans. Walter Kaufmann (New York: Vintage, 1966), sect. 229 and passim. Idem, *The Genealogy of Morals*, trans. Walter Kaufmann (New York: Vintage, 1969), passim. For Nietzsche's ambiguities about cruelty see *Menschliches, Allzumenschliches*, in *Gesammelte Werke* (München: Musarion Verlag, 1923), sects. 43, 88, 100, 633.

32. Hannah Arendt, *The Origins of Totalitarianism* (New York: Harvest, 1973), p. 331.

33. Montaigne, "Of Cruelty," in *Essays*, vol. 1, p. 421.

34. Idem, "Of the Useful and Honest," ibid., vol. 2, p. 257.

35. This is true even of the one recent book that deals with cru-

elty directly and that is, not surprisingly, by a Montaigne scholar. See Philip P. Hallie, *The Paradox of Cruelty* (Middletown, Conn.: Wesleyan University Press, 1969). It is even more true of Barrington Moore, Jr., *Reflections on the Causes of Human Misery* (Boston: Beacon, 1970).

2. Let Us Not be Hypocritical

1. William Hazlitt, "On Religious Hypocrisy," in *The Round Table* (London: Dent, 1964), pp. 128–131. Idem, "On Cant and Hypocrisy," in *Sketches and Essays* (Oxford: Oxford University Press, 1936), pp. 17–29.

2. Joseph Hall, "The Hypocrite," in *A Book of Characters*, ed. Richard Aldington (London: Routledge, 1924), pp. 71–73.

3. Molière, *The Misanthrope and Tartuffe*, trans. Richard Wilbur (New York: Harvest, 1965).

4. G. F. W. Hegel, *The Philosophy of Right*, trans. T. M. Knox (Oxford: Clarendon, 1942), sects. 139–140, pp. 92–103.

5. John Morley, *On Compromise* (London: Watts, 1933).

6. Benjamin Franklin, *Autobiography*, ed. Leonard W. Labaree (New Haven: Yale University Press, 1964), pp. 159–160.

7. I owe much to Bernard Williams' objections to my views. See especially Williams, "The Idea of Equality," in *Philosophy, Politics and Society*, ed. Peter Laslett and W. G. Runciman (New York: Barnes and Noble, 1962).

8. Michael Walzer, *Just and Unjust Wars* (New York: Basic, 1977), pp. xv, 19–20.

9. William Farr Church, *Richelieu and Reason of State* (Princeton: Princeton University Press, 1972), passim.

3. What Is Wrong with Snobbery?

1. Among the entries in Eric Partridge, *A Dictionary of Slang and Unconventional English*, 7th ed. (New York: Macmillan, 1961), there are some neutral and some extremely abusive meanings, but none that has any bearing on present usage. Walter W. Skeat, *A Concise Etymological Dictionary of the English Language* (Oxford: Clarendon, 1961), mentions "a servant, usually in a ludicrous sense; a cobbler's boy." In Danish dialect, it means "a dolt, with the notion of imposter." Finally the *Oxford English Dictionary* says

that in the Middle Ages, snobbery meant sniveling. There is no doubt that the use of the word in its present sense became very frequent only from about 1850 on. See "Appendix" in William Makepeace Thackeray, *The Book of Snobs,* ed. John Sutherland (New York: St. Martin's, 1978), pp. 235–237.

2. William Makepeace Thackeray, *The Book of Snobs,* in *Works,* vol. 22 (New York: Scribner's, 1904), pp. 261–265. This edition has the largest number of sketches, including one on "Radical Snobs."

3. Harold Nicolson, *Good Behavior* (New York: Doubleday, 1956), pp. 280–283.

4. Aldous Huxley, *Music at Night* (London: Penguin, 1955), pp. 145–148.

5. C. Wright Mills, "Introduction" to Thorstein Veblen, *The Theory of the Leisure Class* (New York: Mentor, 1953), pp. vi–xix.

6. Alexis de Tocqueville, *Democracy in America,* trans. George Lawrence, vol. 2 (New York: Harper and Row, 1966), p. 483.

7. Seymour Martin Lipset, *Political Man* (New York: Doubleday Anchor, 1963), pp. 446–449.

8. Samuel Butler, "A Huffing Courtier," in *A Book of Characters,* ed. Richard Aldington (London: Routledge, 1924), pp. 273–274.

9. La Bruyère, *Les Caractères,* in *Oeuvres complètes,* ed. Julien Benda (Paris: Pléiade, 1951), p. 264.

10. See generally Jean V. Alter, *L'Esprit antibourgeois dans l'Ancien Régime* (Geneva: Droz, 1970); and Eleanor G. Barber, *The Bourgeoisie of Eighteenth-Century France* (Princeton: Princeton University Press, 1967).

11. I owe the idea of a distinction between "primary" and "secondary" snobbery, and much else, to Philippe du Puy de Clinchamps, *Le Snobisme* (Paris: Presses Universitaires, 1964).

12. Montesquieu, *De l'Esprit des lois,* in *Oeuvres Complètes de Montesquieu,* ed. André Masson (Paris: Nagel, 1950), vol. 2, bk. 14, ch. 27.

13. John Locke, *Some Thoughts Concerning Education,* in *Works,* vol. 9 (London, 1823), sects. 201–211.

14. John Adams, Letters to Thomas Jefferson, October 9, 1787, and November 15, 1813, *The Adams-Jefferson Letters,* ed. Lester J. Cappon (New York: Simon and Schuster, 1971), pp. 202–203, 397–402.

15. C. Wright Mills, *The Power Elite* (New York: Oxford University Press, 1956), p. 91.

16. Frederick Grimké, *The Nature and Tendency of Free Institutions* (Cambridge, Mass.: Harvard University Press, 1968; orig. pub. 1848), pp. 354–376.

17. Francis J. Grund, *Aristocracy in America*, ed. Perry Miller (New York: Harper, 1959; orig. pub. 1839).

18. See Joseph L. Blau, ed., *The Social Theories of Jacksonian Democracy* (New York: Liberal Arts Press, 1954), pp. 135, 289–300, 142–162.

19. Veblen, *The Theory of the Leisure Class*, passim.

20. Joseph Schumpeter, *Imperialism and Social Classes* (New York: Meridian, 1955), pp. 65–70, 91–98. Max Weber, *Economy and Society*, ed. Gunther Roth and Claus Wittich (Berkeley: University of California Press, 1978), vol. 1, pp. 302–307; vol. 2, pp. 926–940.

21. Blau, *Social Theories*, pp. 31–37.

22. Richard P. Coleman and Lee Rainwater, *Social Standing in America* (New York: Basic, 1978).

23. Sigmund Freud, *The Family Romance*, in *Collected Papers*, ed. James Strachey, vol. 5 (New York: Basic, 1959), pp. 74–78.

24. Harold Nicolson, *Some People* (New York: Vintage, 1957), pp. 57–75.

25. Thorstein Veblen, *The Place of Science in Modern Civilization* (New York: D. W. Huebsch, 1919), pp. 1–31.

26. Richard Hofstadter, *Anti-Intellectualism in American Life* (New York: Knopf, 1963), pp. 182–183.

27. Eric F. Goldman, *Rendez-Vous with History* (New York: Vintage, 1955), pp. 79–81.

28. Kirkpatrick Sale, *SDS* (New York: Random House, 1973).

29. For inspiration, David Riesman, *Individualism Reconsidered* (Glencoe, Ill.: Free Press, 1954), pp. 39–54.

30. Letter to Thomas Jefferson Randolph, November 24, 1808, in *The Portable Jefferson*, ed. Merrill D. Peterson (New York: Viking, 1975), pp. 511–514.

4. The Ambiguities of Betrayal

1. *Ex parte Bollman*, 4 Cranch 125 (1807). I am too indebted for page-by-page citation to James Willard Hurst, *The Law of Treason in the United States* (Westport, Conn.: Greenwood, 1971).

2. Of all possible interpretations that one might put on the material presented by Edward Westermarck in his famous work *The Origin and Development of the Moral Ideas* (London: Macmillan, 1912), one is inescapable: that the stranger is an enemy to most

societies, and that even hospitality is but a way of making a formal exception to the rules of hostility. Kin and stranger are opposites.

3. Bruno Bettelheim, *The Uses of Enchantment* (London: Thames and Hudson, 1975), pp. 66-67, 159-166.

4. Michael Supperstone, ed., *Brownlie's Law of Public Order and National Security* (London: Butterworths, 1981), pp. 230-245.

5. Joost A. M. Merloo, *Total War and the Human Mind* (London: Allen and Unwin, 1944), pp. 17-26. Idem, *Mental Seduction and Menticide* (London: Jonathan Cape, 1957), pp. 233-257.

6. Morton Grodzins, *The Loyal and the Disloyal* (Chicago: University of Chicago Press, 1956), pp. 44-45. I am much indebted to this work generally.

7. James Shirley, *The Traitor* (1613), I, 1; and generally J. Mills Laurens, *One Soul in Bodies Twain* (Bloomington, Ind.: Principia, 1937).

8. E. M. Forster, *Two Cheers for Democracy* (New York: Harcourt Brace, 1951), pp. 68-69.

9. *Haupt v. United States*, 330 U.S. 631 (1947), 646-649. The case of the Rosenbergs is part of the whole problem of political trials. See Judith Shklar, *Legalism* (Cambridge, Mass.: Harvard University Press, 1964).

10. Montesquieu, *Pensées*, in *Oeuvres Complètes de Montesquieu*, ed. André Masson (Paris: Nagel, 1950), sects. 350, 741, 1253.

11. Montaigne, "Of Friendship," in *The Essays of Montaigne*, trans. E. J. Trechman, vol. 1 (New York: Oxford University Press, n.d.), pp. 189-191.

12. Aristotle, *Nicomachean Ethics VIII*, 1161b and passim.

13. Quoted in Grodzins, *The Loyal and the Disloyal*, pp. 142-143; also Edmund Wilson, *Patriotic Gore* (London: Oxford University Press, 1966), pp. 329-335.

14. Floyd S. Lear, *Treason and Related Offenses in Roman and Germanic Law*, vol. 42 (Houston: Rice Institute, 1955), pp. 43-78. John Bellamy, *The Law of Treason in England in the Later Middle Ages* (Cambridge: Cambridge University Press, 1970).

15. Ernst Kantorowitz, *The King's Two Bodies* (Princeton: Princeton University Press, 1957), pp. 24-41.

16. John of Salisbury, *Policraticus*, ed. Murray F. Markland (New York: Frederick Ungar, 1979), pp. 40-41, 44-46, 94-95.

17. John Bellamy, *The Tudor Law of Treason* (London: Routledge and Kegan Paul, 1979).

18. Montaigne, "Of the Useful and the Honest," in *Essays*, vol. 2, p. 250; idem, "Of Physiognomy," ibid., vol. 2, pp. 536–539.

19. John Locke, *An Essay Concerning Human Understanding*, in *Works*, vol. 1 (London, 1823), bk. 1, ch. 3.

20. Niccolò Machiavelli, *The Discourses*, in *The Prince and the Discourses*, trans. Christian E. Detmold, ed. Max Lerner (New York: Modern Library, 1940), bk. 3, ch. 6, pp. 410–436.

21. Quoted in J. W. Lever, *The Tragedy of State* (London: Methuen, 1971), p. 7. See also Julia Briggs, *This Stage-Play World* (Oxford: Oxford University Press, 1983), pp. 190–191.

22. Jean Racine, *Britannicus*, in *Andromache and Other Plays*, trans. John Cairncross (London: Penguin, 1967), act IV, scenes 3 and 4.

23. Montaigne, "Of Different Results of the Same Counsel," in *Essays*, vol. 1, pp. 122–123.

24. Thucydides, *The Peloponnesian War*, bk. 1, sects. 128–138; bk. 5, sects. 43–46; bk. 6, sects. 15–19, 27–29, 60–61, 88–93; bk. 8, sects. 45–89.

25. Josephus Flavius, *The Jewish War*, trans. G. A. Williamson (London: Penguin, 1981), bk. 5, sects. 362–419; bk. 6, sect. 107.

26. For example, Pierre Vidal-Naquet, "Du Bon Usage de la Trahison," Preface to *La Guerre des Juifs* (Paris: Editions de Minuit, 1977).

27. Sallust, *The Jugurthine War and The Conspiracy of Catiline*, trans. S. A. Handford (London: Penguin, 1963), sects. 52–54.

28. Richard Buel, Jr., *Securing the Revolution* (Ithaca, N.Y.: Cornell University Press, 1972).

29. Harold Hyman, *To Try Men's Souls* (Berkeley: University of California Press, 1960), p. 78. Bradley Chapin, *The American Law of Treason* (Seattle: University of Washington Press, 1964), pp. 24–45. Grodzins, *The Loyal*, p. 53.

30. *Cramer v. United States*, 324 U.S. 1 (1944), pp. 1–48.

31. James Randall, *Constitutional Problems under Lincoln* (New York: Appleton, 1926), pp. 91, 96–117.

32. *New York Times*, December 6, 1981, p. 30, col. 8.

33. Rebecca West, *The New Meaning of Treason* (New York: Viking, 1964), p. 34.

34. I am much indebted to John Dunn's unpublished essay, "Trust in the Politics of John Locke."

35. *West Virginia Board of Education v. Barnette*, 319 U.S. 624 (1943).

36. Josiah Royce, *The Philosophy of Loyalty,* in *Basic Writings,* ed. John J. McDermott, vol. 2 (Chicago: University of Chicago Press, 1969), pp. 855–1013.

37. Joachim Kramarz, *Claus von Stauffenberg,* trans. R. H. Barry (London: André Deutsch, 1967); Carl J. Friedrich, *The Pathology of Politics* (New York: Harper and Row, 1972), pp. 109–123.

38. Sebastian Haffner, *The Meaning of Hitler,* trans. Ewald Osers (London: Weidenfeld and Nicolson, 1979).

39. Raymond Aron, Preface to André Thérive, *Essai sur les Trahisons* (Paris: Calman-Lévy, 1951), pp. vi–xxxii.

5. Misanthropy

1. "Letter to Germinus," *The Letters of Caius Plinius,* trans. Melmoth (London, 1878), 8:22, p. 292.

2. John Marston, *Antonio's Revenge,* IV, 1.

3. Cicero, *Tusculan Disputations,* trans. J. E. King (Cambridge, Mass.: Harvard University Press, 1927), IV: 11, pp. 353–355. Pliny the Elder, *Natural History,* vol. 3, trans. H. R. Rackham (Cambridge, Mass.: Harvard University Press, 1942), VII: 19, pp. 558–559. Plutarch, "Antony," in *The Lives of the Noble Grecians and Romans,* trans. John Dryden (New York: Modern Library, 1932), p. 1144. There are good accounts of Timon's historical fortunes in Gerhard Hay, *Darstellung des Menschenhasses in der deutschen Literatur des 18 und 19 Jahrhunderts* (Frankfurt am Main: Athenäum Verlag, 1970); and in Rolf Soellner, *Timon of Athens* (Columbus: Ohio State University Press, 1979). On nonpolitical satire generally, I was helped by Robert C. Elliott, *The Power of Satire* (Princeton: Princeton University Press, 1972).

4. Tacitus, *The Annals,* in *Historical Writings,* trans. Arthur Murphy, vol. 1 (London: J. M. Dent, 1908), bk. 15, sect. 44, p. 487.

5. Friedrich Nietzsche, *The Gay Science,* trans. Walter Kaufmann (New York: Vintage, 1974), sect. 167. Idem, *The Will to Power,* trans. Walter Kaufmann (New York: Vintage, 1968), sect. 939.

6. Karl Marx, *Capital,* trans. Eden and Cedar Paul, vol. 1 (London: J. M. Dent, 1946), pp. 112–113.

7. Antonin Artaud, *The Theatre and Its Double* (London: Calder and Boyars, 1970), pp. 18, 22, 60, 64–67, 77, 79–80.

8. Montaigne, "Of Glory," in *The Essays of Montaigne,* trans. E. J. Trechman, vol. 2 (New York: Oxford University Press, n.d.), pp. 70–80; idem, "Of Liars," ibid., vol. 1, pp. 30–31; idem, "Of

Giving the Lie," ibid., vol. 2, pp. 117–118; idem, "Cowardice is the Mother of Cruelty," ibid., vol. 2, pp. 147–150.

9. Montesquieu, *Les Lettres Persanes*, in *Oeuvres Complètes de Montesquieu*, ed. André Masson, vol. 1 (Paris: Nagel, 1950), pp. 316–317.

10. Montaigne, "Of Presumption," in *Essays*, vol. 2, pp. 108–114.

11. Immanuel Kant, *The Metaphysical Principles of Virtue*, trans. James Ellington (Indianapolis: Bobbs-Merrill, 1964), pp. 134–146.

12. Anthony, Earl of Shaftesbury, *Characteristics*, ed. John M. Robertson, vol. 2 (Indianapolis: Bobbs-Merrill, 1964), pp. 83–84.

13. Montesquieu, *Les Lettres Persanes*, pp. 23–24.

14. Immanuel Kant, "Perpetual Peace," in *On History*, trans. Lewis White Beck (Indianapolis: Bobbs-Merrill, 1963), p. 112.

15. Montesquieu, *Pensées*, in *Oeuvres Complètes*, vol. 2, sects. 831, 892, 935, 1008, 1253.

16. Sidney Verba, *Small Groups and Political Behavior* (Princeton: Princeton University Press, 1961); J. Roland Pennock, *Democratic Political Theory* (Princeton: Princeton University Press, 1979), pp. 470–500.

17. Friedrich Nietzsche, *The Gay Science*, sect. 379.

18. Idem, *Thus Spake Zarathustra*, trans. Walter Kaufmann (London: Penguin, 1978), pp. 198, 209, 214, 218. Idem, *The Will to Power*, sect. 866. Idem, *Ecce Homo*, trans. Walter Kaufmann (New York: Vintage, 1969), p. 309.

19. Idem, *Beyond Good and Evil*, trans. Walter Kaufmann (New York: Vintage, 1966), sect. 199.

20. Montaigne, "Of Repentance," in *Essays*, vol. 2, pp. 262–264.

6. Bad Characters for Good Liberals

1. See especially Aristotle, *Nicomachean Ethics*, trans. Martin Ostwald (Indianapolis: Bobbs-Merrill, 1962), bk. 2, ch. 5, 1105b, and ch. 6, 1106a–1107a; bk. 3, ch. 5, 1114a; bk. 4, chs. 1–2, 1123a–1119a; bk. 10, chs. 7–8, 1177a–1179a.

2. Immanuel Kant, *The Metaphysical Principles of Virtue*, trans. James Ellington (Indianapolis: Bobbs-Merrill, 1964), pp. 39–141. Idem, "Perpetual Peace," in *On History*, trans. Lewis White Beck (Indianapolis: Bobbs-Merrill, 1963), p. 112.

3. Anthony F. Granucci, " 'Nor Cruel and Unusual Punishment': The Original Meaning," *California Law Review* 54 (1969): 839–865.

4. Friedrich Nietzsche, *On the Genealogy of Morals,* trans. Walter Kaufmann (New York: Vintage, 1969), bk. 3, sect. 27, p. 161.

5. Morton Bloomfield, *The Seven Deadly Sins* (n.p.: Michigan State College Press, 1952). Saint Thomas Aquinas, *Summa Theologica,* trans. The Fathers of the English Dominican Province (New York: Benziger, 1947), vol. 1, pts. 1–2, quests. 71–89, pp. 902–990; vol. 2, pts. 2–3, quest. 159, pp. 1844–45. John of Salisbury, *Policraticus,* ed. Murray F. Markland (New York: Frederick Ungar, 1979), pp. 4, 34, 56.

6. Benjamin Boyce, *The Theophrastan Character in England* (Cambridge, Mass.: Harvard University Press, 1947).

*C*redits

Index